Hitler's Last Witness

Hitler's Last Witness

The Memoirs of Hitler's Bodyguard

Rochus Misch

Co-authored by

Michael Stehle, Professor Jörn Precht, Ralph Giordano,
Regina Carstensen and Dr Sandra Zarrinbal

Introduction by Roger Moorhouse

Frontline Books, London

Hitler's Last Witness
First published in 2014 by Frontline Books.
This paperback edition published in 2017 by Frontline Books
An imprint of Pen & Sword Books Limited
47 Church Street
Barnsley
South Yorkshire
S70 2AS

ISBN 978-1-47389-902-5

Publishing History
Originally published in German in 2008 under the title *Der Letze Zeuge*.
This is the first English language edition and includes an introduction
by Roger Moorhouse and a new introduction by Rochus Misch.

CIP data records for this title are available from the British Library
For more information on our books, please visit www.pen-and-sword.co.uk,
email info@frontline-books.com or write to us at the above address.

Printed and bound in the UK by CPI Group (UK) Ltd, Croydon, CR0 4YY

Typeset in 11/14 point Garamond by Wordsense Ltd, Edinburgh

For a complete list of Pen & Sword titles please contact
PEN & SWORD BOOKS LIMITED
47 Church Street, Barnsley, South Yorkshire S70 2AS, United Kingdom
E-mail: enquiries@pen-and-sword.co.uk
Website: www.pen-and-sword.co.uk

Contents

Contents

Illustrations

Acknowledgements

EXCEPT WHERE STATED, THE photographs reproduced in this book are from the private collection of Rochus Misch. The copyright holders for the following photos are:

ACME: 73

akg images: 39

Archiv Alfons Schulz: 22, 43, 54

Archiv preussischer Kulturbesitz: 69

Archiv vereinigte Werkstätten München: 14, 15

Getty Images: 18

Landesarchiv Berlin: 12, 74

Library of Congress: 16

Michael Stehle: 23, 35

National Archives and Records Administration, Washington, DC: 63, 71

Ullsteinbild: 7, 10, 13, 21, 34, 36, 40, 41, 49, 61, 70

With regard to photographs 14, 58, 61, 62 and 72, by the time editing was concluded on the German-language edition the copyright holders of these photographs had not been identified. The publishers therefore request the holders to contact them for the settlement of claims.

Introduction

WHEN THE NEWS BROKE, in September 2013, of the death of Rochus Misch, it made headlines across the world. It was not Misch's vitally important role in the history of the Third Reich that sparked the interest – he hadn't really had one – rather it was the simple fact that he had been the last surviving witness to the grim denouement of Hitler's regime – the suicide of Adolf Hitler in the Führerbunker in Berlin, on 30 April 1945.

Rochus Misch was born in 1917 in the German eastern province of Upper Silesia. An orphan, he joined the SS in 1937, and – mainly due to his height (he was more than 1.8 metres tall) – found himself in Hitler's bodyguard regiment – *SS-Leibstandarte*. After being severely wounded in the Polish campaign of 1939, he was appointed to Hitler's household staff, initially as a 'man-Friday' and later as a telephonist. It was in this capacity, serving his master to the very last days of the Third Reich, that Misch would make his modest mark on history.

Misch never sought publicity or even intended to write his biography. As he explains in his introduction – specially written for this volume only months before his death in 2013 – he wrote this book in 2008 to meet the growing interest that the world had in him, as well as to correct what he perceived as a few popular misconceptions. After returning from Soviet internment in 1953, he had settled into an ordinary and unremarkable life – one that history only caught up with after 2000, when he emerged as one of the few remaining survivors of Hitler's bunker. In time, he became the only survivor.

But, for all that serendipity, Rochus Misch had a story to tell. As a member of Hitler's SS Escort, he would accompany the Führer wherever he went. Whether in the Chancellery in Berlin, on the Obersalzberg or in the Wolfsschanze HQ in East Prussia, he would always be close to Hitler, one of the small group of guards who had to be within sight or sound of the dictator at all times. This naturally afforded him a tremendous opportunity to observe life at the pinnacle of the Third Reich, including the personalities and characters involved – not least Hitler himself, who knew Misch by name.

This memoir is the product of that proximity. Misch saw Hitler's household close up, in action; he noticed the difference between the public and private faces, and got to peek behind the curtain. Sometimes the experience could be alarming, as when he blundered into a guest room in Hitler's private suite one morning, only to find Eva Braun in her nightdress: 'She said nothing,' he writes, 'but merely raised her right forefinger to her closed lips.' Clearly, Misch had the sort of 'access' that historians (and gossips) would have killed for.

On one level, then, Misch certainly delivers. His memoir is full of details, asides and digressions, which allow the reader a rare and fascinating insight into the Third Reich's inner sanctum. Hitler, he says, was just 'the Boss', a 'normal, simple man' who was 'neither a monster nor a superman'. Eva Braun, meanwhile, was 'gay and carefree, almost childlike', with a 'zest for living'. Goebbels was popular with the staff, while Bormann was not. Misch overheard conversations, watched the comings and goings and was a keen observer of events. He was present, for example, when Hitler received news of Hess's flight to Britain in May 1941; he listened in when Hitler spoke on the telephone with Major Remer in the aftermath of the 20 July bomb plot, inspiring the latter to lead the crushing of the Stauffenberg coup in Berlin. He was as close to being a 'fly on the wall' as one could get.

Yet, for all that, Misch's view of events is a curiously myopic one. For one thing, the rarefied, claustrophobic atmosphere of the Führer's headquarters was clearly not the ideal location from which to gain a rounded perspective. Misch barely *saw* the world outside, much less was able to make sense of it. The eye of the storm, one could surmise, is rarely the best place from which to view the resulting carnage.

Another inhibiting factor was Misch's own nature. He was, in essence, a simple provincial lad – someone who joined the SS because he saw it as a short cut to a secure career in the service of the state, and was given the job in Hitler's household as he was considered someone who would 'give no trouble'. Misch, certainly, was that man. He kept his head down, did his job, didn't gossip, didn't ask questions and didn't speak out of turn. He was essentially apolitical – naïve even. As this memoir demonstrates, he was clearly no fanatic, and was no militarist – naturally preferring the soft leather boots and tailored uniforms of headquarters to the mud and blood of the front. He was not even a member of the Nazi Party, and claimed that joining the NSDAP (National Socialist Party) 'never even occurred to [him]'.

Consequently, most of what we now understand as the dominant narrative of Nazi Germany seems to have passed Rochus Misch by entirely. He claims to have first heard about the Holocaust, for example, only after returning from Soviet internment in 1953. And, astonishingly, he wonders aloud in these very pages whether he ever noticed that Hitler 'hated the Jews'. To our modern sensibilities, this is baffling, and it is easy to assume that Misch is simply dissembling, by hiding his own knowledge of, and perhaps even complicity in, Nazi Germany's most heinous crimes. But, I would suggest that this assumption should be resisted. To my mind, this is not an example of a cunning memoirist airbrushing his own memories (Misch had many character traits, but one does not get the impression that 'cunning' was among them). Rather, I would argue that such apparently glaring omissions are the result of Misch's own rather unquestioning nature combined with the blinkering effect of his close proximity to Nazi power. The omissions are also a useful corrective – an example of the tremendous benefits afforded by hindsight and a reminder of the adage: 'The past is a foreign country, they do things differently there.'

What is more genuinely surprising about this memoir is the author's evident lack of any real perspective on the events to which he was a witness. Despite the intervening years, Misch comes across as strangely unreflective, even unrepentant in nature. His comments about Hitler's would-be assassin – Claus von Stauffenberg – are a good case in point. With seven decades of hindsight, one might have expected Misch to have developed a more nuanced, sympathetic view of the assassin and what he was trying to achieve. But no; Misch voices a similar opinion here to that which he might have given back in 1944; Stauffenberg was 'a murderer of his colleagues,' he writes. 'There was really nothing worse.' There is no hint of contrition in Misch; no expression of the collective *mea culpa* voiced by Hitler's secretary Traudl Junge, for example, nor even of the sense of retrospective regret expressed so eloquently after the war by Hitler's former foreign press chief, Ernst Hanfstaengl, who said: 'You get on a bandwagon and it turns out to be a dustcart.'[1] This is perplexing and a little disappointing, but in Misch's case one senses that it is motivated more by a simple lack of imagination than by any lingering ideological fealty.

Yet, despite his limitations, one should not assume that Misch is an uninteresting or unenlightening source. He is neither. His observations, certainly, are more 'kitchen sink' than 'kitchen cabinet', but that does not invalidate them; they still have much to teach us. Purists can sometimes get rather sniffy about 'human interest' in history – complaining, for example, that the fact that Hitler kissed ladies' hands, or chatted amiably with his secretaries tells us nothing of substance about the Third Reich. On the superficial level, they are right of course. We are brought no nearer to understanding the Holocaust by knowing Hitler's dietary habits. And yet, I would suggest that such

---

1 Quoted in Peter Conradi, *Hitler's Piano Player*, London 2005, p. 325.

information does play a role. It is of interest in its own right, of course, but it also serves a more profound purpose: not only that of explaining the dynamic provided by Hitler's personal charisma, but also that of reminding us of our shared humanity with an otherwise rather two-dimensional monster. It is too easy, in my opinion, to dismiss Hitler as a breed apart – not like us. Acknowledging his humanity, in contrast – the hand kissing, as well as the hatred – makes his crimes all the more horrific.

In addition, it is Misch's very ordinariness that makes his account rather instructive. Though his rather cosseted, privileged war was not the same as that of the average Berliner, his views, prejudices and blind spots most certainly were. Consequently, his recollections are almost as interesting for the things that he doesn't say as for the things he does. One gets the impression, indeed, that Misch represented the kind of rather bovine, uncritical, unthinking type that provided the very backbone of the Nazi regime – being obedient, unquestioning, 'making no trouble'. Without Misch, and many thousands like him, the Third Reich would simply have been unable to function.

When Rochus Misch died, the media was primarily excited by the fact that he was the last surviving witness of Hitler's final days. With his passing, the sole living link with the tumultuous, bloody demise of the Third Reich was finally severed. This was certainly true, but Misch signified a lot more than just an accident of longevity. For all his blind spots, he gives us vivid detail about everyday life in Hitler's innermost circle, and by extension provides an insight into the thoughts and feelings of a generation of ordinary Germans. He was a remarkable eyewitness to a fascinating period.

© Roger Moorhouse 2014

Author's Introduction

I NEVER INTENDED TO write my biography. In the course of my life I granted countless interviews to authors, newspaper reporters, historians and television teams from all over the world, rather fewer from Germany. It has all been said, so I thought. The fact that the questions reaching me by post and telephone over the last few years have increased, and not the opposite, taught me otherwise. The letters are overwhelmingly friendly and interested, and they come mainly from young, often very young people. I have a bad conscience about having left so many unanswered. I am an old man and can no longer handle the onslaught. Not long ago I decided to go ex-directory, because many international telephone calls came at night, because of the time lag. For decades my telephone number had been in public directories, but now the interest in me has grown so large that I have had to protect myself in this way.

Why has this interest expanded? I think that with the increasing passage of time since the 1933–45 period, young people simply have fewer worries about digging up the past than the previous generation. For them, it is perfectly clear that one can only learn from history if one knows it. And what is written in the history books has for some time not answered everything. In addition, I have to state this soberly and with resignation – there is the race against time. The opportunity will not exist much longer to put questions to such eyewitnesses as myself.

This book is, therefore, for me first of all an unburdening of my workload; henceforth, I can refer interested people to my memoirs. From very recent documentaries about events of which I am today the last surviving witness, I have become aware that my impressions may be an important source for understanding. I observe that certain representations which I know for certain to be false, or that in any case I saw, perceived or recall the basic events and circumstances differently, threaten to become historical fact. I would now like to explain what I mean.

As a result of my involvement with the American film-makers of the Hollywood drama *Valkyrie* in the summer of 2007, I became aware that numerous errors of fact were presented in the public domain. This was a film about the failed attempt on Hitler's life on 20 July 1944. I was asked all things imaginable, from routine security measures to Hitler's habits. The team appeared well informed, yet I was surprised at so much incorrect presentation.

I noticed this particularly some time before in connection with the sensational world release of *Der Untergang* (*Downfall*) – an important film, if a comic-opera type tragedy. 'I' was to be seen in a couple of scenes: the representative of my person did not have a speaking role. It was shown how this actor discovered the bodies of the generals Wilhelm Burgdorf and Hans Krebs after their suicides. Why was I not asked how it really happened? Then they might have learnt that I did not react in the least in a calm, almost business-like way, as the film showed. On the contrary, I was extremely agitated to find that Burgdorf, whom I touched gently to tell him he had a telephone call waiting for him, had not nodded off, but was dead. I went off immediately to report the deaths of the two generals. A detail. Nevertheless, it gave a false impression, for I was anything but composed at that moment.

In the final hours in the Führerbunker, one thought above all others made me panic, and it had nothing to do with the Russians or the dead Hitler, but Gestapo Müller! I had seen the head of the Gestapo at RSHA (SS-Reichssicherheitshauptamt/Reich Main Security Office) in the

New Reich Chancellery. His presence was completely strange. Hannes – a technician who also had remained to the last in the bunker – and I speculated whether we would now all be eliminated. Maybe they would blow up the bunker? Better to destroy everything than have it fall into the hands of the Russians – and we had to reckon that that might go for us too. Was nothing and nobody to escape the Führer bunker?

During April 1945, silence – a deathly silence – reigned in Hitler's bunker flat below the garden of the Old Reich Chancellery. There was no excited coming and going. The actual Führerbunker consisted of a couple of small cell-like rooms. Apart from Eva Braun, only Hitler's valet and his physician Dr Morell had rooms in which they lived; later, Goebbels moved in with the doctor. All other rooms were for official purposes. Only by my small telephone switchboard was there a 'public' sitting area to offer anyone. The portrayed hectic scenes before the end in *Der Untergang* – most of them occurred in the cellars of the New Reich Chancellery, many in the ante-bunker. The film had almost everything played out in Hitler's bunker apartment, to which only a few ever came, if summoned to 'the boss'. In the Führerbunker, deeper underground than cellars and the ante-bunker, death had already taken up lodgings long before Hitler put the gun to his head. The war could only be heard from the ante-bunker and in the Reich Chancellery cellars. In Hitler's domain there was only some shaking and dull noises to be felt and heard. On the other hand, it was not possible to know about events in the deep bunker if one was in the ante-bunker or in the remote cellars of the New Reich Chancellery.

The day before the release of *Der Untergang* in Berlin, I received a telephone call in the late evening. It was somebody from the production team letting me know that I had been requested not to appear at the première. No reason was given. Five weeks later, producer Bernd Eichinger visited me at my Berlin house. He was researching something new. Mentioning *Der Untergang*, Herr Eichinger referred to the book of the same name by Joachim Fest, which had been the basis for the film. They had set store by it, and my role was based on it. Yet Herr Fest had never spoken to me personally.

I was barely twenty-eight years old when the Third Reich went down. After Hitler's death I maintained the telephone connection to the Russians, and after my official release by Reich chancellor Joseph Goebbels I removed all the plugs from the telephone installation. For five years – the last five years of Hitler's life – I lived wherever Hitler lived: in the Führer-apartment in the Old Reich Chancellery, in the Führer-HQs and finally in the Führerbunker.

I am an insignificant man, but I have experienced significant matters. Many thought – in connection with their relationship to Hitler – they should make themselves seem less or more important according to how the information was to be used. I saw no reason why I should do any such thing. I was always an apolitical person.

Completely in contrast to my wife, who was an SPD (Social Democratic Party) politician, even at one time a member of the Chamber of Deputies in Berlin, I was never a Party member, neither of the SPD nor of the NSDAP (National Socialist Party). I never volunteered for the Waffen-SS. I was recruited for the SS-Verfügungstruppe (VT), enticed by the possibility of state service. I would like to have gone into the Reichsbahn (state railways). Only later did the SS-Verfügungstruppe become the Waffen-SS.[1]

Having recovered from a serious wound in the Polish campaign and back with my unit, one day my company commander chose me for a post at the Reich Chancellery. I went there as ordered, and the following day, either 1 or 2 May 1940,[*] I began service there. My new boss was Adolf Hitler.

---

1 The SS-Verfügungstruppe (VT) was the forerunner of the Waffen-SS: after the outbreak of war the Waffen-SS came into being by a merger of the VT with the SS-Totenkopf units.

* Rochus Misch contradicts himself concerning the exact date he started work with Hitler. In fact, both 1 and 2 May were holidays in 1940. According to Russian reports, he began on Monday 6 May 1940.

Today there are long debates about whether Hitler can be portrayed as a 'private' man at all, even as 'a person', but it is very difficult for me to separate the two. I knew him only as a person. A person who was my boss and to whom my welfare was important. He was a boss who had his own physician examine me when I felt bad, who spontaneously gave permission for me to be absent to see a girl, who upon my marriage sent me two cases of the most select wines and made a special payment assuring my life in the enormous sum of 100,000 Reichsmarks, and who never shouted at me. If nevertheless I felt a little uneasy in his presence, that was simply because he was 'my boss'.

I tried to carry out all my duties to the best of my ability, as was expected. While doing so, I enjoyed the many liberties my service often brought in its train, and I played pranks on those colleagues with whom I had a good relationship. I was careful to avoid blunders, such as made by two of my colleagues when they created model panzers for their children after seeing a demonstration of new weapons; this got them sent back to the fighting front. Heavy field boots sinking into mud and filth instead of extra light, dazzling made-to-measure boots on thick carpet – no thank you. Conscious of the front, I was careful to present myself exactly as the man who had been selected expressly for my task – somebody who gave no trouble.

I did not like being a soldier; having a rank was not something that mattered to me. Throughout my service I was in the lower ranks (finally Oberscharführer).[2] The possibilities of promotion to higher rank for a member of the Führer's personal bodyguard were in any case limited. Because of that, five close friends volunteered for the front – and only two came back, one of them Otto Günsche, who then became Hitler's adjutant.

Well, for me the front was far away, marriage near, work in the bodyguard rich in variety and, in comparison to a soldier's lot, a relaxed life. As long as we made sure that the shifts were covered, we

2 The SS rank Oberscharführer was the equivalent of sergeant in the German army.

could change them as we liked. At the Berghof (Obersalzberg), which had its own telephonist, it was like being on holiday.

Obviously I am aware that I am not speaking of any old job and just any boss. It was clear to me then that I was in a special place among people in a genuine position of note. I know – today – what went on in Germany and elsewhere in the name of Germany while I was serving Leni Riefenstahl tea, sitting with Erwin Rommel at the cloakroom table looking at his Afrika Korps photos or hearing from Hitler's study the fine voice of the Jewish chamber singer Joseph Schmidt, whose gramophone records the boss loved so much. At that time I did not know.

I neither attended the military situation conferences nor was I a personal conversation partner of Hitler's, unlike the adjutants. So what can I describe? In my experience of the last few years it is young people who ask me, not to confirm long-known facts or find out about Hitler as 'a person', but how did one get into his closest circle? How did one get to be his telephonist in the bunker? What was everyday life like in the power centre of Hitler's Germany for people such as I? What were my feelings about the course of the war and the defeat as perceived from where I stood? These are the questions of many young people, which I attempt to answer in this book.

It certainly remains a matter of interest what went on in the last days of Hitler's life, what the bunker looked like and what details and facts I remember which belong to the world history of today. However, the things that have stuck in my memory, which at the time seemed important or an invaluable experience, inevitably do not always coincide with what was important historically. It is not easy to put myself back into the centre of my experiences.

For this biography I have separated out much that would interfere when reporting on things as I perceived them. The following account aims to be as free as possible of retrospective assessments, now that I know the extent of the horror, but, like many others, I was not aware of until long after the end of the war. Only then can I become again the Rochus Misch of his mid-twenties, a man who has not existed for more than sixty years.

This book is not a justification. I was given the post with Hitler because my company commander was certain that I would not cause trouble. I took the post because I was a soldier, and I kept it because my company commander was right.

I do not reproach myself today that I did my job under the circumstances that then existed, that I always did it in an orderly and conscientious manner even when I realised in 1943 that the war would be lost, even when it had long been lost, and even as Hitler's body burnt. No, I do not reproach the Rochus Misch of that time because he didn't make trouble.

All the same, because events at that time were so self-evident they do make me reflective. I used to listen to my father-in-law talk about the old SPD times, hear enemy radio broadcasts with him – and then off I would go to work again at the Reich Chancellery. I managed to get Uncle Paul out of a concentration camp – and then I went back to Hitler. In July 1944, I paid no further heed to talk of Final Victory, but when, after the assassination attempt, the telephone connection to the living Hitler at FHQ Wolfsschanze was restored, I felt at that moment relief, if only because the nerve-tearing tension about the uncertain command situation was ended.

It was never necessary to compel myself to fulfil my duties unconditionally. I never struggled inwardly over them – never hesitated. Only at the very end, overwhelmed by worry about my wife and daughter, only then did I consider doing something contrary to my oath. But then I remained at my post in the bunker until the new Reich chancellor Joseph Goebbels released me officially as the last man. I was a soldier. I had my duty, my instructions, my place to be. And I had a good place to be, in contrast to my comrades in the field. I brought mountains of despatches to Hitler and relayed countless conversations, but I never saw the whole thing again nor looked for it. I did not bother. I asked no questions when it was best to ask none, but I also raised no questions when I could have done. I tell it as it is: the young Rochus had few queries.

As one of Hitler's bodyguards, I spent most of the time standing around; as his telephonist, I pressed buttons at the switchboard; and as a courier, I transported paper across the district. In the future that would be condemned by the Russian authorities as 'support for the Nazi regime'. Who of my generation, however, did not make himself guilty in this sense?

When I am asked what my duties were for Hitler, I frequently answer: 'Simply to be there.' I am very pleased about that today. Nothing else was required of me but to 'simply be there'. And what if it had been different? How far would my sense of duty, obedience and the oath to Hitler have stretched? I am glad I escaped the test. Many comrades were not so fortunate.

I am also relating my story to young people so that they do not neglect to ask the right question at the right time. To put people on the right track as to why I and so many others failed to do this, where possible I report things as I saw them then.

I want to portray my path as it happened: from Silesia via the Oberlausitz and the Black Forest to Berlin into the Reich Chancellery; from Obersalzberg into the East Prussian FHQ Wolfsschanze; then direct from the Führerbunker into the torture chamber of the NKVD (Soviet secret service) at Moscow's Lubyanka prison; the various work camps at Karaganda (Kazakhstan), Borovichi (Oblast Novgorod), Sverdlovsk (Ukraine) and Stalingrad; and finally after almost nine years as a prisoner of war (POW) back to Berlin again. My notes, which I wrote in February 1954 with the help of my wife after my return from the Soviet Union, support my memories which I have repeated orally in extensive conversations and are now sketched in this book.

When my memoirs appeared in book form in Germany in 2008 I did not anticipate anything like the enormous interest they would generate in the public. I was simply content that I could now refer many enquirers to the book. Extracts from it appeared in the important magazine *Bild* in Germany in a preview a week before publication. This was a five-part series expected to reach 40 million readers. Diverse reviews followed in the press and online, and very soon the book became a German-language bestseller. As a result of its great success, a reprint came out a year later as a paperback edition.

From the outset foreign interest in my memoirs was very great. Almost daily I continued to receive a large postbag from all over the world, and people rang me from abroad. Often the language barrier prevented me from talking and answering the questions they had about those past events.

In the summer of 2011 the 'James Bond' director Roger Spottiswoode visited me from the United States with a plan to present my German memoirs in an international film using a team of authors and translators. Often my small living room was 'bursting at the seams'. Special lighting effects would be set up, details recorded by camera. I continued to be asked by newspapers and television companies from all over the world for interviews. Because of my age, as I have said it is ever more rarely possible for me to agree to these requests.

In 2006 I was visited in my Berlin home by the Überlingen agent Michael Stehle. After many meetings with him and his assistant Dirk Mosel, I decided in 2012 to allow their agency to handle all enquiries addressed to me. Shortly after taking this decision, I was extremely pleased when Michael Stehle informed me that work would soon be under way for an English-language translation of my book.

As the last surviving eyewitness to Hitler's demise in the bunker, it pleases me that the many English-language speakers with an interest in that historical period will now have the opportunity to read my memoirs. Although I was not present at the conferences in which Hitler's political decisions were taken, perhaps the lesser 'historically relevant' details perceived by a man in his mid-twenties during his everyday duties may make things clearer. I asked no questions back then. But asking questions about that past may perhaps help us today, to ask the right questions at the right time.

Rochus Misch
June 2013

Chapter 1
My Childhood: 1917–1937

'But he thanked God for allowing him to experience all kinds of misfortune, and spent five whole years in the dungeon.'

Johann Wolfgang von Goethe, 'Sankt-Rochus-Fest zu Bingen' (The Orphan Boy from the Village)

THE VENERABLE SANKT ROCHUS is honoured in Europe as a curer of the plague. Born in Montpellier in the thirteenth century, he had the gift of protecting people against epidemics. On 16 August 1814, Goethe attended the dedication of the Rochus Chapel at Bingen on the Rhine, in honour of the saint, and in his essay 'Sankt-Rochus-Fest zu Bingen' he described his impressions of that day. The name Rochus itself comes from the Old High German word *rohon* (roar) or from the Yiddish terms *rochus* and *rauches* (annoyance, anger), and the French *rouge* (red). As it so happens, the venerable Rochus was born with a red cross on his chest – a sign of his divine selection.

I found all this out a long time ago when I developed an interest in my uncommon Christian name. Whether my mother knew the story when she named me I have no idea. Equally, I do not know if my grandparents intentionally chose the plague-healer as patron of their son, my father. Rochus was my father's name, and it was also mine. Probably I would not have been given it had my father survived my birth. After my elder brother Bruno, I am the second son of Rochus and Victoria Misch, and had my father wished to pass on his name he would surely have given it to his first-born son. However, my mother wanted me to have the name of her dead husband.

My father was a builder, while my mother Victoria worked for the Berlin public transport. Bruno was born when my parents lived on the Händelplatz, Berlin-Steglitz, but shortly afterwards, when the First World War began, the family moved to Alt-Schalkowitz[1] near Oppeln in Upper Silesia. My mother's parents lived there. I assume she did not want to spend the war alone in Berlin, as my father was quickly sent to the front.

In July 1917 my mother was very advanced in her pregnancy with me. My father was in a field hospital at Oppeln. He had been returned from the front seriously wounded, shot through a lung and missing his thumbs. Shortly before the expected date for my birth, he was allowed to leave hospital. He therefore went home, where everybody was awaiting my arrival. One night, my father suddenly had a haemorrhage and died next morning. The undertakers came to fetch him, and my mother wept and shouted as they carried the coffin past her. The midwife was already in the house and stood by helplessly. A few hours later, on that 29 July 1917 I was born.

When I was two and a half, my mother died of pneumonia following influenza. My brother Bruno met with a fatal bathing accident on 2 May 1922. His right side was stiff, probably as the result of a stroke brought on by the ice-cold water in our small brook. It took fourteen days for him to die.

Now I was quite alone with my grandparents. I was still too young to understand that I had lost my whole family within the first five years of my life: father, mother, brother. My grandparents Fronia, my mother's parents, spoke little of their daughter. They did not even have a photograph of her hanging somewhere. So I grew up without even

---

1 In 1936, as a result of the National Socialist policy of Germanising Polish-sounding names, Alt-Schalkowitz was renamed Alt-Schalkendorf.

having a picture of my parents. Nevertheless – or perhaps because of that – I did not consciously miss my father and mother. At first, my grandmother was my guardian. Later, in the 1930s, when she was too old for it, the duty was transferred to my mother's sister, my Aunt Sofia Fronia in Berlin.

Despite this tragic start in life, I have only good memories of my childhood. However, I must have been very ill once as a small boy. I was told I had had the English Disease.[2] I remember that I was taken to a special hospital in the Altvatergebirge mountains for treatment, but I do not know how I got there and how long I stayed. Apparently, they knew how to treat it.

After eight years of elementary school, my grandfather wanted me to learn a trade. He would tell me interesting stories, and in Berlin he had worked on the building of the Teltow canal. This was a big project, which had opened in 1906 – no fewer than 10,000 men had worked on it. It was very important for him that one did something 'with one's hands', develop one's talent for something. Thus, he got me to learn the mandolin. The master tailor in the village taught me this instrument.

I well remember my grandfather having a big row with the school director Demski, when he took me out of school. The director was adamant that I should continue my education and go to a higher school in Oppeln – I had good grades. However, grandfather had decided against it, even though the director visited us at home in an effort to convince him. To no avail. It was obvious to my grandfather that I should learn a trade. To his great joy, I had an 'A' in Art, and so it was quickly decided that I should be a painter. Grandfather would brook no opposition, being a thorough-going Prussian authoritarian, but in any case I had no objections.

My cousin Marie from Hoyerswerda, who happened to be visiting us when my grandfather had this row with the school director, obtained for me in 1932 through her husband's contacts an apprenticeship with

---

2 The 'English Disease' was rickets, an illness caused by vitamin D deficiency.

the firm Schüller and Model. During the first two years, I lived with my instructor Schüller. He also had a son, Gerhard. My instructor was a kind of foster-father to me, but ultimately I was left to my own devices, although I was not given a key to the house. If nobody was home, I had to wait somewhere. This was not too bad – I was a loner and could always find something to do.

I had great fun as an apprentice. I may say that I was specially gifted, and from early on I was given many interesting things to do. We painted cinema placards and gigantic advertisements on walls. For example 'Persil – for all your washing only Persil' stood in letters as tall as a man at a neighbouring station, the name of which I can no longer recall.

When Hitler became Reich chancellor in 1933 hardly anybody in Hoyerswerda was interested. There must have been some sort of event on the marketplace, but if there was I never noticed; at the time, the name Adolf Hitler meant next to nothing to me. Hoyerswerda, a small town, was rather left-wing because of its many mine workers. Even the Schüller family had nothing to do with the National Socialists. The boys of my other boss, Herr Model, however, were in a Nationalpolitische Erziehungsanstalten[3] (National Political Education Institute; 'Napola' for short); and a neighbour's son joined the Hitler Youth, but all that passed me by. Subsequently, I never observed any oppression, arrests or other measures against people, which could be traced back to the new regime.

In 1935, the year before the Berlin Olympic Games, Schüller and Model received an especially important commission from the local shooting club: at every festival a painting would be prepared as a prize, and this time the theme had to be the Olympic Games. Our talented master Schrämmer wanted to paint it, but scarcely had he begun than he fell seriously ill. Therefore, at just eighteen years of age and not

---

3 The official abbreviation of the Nationalpolitische Erziehungsanstalten was NPEA, which became Napola colloquially. The schools had the task of educating the future National Socialist ruling elite.

yet even a journeyman, I was chosen to finish it. It was actually two pictures: one as a prize for the victor in the main competition, and one for the junior champion. The first work showed the Olympic stadium; the other was of a torch bearer, with the countries through which he would run, in the background.

I received 300 Reichsmarks for the big painting, and 190 Reichsmarks for the smaller one. I was rich. This was really a lot of money. My instructor contacted my grandparents in order to make sure I did something sensible with it. My continued training was considered a good investment by both my grandfather and my instructor.

Therefore, for six months I was able to attend the Masters' School for Fine Arts in Cologne. Note, this was as a trainee. As I was not a journeyman, naturally I could not become a master even though I had passed all my examinations. There were about forty master-instructors at the school from all regions of the German Reich. I learned many interesting creative techniques, such as gilding and varnishing processes, also stage design and much more. I went about the job with a will.

When our school was commissioned to design a set for a Cologne theatre in the cathedral office, I noticed that the stage manager cast frequent looks at my work. One day he asked if I would like to be an extra in a play about the building of the cathedral, as a stone-cutter, because it would be better if the actor already had the movements for the part. At first, I was not particularly enthusiastic. I did not see myself on the stage. After some hesitation, I let myself be persuaded. Thus, I became a thirteenth-century stone-cutter with a boy's head and leather apron forced to do compulsory labour on the cathedral building. It was a speaking role, in which I had to say: 'Maria'. Although I liked acting in the end, without doubt I preferred the five Reichsmarks, which I received per performance, more. One day in the future I would have to do forced labour for real: as a POW in Russian work camps, I painted shields for building sites. This macabre parallel is only one of the many strange things that Fate had in store for me.

In Cologne I lodged at the Kolpinghaus youth hostel on Breite-Strasse. One could live very comfortably there, and a meal was to be bought for only forty pfennigs. At the beginning of March 1936, I saw German soldiers on the Cologne streets, moving out to occupy the demilitarised Rhineland. At the time, this was not a special experience for me. It was during the famed Cologne carnival, and the city was in a state of high excitement – just as it used to be in its 'wild days'. There was music and dancing everywhere. I was fascinated by the great city, the legendary gaiety of the Rhine and naturally the girls of Cologne. I felt free and had a lot of fun. After this six-month excursion I went back to Hoyerswerda to continue my training.

I was soon able to put to good use what I had learnt in my advanced training. In the whole town I was now the only person who could gild competently. Most people thought it was dreadfully expensive, but it never was. I knew that one could go a very long way with a bag of gold dust for thirty-seven Reichsmarks. In Cologne I had learnt that, with a little pile of gold dust sufficient to cover a five-mark coin, I could gild a whole horse. When they wanted to use bronze for the clock on an evangelical church tower at Hoyerswerda, I made it clear that the bronze would soon darken. Thanks to my skill in persuasion they used gold instead. And so I gilded not only this clock, but also the background of the fourteen stations of the cross in a Catholic church. At Moritzburg Castle near Dresden, Schüller and Model restored the gilded picture frames. The remains of the gold I preserved carefully in silk paper. A short while ago, I gave away my last packet of it.

Olympic Games: 1936

In the spring of 1936, at the shooting festival for which I had done the painting in 1935, I took part in the actual rifle competition. I was the third-best Silesian in the youth competition, for which I received a small bronze medal with the official Olympic logo and the inscription: 'We call the Youth of the World – Berlin 1936', a diploma and a free ticket for the opening day of the Berlin Olympic Games.

15

Thus, on 1 August 1936, there I stood, the young man from the village with my Aunt Sofia in the crowd before the Reich stadium. The tension, the masses of people, the theatre – it was tremendous.

The entry of Hitler made the greatest impact on me. As luck would have it, just at the very moment that my aunt and I stood very close to the carriageway for the guests of honour, Hitler came past, at the head of the triumphal convoy of officials and guests of honour, which had driven from the Reich Chancellery through Berlin. He stood up in the open limousine saluting the crowd, surrounded by members of his personal bodyguard, who rounded off the picture perfectly in their black uniforms with white belts. The crowd was beside itself. Everybody was now looking in one direction, all eyes were on this man. Not ten metres away from us, the limousine slowed. Before it came to a stop, the men of the bodyguard party had jumped off the running boards elegantly and threw their whole weight into holding back the surging throng of spectators. The public pushed and shoved. Whoever managed to get through the cordon clung to the vehicle like a drunkard and had to be dragged away. All was jubilation and cries of joy – it was deafening.

I was completely swept up in the emotion; tears welled up in my eyes. 'What is wrong with you?' my aunt asked. I was dreaming, imagining myself standing on the running board of the car, a member of the bodyguard squad, in one of those smart uniforms. Man, they were just normal soldiers, how lucky they were. I never considered that my daydream would one day become reality.

My ticket allowed me to go much further into the Olympic stadium, but I did not use it. After experiencing the entry of Hitler at such close quarters, I was so full of impressions that all I wanted to do was return home. Go any further into this frenzy? No, I was not in a state to do so. It was simply too much for me. And, anyway, my aunt could not have got in without a ticket. Never again did I experience anything comparable to this spectacle. Berlin sank into a sea of flags. One could hardly make headway through the streets.

For days and weeks after that event I was still totally gripped if I thought back to it. The overwhelming entry of Hitler had not brought me nearer to the Nazis and their policies. What they wanted, to where they were moving our country, who did what within the regime – people talked about it but I never took part in these discussions. I was interested in my work, and besides that only sport. I loved playing football, which my boss at work did not look upon kindly, for fear that I might be injured. After watching me play once, however, he relented. Apparently, he was a little proud of his apprentice, for in contrast to his son I was a really gifted footballer.

In December 1936, my apprenticeship terminated. My journeyman piece, some advertising for a travel company, was never finished. Scarcely had I started on it than my boss told me to leave it. 'The others are no match for you, Rochus.' My practical work was therefore waived; I received only the highest marks.

After some time as an assistant painter at Hoyerswerda, one of the older colleagues at Schüller and Model, the master-painter (arts) Schweizer from Hornberg in the Black Forest, brought me to his home town, where he wanted to set up his own business. He was hoping to receive commissions under a programme aiming at beautifying Germany, which attracted state subsidies of up to forty-five per cent. Therefore, I completed designs for public buildings in Hornberg, Triberg and Hausach, three pieces each, and then the public commissions really began to roll in. We also painted advertising boards, among others for an important exhibition in Brussels. I earned ninety-five pfennigs an hour.

In the Black Forest, I quickly made friends, and in my spare time I was mostly with three or four people of my own age. One of them was a technical draughtsman in a neighbouring business. We often went to a rustic inn, offering glorious Black Forest ham. Before our eyes, breath-fine slices were cut from a giant ham with a very sharp knife, and we relished them with black bread and mustard. We went a lot to dances and the swimming baths. There, I got to know a miller's two daughters and tried to impress them with my virtuosity on the mandolin. One of them became my first girlfriend. Best of all, I liked going with my friends to Überlingen at Lake Constance at the weekends. I packed the mandolin and bathing trunks, and then off we went. The best memories of my youth are from this time.

Of course, we got up to all kinds of mischief. We boys were able to roam freely and unsupervised – the opportunity had to be seized. Once, in Überlingen, we came across a defective cigarette machine, which simply could not stop spilling out cigarettes. 'Try to leave some behind,' my friend warned me – his pockets already stuffed full with packets of them.

None of us knew then, of course, that the carefree times for our generation, as for so many others, would soon come to an abrupt end.

Chapter 2

Conscripted Soldier: 1937–1939

I N 1937 I RECEIVED my call-up notice. I had to become a soldier.
There was no choice.

A few weeks after my twentieth birthday I took the train to
Offenburg, together with my friend of the same age, Hermann, for
assessment. SS men had set up a small table in the open and were
pressing fairly hard for volunteers to do their national service with the
Verfügungstruppe.[1] The lure was four years' military training while
avoiding the compulsory RAD (Reichs Arbeits Dienst/Reich Work
Service). It counted as full discharge of the general obligation and
could provide direct entry into state service.

For my friend Hermann the matter was soon clear: normally
conscription and RAD, plus a break in-between, took three years.

---

1   At the instigation of Heinrich Himmler, the SS-Verfügungstruppe (SS-VT) was
joined to the Schutzstaffel (bodyguard) as an armed component. In 1934, Hitler
approved three armed SS regiments, which would undertake the role of state fighting
police. When Misch was called up, the structuring of the SS-VT was already well
advanced. In high summer 1936, Hitler appointed SS-Brigadeführer Paul Hausser as
Inspector of the VT. Subsequently, in Munich from three companies of stormtroops,
the SS regiment *Deutschland* came into being, in Hamburg SS regiment *Germania*,
in Berlin the *SS-Leibstandarte* was expanded into a motorised infantry regiment, and
in Vienna in 1938 the regiment Der Führer was formed. It was not until 1940 that
the Waffen-SS came into being by the amalgamation of the VT with sections of the
Totenkopf units: see Heinz Höhne, *Die Geschichte der SS*, Augsburg 1992 (first edn
Munich 1967) pp.404ff.

Here one had the opportunity to hang an extra year onto that, but then afterwards go directly into public service and rise to be an official much earlier than would otherwise have been the case. It appealed to Hermann: 'Man, Rochus, I'm joining.' This way he saw his path eventually into the newly formed Reich autobahn police, and already he envisaged himself roaring up and down the brand-new motorways on a BMW motorcycle.

Initially, I was not as enthused as Hermann, because it was very important for me to avoid any kind of office work and I feared that was what above all awaited me in public service. I cast my doubts aside, however. Why not become an official? Perhaps there would be something in the Reichsbahn involving travel, or I could work for the state as a graphic artist. In any case, Hermann and I both filled out the necessary application forms for the SS-VT at Offenburg and then went back home. Some time later, I was invited to attend another assessment for the SS-VT – this time in Munich. It was an unspectacular affair – do a few exercises, how much did I weigh and how tall was I? My height interested them in particular – I heard it said that one had to be at least 1.78 metres. There were 139 young men called up for the SS-VT, and together with eleven colleagues I was 'specially selected' for the *SS-Leibstandarte*.[2] That same evening I received the official conscription notice for 1 October 1937. I lost sight of Hermann that day and never saw him again.

---

2 On 17 March 1933, SS-Gruppenführer Josef (Sepp) Dietrich received the assignment from Hitler to form a new Stabswache (HQ guard). Six months later, at the Nuremberg rally, the Stabswache, now of regimental size, was officially named *SS-Leibstandarte Adolf Hitler* (LAH). Although nominally under Himmler's control, commander Dietrich was in fact answerable only to Hitler. It was an elite bodyguard, which stood guard in front of government buildings and played a representative role on state visits, state events and similar. The *SS-Leibstandarte* was one of the units that made up the VT. Because of its predominantly ceremonial duties, it concentrated more on sport than military training and so was known sarcastically as the *Vergnügungstruppe* (the Enjoyment company).

'Specially Selected'

So it was that I went into the 5th Company of the *SS-Leibstandarte*, into the old Prussian cadet academy[3] at Berlin-Lichterfelde for military training. Everybody in the 1st Company was around two metres tall. I was among the smaller soldiers, having a height of 1.85 metres.

When exactly I swore my oath of allegiance to Adolf Hitler I cannot remember. It was definitely not in Berlin but in Munich, in front of the Fernherrnhalle. The oath taken by SS men was this:

Ich schwöre Dir, Adolf Hitler, als Führer und Kanzler des Deutschen Reiches, Treue und Tapferkeit. Ich gelobe Dir und den von Dir bestimmten Vorgesetzten Gehorsam bis in den Tod. So wahr mir Gott helfe.

(I swear to Thee, Adolf Hitler, as Führer and Chancellor of the German Reich, loyalty and bravery. I promise to Thee, and to those placed by Thee above me, obedience unto death. So help me God.)

This was, by the way, the only time I ever addressed Hitler by the familiar form of the pronoun for 'you'.

My military period was mostly spent in a sports camp. Running and exercises of all kinds filled the days. Almost without exception everybody in my company was a sportsman or had obtained his school-leaving certificate (the passage to university). I got on well with all six colleagues in my squad room. We had a large number of successful high-level sportsmen in our ranks, including Olympic competitors and medal winners from 1936, such as the shot-putter Hans Woellke. The *SS-Leibstandarte* had also recruited track athletes and rowers. I did not do so badly when pitted against them. My speciality was the 400 metres. I was the fastest in my company, my time without any

---

3 The Prussian main cadet training institute taken over by the *SS-Leibstandarte* in 1933 was formerly the officer-training school of the Prussian army. (Previously the SS-Stabswache *Berlin* had its quarters in the Alexander barracks near the Friedrich-Strasse tram station.)

training was just over fifty seconds. In the 5,000 metres I came second, behind the specialist.

I also enjoyed boxing. That was the world of Herbert Kleinwächter and Adolf Kleinholdermann. These two became famous boxers. Kleinwächter was a light heavyweight, while Kleinholdermann, one of my squad room companions, a heavyweight. He had fought against many of the great boxers of the time and knew Max Schmeling well.[4] Kleinwächter and Kleinholdermann continued their careers after the war. Thus it came about that Kleinholdermann became the first German to box a US-American, the black boxer Gene 'Tiger' Jones, after the war, on 14 May 1950. A German Adolf against a black boxer – that was really something so few years after the Second World War. Kleinholdermann lost and was counted out in the fourth round by Max Schmeling, acting as referee. When this was being fought out at the Berlin Waldbühne, I was in the torture chambers of the Soviet secret service. Kleinholdermann was a nice guy. Through him after the war I became a peanut butter producer. But it is a long story until then.

Sports, sports and yet more sports. The cadet academy had one of the most modern swimming pools in Europe. One day, shortly after we finished some building work, the Spiess (CSM) came into our squad room with a bucket and scrubbing brush and grinned: 'Who's for a swim?' The pool had to be cleaned of all sandy residue, he explained, before being filled with water. He did not need to ask twice. We grabbed the cleaning gear and scrubbed the tiles. Then the pool was filled with water. The high-diving tower was still rusty, but we wanted to stare down from there into the depths. So we began climbing up, and the higher we got the less jovial the troops became.

We were all standing at the top when we heard voices. The commander, Sepp Dietrich[5] in person, entered the hall with the actor

---

4   Max Schmeling (1905–2005) heavyweight boxer, world champion 1930–2.

5   Josef ('Sepp') Dietrich (1892–1966), commanding officer *SS-Leibstandarte Adolf Hitler* from 15 August 1938 to 7 April 1943.

Mathias Wiemann[6] and some generals. Dietrich described the place with sweeping gestures and all kinds of superlatives. Meanwhile, I had pressed myself long and flat like a postage stamp along the springboard so as not be seen from below. But not quickly enough. 'Have you people being doing any jumps from up there?' Dietrich's challenging voice rang out. It was obvious that the situation could now only be saved in the truest sense of the word by jumping into the cold water. It was the first and last time that in deadly fear I made a classic arse-bomb into the depths from a ten-metre high tower. An arse-bomb for the commanding general. What do you think of that?

Besides sports, there was hardly time for anything else. The most uncomfortable duty was at the barrier to the chapel. This was open to all those attending religious services and was situated in the academy grounds. There was one service a week – the evangelical alternating with the Catholic. When the service was about to begin, I would have to open the barrier and wait there until it ended. It was an unbelievable bore. Aunt Sofia was a very devout woman and went to church every Sunday. She was living then in Lichterfelde. Like our whole family, I am also Catholic and have never tried to make a secret of it.[7]

Real military training was much too short, and many of us would have bitter regrets about this. In the first two years, we spent only two ten-day periods on the exercise grounds. Instead, we were parade-soldiers, disporting ourselves as extras in film and theatre productions. For the UFA film *Die Gelbe Flagge* (The Yellow Flag – 1937) we filmed near Berlin. Hans Albers played the star role, his partner was Olga Chekhova. Also at the Deutsches Theatre three colleagues and I in one performance played soldiers of Frederick the Great. I never

6 Mathias Wiemann (1902–1969), German theatrical and film actor.

7 Misch often mentioned that both during his time with the *SS-Leibstandarte* and as a member of the SS bodyguard he attended religious service throughout infrequently. It is noteworthy in that it has often been reported that VT men were forced to leave the Church. See Heinz Höhne, *Die Geschichte der SS*, Augsburg 1992 (first edn Munich 1967) p.417: 'The VT became a stronghold of SS godlessness ... at the end of 1938 53.6 per cent of VT soldiers had left the Church.'

took part in any major parades or as an honour-guard before the Reich Chancellery; that was reserved for men of more impressive height. I marched past the Führer-balcony in the Wilhelm-Strasse twice, however.

I was very averse to all this. I was an enthusiastic sportsman, being a soldier was of no interest to me. The fact that I had been selected for the *SS-Leibstandarte* from among so many, even now I did not have a bad conscience about it. Although we had had it explained to us that we were the Führer's elite, I still did not know much about this Hitler. On the barracks blackboard were listed those of us who were NSDAP members – few.[8] There was no kind of pressure to join the Party – it never even occurred to me. Instruction in the 'world view' was given in the form of speeches, which enjoyed the same type of inattention as the German language lessons at school – the dry swotting of grammar. It was easy to see, however, that the political situation in Europe was changing, and many enthused over Hitler's policy of strength to oppose the Versailles dictates.

When the order came – 'Buckle up "apes",[9] on the vehicles!' – we didn't ask much. In March 1938, we headed for Vienna. For the annexation of Austria, one of the so-called Flower Wars ('There were flowers, flowers everywhere'), I was present. The people of Vienna received us ecstatically. In jubilation, people edged the streets and bombarded our vehicles with flowers. We were equally in a relaxed mood, and when we were given quarters in a nunnery we kept on celebrating. We put a piano in the courtyard and made music and danced until late in the night. We intoned cheerful songs loudly in the manner of Russian folk songs for especially impressive intermezzos. The nuns, who had at first retired in horror, now looked out from their

---

8 The official statistics for the SS-VT on 1 July 1937 show that twenty-seven per cent were non-NSDAP members, and twenty-nine per cent of SS-Totenkopf units were not. Although only 'a few' of either was an NSDAP member, the figures are striking. Heinz Höhne, *Die Geschichte der SS*, Augsburg 1992 (first edn Munich 1967), p.64.

9 The 'ape' (Affe) was the field pack.

windows in curiosity and occasionally they came down to us in the courtyard. 'Where there is singing, one can go below in tranquillity, evil people know no songs,' they might have been thinking! Finally, at almost midnight, we set up our night camp in the dining hall of the nunnery. The nuns threw mattresses for us down the staircase.

We stayed three or four days in Vienna, during which we tasted the world-famous Wiener Schnitzel. We were recommended a good restaurant, but everybody fell quiet when we were told that the original Wiener Schnitzel was made from udder skin.

Once back in Berlin, everything continued as usual. On 11 July, I went with some colleagues to a police festival in Treptower Park. I wasn't keen on going but allowed myself to be persuaded. When one of my friends went up to a girl to ask her to dance, her friend remained seated. I went up to her and thus I got to know Gerda Lachmund, my wife-to-be. She had had her eighteenth birthday on 3 July 1938, and this was her first time out alone. She was 1.78 metres – taller than most women there and many of the men. She seemed a bit serious, like a schoolteacher. She was a pretty girl with short hair. I did not fall in love with her straight away, but I must have made an impression. Before we parted, she invited me to her home for the coming weekend.

After that, we met ever more frequently, although often only by chance, because Gerda could not be reached by telephone. Frequently, I would spend the whole afternoon with her parents because Gerda had gone out with a friend. I would make myself useful then. My later father-in-law was unable to move one of his thumbs properly, after an industrial accident. He was very happy for me to take an interest in his garden, and quickly took me to his heart, although not just for that alone. He stood well to the left politically: all his life he had fought for the rights of the labouring classes, and he had been a member of the USPD[10] in the First World War. His wife had joined the SPD (German Socialist Party) in 1916.

10 In 1917, former SPD members who during the First World War had voted against approving war credits formed the USPD (German Independent Social

Gerda's parents' house was located in a typical working-class district of Berlin. Nearly all its inhabitants were factory workers – many large organisations, such as the Henschel aircraft works and AEG, having settled in the neighbourhood. One might think that an SS man was not quite what these families would have had in mind for their daughter. My later father-in-law understood, however, that my path was nothing but a soldier's destiny. I was not in the Party, and he knew how I had come into the *SS-Leibstandarte*, and later to Hitler. Hitler and the Nazis never came between us. I was a soldier – that explained everything, even for my future father-in-law.

Gerda's father often took me to see 'Uncle' Paul, a so-called uncle, and a very good friend of the family. He was also a convinced Social Democrat and active trade unionist – as long as it was not dangerous but occasionally beyond. He got into trouble with the regime later, and I was able to help him.

Gerda and I used the formal 'Sie' (you) to address each other for two years. When my colleagues hinted at a 'fried potato relationship,'* I corrected them, 'tomato relationship' – Gerda's mother made an outstanding tomato salad. It was very unusual, but my relationship with Gerda developed basically in the shadow of the ever-closer relationship between myself and her parents. I was an orphan, Herr and Frau Lachmund were less the parents of my bride than my substitute parents.

I knew nothing of Reichskristallnacht, on 9 November 1938. It may be that we were confined to barracks to keep us from asking

---

Democratic Party). In 1920, most of the USPD joined up with the KPD (Communist Party). In 1922, the rump of the USPD rejoined the SPD, although a few USPD remnants led the USPD as a splinter party until 1931. In the framework of *Gleichschaltung* ('the streamlining of Parties') the SPD was outlawed on 22 June 1933.

* That is, the relationship was little more than a meal ticket.

questions.[11] Hitler's valet at that time, Karl Krause,[12] told me much later that Hitler was beside himself with rage about the events of that night. 'What have you set in motion again!' he shouted and would not be calmed by being informed that Goebbels had approved it.[13] He then drove with Krause to a burning Munich synagogue in order to see it for himself from a distance. After that he was taken home and went into his room in a rage. In a daze, Krause shrank back. Hitler then opened the door a crack and told Krause tersely when he wished to be woken the following day.

I remember the two years before the outbreak of war as very fine ones. The invasion of Czechoslovakia in March 1939 and the occupation of the Sudetenland six months earlier did not involve war-like confrontations for us. We crossed the mountains to arrive in the Slovak part of Czechoslovakia, as far as Zilina. It had snowed and was very cold in the mountains. When the sun came out, the snow was so blinding that we could hardly see. Our company commander, Wilhelm Mohnke, distributed zinc salve: 'Here, everybody smear this over your noses, otherwise you'll get terrible sunburn.' I did as I was told, my nose as white as the snow from the paste. At Zilina we were given a friendly reception by the inhabitants.[14] We were allocated

---

11   On Himmler's orders the SS were told officially to stay clear of events. (Ian Kershaw, *Hitler 1936–1945*, Stuttgart 2000, p.197). The commander of the 5th Company of the *SS-Leibstandarte*, Wilhelm Mohnke, was quoted as saying that a curfew had been imposed on the Berlin-Lichterfelde location as from the afternoon of 8 November 1938. Thomas Fischer, *Die Verteidigung der Reichskanzlei*, Zweibrücken 2007, p.68.

12   Karl Wilhelm Krause (1911–?) was Hitler's valet from 1934 until 10 September 1939.

13   The pogrom began before 9 November 1938. It was stirred up by the Reich Propaganda Ministry and partly directed from there; Hitler held back from it at least outwardly but was kept informed on the course of the action by Goebbels (Ian Kershaw, *Hitler 1936–1945*, Stuttgart 2000, pp.194ff.)

14   Company commander Wilhelm Mohnke was quoted as saying: 'The troops were welcomed with jubilation by the inhabitants of German stock, the Slovaks were friendly, but the Czechs very reserved.' Thomas Fischer, *Die Verteidigung der Reichskanzlei*, Zweibrücken 2007, p.73.

quarters with civilians, and, on departure, a local family even gave me a fine knitted jacket with expensive embroidery for my girlfriend. Gerda wore it often for a long time. I remember being very impressed on a visit to a rolling mill at Vitkovice. I had never seen how steel was formed before.

In the summer of 1939 we came to Berchtesgaden for six weeks and stayed in the barracks at the Berghof. Hitler had a kind of summer retreat there. We were divided up into Führer protection squads on the Obersalzberg, had patrol duties and received further military instruction. I still had no idea under what circumstances I should soon return to this imposing and idyllic mountain world.

Chapter 3

The Outbreak of War: 1939

B Y THE END OF August 1939 I had been promoted to
SS-Rottenführer* and now we were moved by train once more
to an unknown destination. We passed through Silesia to the
Polish border. To the very last moment all of us expected this to be an
exercise. Thus the Polish campaign began for us without the least hint.
My company was attached to a Wehrmacht unit.[1] I never experienced
heavy fighting in all my service. The fighting in Poland was for the
most part widely disposed in favour of ourselves – major encounters
being handled by the Wehrmacht units.

Nothing led us to suspect that this Polish campaign would bring
in its train something that had no similarity to 'flowers, flowers
everywhere'. We did not see in it the seeds of a world war, and considered
the intervention as inconsequential – as had been the annexation of
Austria or the invasion of Czechoslovakia. But we were wrong.

During the advance on Warsaw we came to a fruit farm. Boxer
Adolf Kleinholdermann was No. 4 gunner, I was ammunition carrier

---

1 The SS infantry regiment *SS-Leibstandarte* was attached to XIII Army Corps
(commander Maximilian von Weichs), part of Eighth Army (Johannes Blaskowitz)
making up Army Group South (Field Marshal Gerd von Rundstedt).

* The rank of SS-Rottenführer carried the authority equivalent to a British lance-
corporal but was not of NCO status. Misch was promoted to Unterscharführer (full
corporal) in early May 1940. (TN)

and No. 3 gunner of a four-man machine-gun squad. Suddenly we came under fire. The Poles were in the trees, and all at once let loose. Kleinholdermann and I were unharmed, but our comrade Kolditz, who came from Lake Constance, was shot in the head and fell to the ground. Everything happened so quickly that what occurred immediately after the exchange of fire has been erased from my memory. I have no idea if Kolditz died at once or not. It was like a car crash – everything up to the moment of impact is remembered precisely but what follows is a blur. In any case, I realised that it was not necessary for there to be a great battle for one to die in war. It can simply happen in the blink of an eye in a beautiful fruit farm. A little later, I escaped the same fate by a hair's breadth – no, by two centimetres.

Close to Warsaw, towards the end of the campaign, on 24 September 1939 with three of my colleagues I was selected by my company commander, Hauptsturmführer Mohnke,[2] to parley the surrender of the Modlin fortress.[3] My later destiny would be linked to Mohnke. Mohnke had assumed that as a Silesian I would be able to speak a few phrases of Polish. I told him that my knowledge extended to pidgin-Polish, which consisted of trying to make German words sound like Polish. Mohnke was not impressed, but I remained selected.

Together with my platoon leader Lindner and two other men I set off. Unarmed and with a white flag unfurled, we made our way over infantry trenches towards the old fort and got to the bunker of the Polish position. No negotiations were possible, because the Poles said they had no negotiator, and their soldiers refused to be encumbered with making the decision to surrender. It seemed to us that this was a

---

2 Wilhelm Mohnke (1911–2001) received the Iron Cross I and II Class for his service in the Polish campaign.

3 The Modlin fortress (about fifty kilometres northwest of Warsaw) was one of the most important Polish defensive positions before Warsaw. The 'Modlin Army' was supposed to prevent the German attackers reaching the capital, but on 13 September a part of the army was trapped inside by an encirclement. Sixteen days later, on 29 September, the fortress surrendered after a Luftwaffe attack. Janus Piekalkiewicz: *Polenfeldzug*, Herrsching 1989 (first edn Bergisch Gladbach 1982), p.224.

delaying tactic, and, after spending a few hours making a circuit, our platoon commander decided to return empty-handed.

On the way back we struggled through barriers and wire entanglements and were about eighty metres from the fort when the Poles opened fire on us. We were unarmed, and they opened fire with everything they had. I felt a dull hard blow in the back, which I can still feel today when I think about it. Hit by several rounds I collapsed. The first round had gone through my back and tore through my body to within two centimetres of my heart. A straight shot went through one lung. Two centimetres from death. A second round lodged in my arm. My comrade was also wounded in the arm. I felt the blood rise to my mouth, pour out from my lips and run down my neck. I was gripped by mortal anguish. At some point I lost consciousness. My comrades carried me to the main dressing station. There and later in the hospital at Lodz, I received several blood transfusions. As all Waffen-SS men I had my blood group tattooed under the upper arm. The second bullet had hit me there. They could still make out the type 'B'. When I regained consciousness, I cannot remember what was running through my head.*

After several weeks in the field hospital I was transferred to a hospital at Bad Berka near Weimar, and after that I spent six weeks at a convalescent home in the Alps. One has to admit that the first people to be wounded in that war were really well looked after. There were not very many of us, and we received the full attention of the doctors and other staff.

Soon Gerda visited me. Both of us now felt that there was more between us than our 'tomato relationship'. It was here in the hospital camp at Bayrischzell that we kissed for the first time.

It soon struck me that prisoners were working in the spa clinic. Opposite the clinic was a barrack camp guarded by soldiers. From our

---

* Rochus Misch was awarded the Iron Cross Second Class (EKII) for an act of bravery near Modlin Fort on 24 September 1939. He was probably the first *SS-Leibstandarte* man to be decorated in the Second World War. Apparently modesty forbade that he mention the circumstances of the award. (TN)

terrace we watched these prisoners fall in, morning and night, for roll call. One day, one of these men was cleaning the radiator in my room, and I asked him about the barracks. He told me that it was an outlying annexe of Dachau concentration camp with two hundred inmates. He was a 'bible student', people known today as Jehovah's Witnesses. In reply to my question why he was in a concentration camp, he replied that he was being detained there until such time as he signed a document distancing himself from the community that shared his beliefs. If he signed he could go home, but he would not do so.[4] It was the first time that I knew anything about concentration camps which was not hearsay.

Back at Lichterfelde barracks I was assigned to the Convalescent company. Apart from a few circuits of the terrain there was nothing to do. I re-met Mohnke among the convalescents, having last seen him during the skirmish at Modlin. He had also been wounded and enquired where I wanted to go next. I had no idea what he was getting at and merely shrugged my shoulders. Apparently, I was likely to be sent into supply, possibly as a kitchen hand in the rearward area of the front. Having little enthusiasm for a return to the fighting front, I did not like the sound of that much either. If Mohnke wanted to protect me from the fighting I cannot say. He knew I was an orphan, and he

---

4   In 1936, the Gestapo formed a special squad to root out Jehovah's Witnesses (whose organisation in Germany had been disbanded in 1933) and enforce the prohibition of the spreading of their religious texts. Because Jehovah's Witnesses appeared 'totally ideal' to the SS leadership (as Himmler expressed it in a letter in 1944 to the head of the RSHA, Kaltenbrunner), and they were, in pursuance of their convictions, 'industrious, tolerant, honest and not burdensome', a major effort was being made to turn them away from their beliefs. Imprisoned Jehovah's Witnesses seldom attempted to escape, which was why they were often sent out to work in areas where it was difficult to guard prisoners effectively. The document mentioned by Misch may have been the so-called Verpflichtungsereklärung (Declaration of Obligation), in which believers recanted their religious belief and acknowledged loyalty to the state in order to avoid being placed in protective custody. Alternatively, it may have been the Wehrpass (service record book), which many believers refused to sign as conscientious objectors. Stanislav Zamecnik, *Das war Dachau*, Frankfurt/ Main 2007 (first edn, Luxemburg 2002) pp.227f.

probably considered a task with a 'family connection' to be the right thing for me.

Meanwhile, battalion commander 'Teddy' Wisch[5] was looking for somebody to help out on his brother's farm. The brother had just been called up, and his wife, pregnant with their fourth child, needed land workers urgently. The farmstead was at Dithmarschen in Schleswig–Holstein, near the then Adolf-Hitler-Koog.[6] Therefore in the spring of 1940 I spent about four weeks on a farm working shoulder to shoulder with a Polish POW and a girl. There was much to be done, and I did my share everywhere, to a certain extent I was a jack of all trades. There really was nothing I did not put my hand to. One night I took the farmer's wife, who was in labour, to the hospital and also dug trenches against low-level British fighter attacks.

It was here that I experienced the first British bombing raids. Cuxhaven opposite the Koog was an important naval base. One could see flames flickering in the distance while RAF fighters howled overhead. They fired on farms deliberately, leaving two of them burning at Wesselburen. So I stayed in my slit trench alongside a Pole! I wrote to my Aunt Sofia in Berlin: 'Aunt, we are in the thick of it here. I came to convalesce, but now I'm back in the war!' National Socialist propaganda ensured that the German civilian population heard little about it. Nobody was to become alarmed.[7]

---

5 Theodor 'Teddy' Wisch (1907–1995) was a brigadier and led 1st Company, SS-Leibstandarte from October 1933. From December 1939 he took command of the new 4th (Watch) Battalion.

6 Koog was reclaimed from the North Sea in 1935 to become a model terrain within the framework of the National Socialist policy of 'Blood and Soil'. Until 1945, it was settled only by SS officers. After the war Adolf-Hitler-Koog was renamed Dieksander-Koog. Theodor Wisch came from the area, being a native of nearby Wesselburenerkoog.

7 Early RAF attacks and individual bombing raids were intended primarily for military targets such as the shipyards of North Germany, shipping convoys in the English Channel and airfields on the North Sea islands but some attacks did occur against Cuxhaven, Wilhelmshaven, the naval air base at Hörnum on Sylt island and the naval town of Kiel.

Chapter 4

Hitler Needs a Courier

ABOUT TWO WEEKS AFTER my return to the Berlin-Lichterfelde barrack, while I was still assigned to the Reserve company, a young man was being sought for the personal bodyguard of the Führer. This involved being a telephonist, courier and bodyguard for Hitler, personally. His chief adjutant Wilhelm Brückner[1] had let battalion commander Teddy Wisch know that an absolutely reliable man was being sought – a person who would give no trouble. It was urgent.

Wisch passed the requirement to company commander Mohnke, who had suggested me. I had returned seriously wounded from the front and was moreover the last surviving son of my family. It had been ordered by the Wehrmacht High Command that the last surviving son of a German family had to be spared for the future and not sent to the front. He, Mohnke, was to assess my devotion to duty.

Wisch recalled having heard only good things from his sister-in-law on the Schleswig–Holstein farmstead and so accepted Mohnke's recommendation. I had to present myself at once to Wisch, who then informed the Reich Chancellery that a suitable young man had been found. I was therefore appointed, and in less time than it takes to tell I was seated alongside Mohnke in his car heading for the Führer-

---

1 Wilhelm Brückner (1884–1954) was Hitler's chief adjutant until the end of 1940.

apartments at the Reich Chancellery, Wilhelm-Strasse 77. This was on 2 or 3 May 1940.*

On arrival at the Reich Chancellery, Mohnke spoke briefly to a guard at the entrance and then left me to my destiny. The guard accompanied me to the upper floor, directly into Brückner's office. He had been Hitler's regimental commander in the First World War. My heart pounded – before me stood Hitler's chief adjutant. Brückner looked me up and down. He got straight to the point. It was his intention, he explained tersely, to employ me as a messenger, distributing despatches and newspapers in the adjutants' wing. Now I should return to my barracks to fetch my personal belongings.

An hour and a half later I stood once more in the Reich Chancellery hall, grasping my suitcase. A different guard from the first one indicated that I should follow him. He showed me into my service room on the upper floor of the adjutants' wing, then left me alone. Cautiously, as if I might damage something, I put down my suitcase and looked around. The room was simply furnished: two beds, a military locker, a hand basin.

Me, here? In the Reich Chancellery? In the Führer-apartments? Why me? I was not even a Party member! I could not think clearly, saw before my mental gaze the cheering crowds in the Olympic stadium and Hitler driving past me with his arm outstretched.

I went out into the corridor and met two middle-aged men of the Watch. Both showed me round. I was desperate to know the various offices, but it would be some time before I really knew my way around. The most important thing, the two elder colleagues advised, was to become familiar with the rules of behaviour to be observed here in the Reich Holy of Holies. The most important of all was: 'If you run across the Führer, stand aside and do nothing! Either he will speak to you of his own accord, or equally he will not.' To my many questions, their response always was: 'Stay close to your comrades! Watch closely what they do; it will become clear.'

Next day my work began.

---

* See footnote on p.4.

In the SS Bodyguard

There were about twenty of us and we worked three shifts around the clock: from six to two; two to ten; and ten to six (the night shift). Each shift had one senior and three men on detached duty, a messenger and two men on watch duties. In order to raise alertness, the watch, telephone, courier and messenger duties were alternated.

One of us would sit on sentry duty at a small table downstairs, at the kitchen entrance to the Old Chancellery. From there, a stairway led directly up to Hitler's suite, twenty-two steps in all. It was guarded by just one man. In my first days, the sparse security precautions struck me. Before going on duty, I had a long walk through the New and Old Chancelleries, from which it was easy to notice that the security watch on the head of state was not especially thorough.

I was living in Gerda's parents' house, sleeping in a tiny room, and continued to do so until Gerda and I were married. Every morning, unless I had been on night shift, I went from Rudow by tram to the Potsdamerplatz, then through the Wertheim department store on Leipzigerplatz, leaving by the deliveries door on Voss-Strasse. The nearest entry into the complex of buildings was at Voss-Strasse 6, the entrance into the president's Chancellery headed by Otto Meissner.[2] In the reception foyer there would be somebody seated in a glass box, but he had only the usual information function. One did not have to report to him or explain oneself. From there one proceeded through the interior to the New Reich Chancellery. I walked along endless corridors until I reached the adjutants' wing in the Old Reich Chancellery. On leaving the Great Reception Hall behind me, I crossed the 150-metre-long Marble Gallery, with long strides. Leading off from it was Hitler's study, which incidentally he never used as such; it was only occupied as a reception room. Then one reached the two floors of offices occupied by assistants to Hans Heinrich Lammers, Hitler's head of the Reich

---

2 Otto Meissner (1880–1953) was from 1919 to 1945 head of the Berlin presidential office.

Chancellery throughout all his time in government. On again through the Dome and Mosaic Hall to the dining room, and the steps leading down into the Old Reich Chancellery. In contrast to the New Reich Chancellery, the ground floor was level with the ground outside. The Führer's Chancellery[3] was in the building between the Old and New Chancellery, the area being called Borsig Palace.[4] I cannot recall having met a security man once on the whole walk. There was simply nobody about. The Reich security service SD used to stroll round to make sure everything was as it should be, but no more than that.

My room in the Old Reich Chancellery had a view of Wilhelm-Strasse and was situated in the adjutants' wing, not more than twelve or fifteen metres from Hitler's private rooms. Nearby was a room for laundry; the toilet and shower were along the corridor. Dwellings had been built on the garden side of the New Reich Chancellery for those employed in the Reich Chancellery, but when I joined the bodyguard they were all taken.

In the five years that I was with Hitler I got to know five of his servants: Hermann Bussmann,[5] Willy Arndt, Hans Junge, Fehrs Linge and Heinz Linge. Karl Krause, Hitler's first servant, already had another function when I came to the bodyguard. Hitler did not have his own valet from the outset – the job was initially rotated between members of the bodyguard. It became obvious that it had to be somebody's sole responsibility, so that 'the boss' always had the right clothes to hand. A valet was employed. At first, this was the naval rating Krause, who

---

3 The Kanzlei des Führers der NSDAP was his private Chancellery to which mainly private petitions, requests and enquiries would be made. From 1939, the front organisations of the euthanasia programme were subordinated to the Kanzlei des Führers.

4 Named after the industrialist Johann August Friedrich Borsig (1804–1854), who had a house built for himself here at Voss-Strasse 1. Albert Speer blended the 'palace' into the structure of the New Reich Chancellery.

5 According to Heinz Linge, the servant and bodyguard member was Eugen Bussmann. See Linge, *With Hitler to the End*, London 2009, p. 20 n.

took up his duties having watched training films at the Servant School, Munich-Pasing.

Krause was a really droll type. I believed him immediately when he recounted liberties that he had taken with Hitler pre-war. He said that once he planted himself before him, and in a tone of voice that brooked no contradiction stated: 'Mein Führer, today you have to wear the black shoes, I have forgotten the brown ones.' When on another occasion Hitler did not really want to accept an invitation to the opera, he asked Krause what he should wear. The servant suggested he should toss for it. Hitler lost. Krause fetched the dress uniform and 'the boss' resigned himself to wearing it without a word.

This composure disappeared when the war broke out. During the Polish campaign Krause fell out of favour when he gave Hitler spring water instead of the Fachingen cure water he always took, and lied when asked about it. Martin Bormann[6] insisted on consequences, stating that Krause was unreliable, was not to be tolerated in Hitler's immediate entourage and that Hitler could have got sick drinking spring water. Krause swore to the effect that everybody without exception had drunk the spring water and additionally he had asked the doctor if it would be all right to give it to Hitler. Somebody even suggested he had wanted to poison the Führer; this was downright nonsense. Krause often complained that he attracted undeserved criticism, and that day during the Polish campaign when Hitler had received a bad report[7] was a prime opportunity for him to feel Hitler's wrath.

Krause was transferred to working in the Reich Chancellery kitchens, but returned to the Kriegsmarine at his own request. Some time later he was back, after Hitler enquired of Krause's wife, who had continued to be employed at the Reich Chancellery, where her husband

---

6 Martin Bormann (1900–1945) was from 1933 chief of staff to Rudolf Hess; from 11 May 1941 head of the Party chancellery; and from 12 April 1943 Hitler's secretary.

7 In all probability this was the report of high casualties among the *SS-Leibstandarte*.

was at present. She told him that he was in a military hospital after the destroyer on which he had been serving had been sunk. This was the third sinking that had happened to Krause. On hearing it, Hitler recalled him to his personal staff, though he never again served as his valet. Krause enjoyed relating how, in their first conversation after his return, the Führer had said to him: 'Krause, I had to take you out of it, every one of the ships on which you were serving has been sunk. Better you are here than that you sink my whole fleet all by yourself.'

The temperament of the former valet soon did for him again, however. One day in our restroom he was boasting about his shooting prowess, and his colleagues – I was not there – scoffed at him until he jumped up and shot the hanging lamps with his service pistol. That was the end of his service with Hitler. Later, we heard that Krause had been enormously successful in the SS flak section of his division and finished the war highly decorated. So he was probably not such a bad shot after all.

I was also quite good at shooting, as my placing at the 1936 rifle festival confirmed. Once I had to provide my comrade Max Wünsche[8] with shooting instruction at the cadet establishment. The most important thing is a steady hand. I got Max to keep lifting a bucket filled with sand and then pick up the weapon. This gives you the feeling that the weapon is light as a feather, and one can control it easily.

In the early days at the Reich Chancellery, my main job involved messenger duties inside the building complex. My rounds took me mostly to Hans Heinrich Lammers, Otto Meissner, Walther Hewel, the liaison officer to the Foreign Ministry headed by Joachim von Ribbentrop, and to Otto Dietrich, Reich press chief, for whom Heinz Lorenz and Helmut Sündermann worked. Since the outbreak of war, the traffic in paper between all these important functionaries had significantly increased; this was also one of the reasons for my employment there.

---

8 Max Wünsche (1915–1995) served with the bodyguard from 1 October 1938 to December 1940 with one short break.

But what if I unexpectedly ran across Hitler – 'the boss' as he was always called. I kept wondering. I could not imagine it happening, but I was sure I would do something wrong at that moment – and the idea panicked me. Let anything happen, but don't run across the Führer. However, I now lived in his immediate vicinity.

My new colleague Hauptscharführer Erich Kraut shared my fear and advised me to avoid the lobby. The way through the courtyard and the personnel entrance was 'safe'. I accepted his advice gratefully and made every detour necessary to escape a meeting. I could see that this was ultimately inevitable, but I convinced myself that I had to work my way into the new environment a little before I would feel ready for the inevitable encounter. In reality, I would not have had the courage to plan a chance meeting even then, but when it came, luckily, it was totally unexpected.

'The Boss'

Around a week after I began my service – it must have been 8 or 9 May 1940[9] – my meeting with Hitler finally came about. It occurred in connection with a friendly talk I had with Chief Adjutant Brückner. In his office we discussed my comrades-in-arms and the decorations I had received during the Polish campaign – the Iron Cross Second Class and the Wound Badge, and the fact that I had also been promoted to NCO as an Unterscharführer.* He also mentioned my turnout. I should change my footwear as soon as possible. 'The boss does not like to see them' – by this he meant the deep impressions on the thick carpet made by heavy military boots. We went together to the door, which I, a well-drilled soldier, opened smartly to allow Brückner to pass ahead. He made no move. I followed his stare in surprise. In the doorway, holding a letter in his hand, stood Hitler.

9   Hitler left Berlin on the evening of 9 May 1940 to travel to his temporary headquarters code-named Felsennest, near Bad Münstereifel in the Rhineland, from where he oversaw the Western Offensive, which began on 10 May.

*   Unterscharführer = Unteroffizier (corporal), the basic NCO rank. (TN)

While Brückner was introducing me as a new man, Hitler glanced at me briefly but seemed not to be interested in what Brückner was telling him about me. Apparently, he had heard the last part of our conversation near the door. I went hot and cold. Hitler turned to his chief adjutant: 'Where does the young man come from?'

'Silesia, I think,' Brückner answered.

Hitler looked at me: 'Is that so?'

I replied: '*Jawohl*' – forgetting to add '*Mein Führer*' – 'from Upper Silesia, near Oppeln.'

Turning to Brückner again, Hitler asked: 'Do we have any more people from Silesia among us?'

'I do not believe so,' Brückner said.

'Well, the young man can do something for me,' Hitler went on. Handing me a letter he said: 'Take that to my sister in Vienna.' With that, he turned and went out.

A heavy weight dropped from my heart. Now I had it behind me. He was for me, as for most of the German people, 'the Führer'. I do not know what I had been expecting, but it had all been quite mundane, no trace of anything extraordinary. I had seen neither a monster nor a superman. This first impression was confirmed over the years. The private individual Hitler was a normal, simple man, the simplest man I ever knew. Only outside did he slip into his Führer role; only then did everything have to go according to protocol – the stage settings perfect. Privately however, and we of the *SS-Begleitkommando* (bodyguard) belonged to his private life, he was uncomplicated. Larger than life and dominating, that was the statesman and everybody who surrounded him in this function. In himself, as a private person, Hitler was extremely unpretentious. After this first meeting I felt relieved. Now ten Hitlers could come; my fears had gone.

House administrator Arthur Kannenberg gave me a package to go with the letter I had been handed. There were some sweets or coffee in it. After receiving a provisional identification paper with Hitler's signature, I took the night train for Vienna, travelling in the separate couriers' compartment. On arrival, I went to the fourth floor of a block of flats and pressed a door bell with no name tag.

Paula Hitler[10] was expecting me. She was pleasant and considerate, gave me tea and biscuits. I thought she looked like Hitler – she had the same facial structure. While nervously sipping my tea, she asked after her brother. She wanted to learn something about him – from me, his courier. Proudly and little self-consciously I told her that I had only been a short time in his service, and was therefore unable to tell her much. Nevertheless, I spent a good half hour with her. I only saw her on one other occasion, at the Berghof, when she visited her brother.

I also got to know Hitler's half-brother Alois.[11] He was the landlord of the inn Zum Alois on Berlin's Wittenbergplatz. This was not far from the Kaufhaus des Westens (KaDeWe) department store, which had opened in 1907. The inn suited Alois, or Alois suited the inn. In keeping with his peasant background, he had had the place done up in rustic style; it was all very cosy. I only ever went there twice, bringing some envelopes at the behest of Albert Bormann,[12] which I assumed contained cheques. Then I would stay for a beer. Today, there is still an inn on the site – the taproom and the bar on the back wall are the same as they were.

In Dresden, I occasionally visited Angela Hammitzsch, Hitler's half-sister, whom everybody continued to call Frau Raubal although she had remarried. Each time she would give me fruit tarts for her brother, which I would deliver to house administrator Kannenberg.

After fulfilling my mission at Paula Hitler's I was expected to spend the night in Vienna. At the imposing Hotel Imperial[13] three rooms

---

10 Paula Hitler (1896–1960) was Hitler's only (full) sister.

11 Alois Hitler (1882–1956) was Hitler's half-brother by their father.

12 Albert Bormann (1902–1989) was head of Adolf Hitler's private Chancellery, and brother of Martin Bormann.

13 On 15 March 1938, after the annexation of Austria, Hitler stayed at the Hotel Imperial and went from there to the Heldenplatz. From there, he announced to a quarter of a million people: 'the entry of my Homeland into the German Reich'. On 11 September 1945, the Allied Control Council founded by the Allies for Austria

were constantly reserved for state visitors and anyone attached to the Reich Chancellery. The hotel was much too grand for me, and I lacked the confidence to go in.

Before I left for Vienna, Brückner had indicated that I could attach three days' leave at my grandmother's to my courier trip, so I decided to go straight to the railway station and take the next train for Breslau. 'It's not far from there to your home province,' Brückner had told me. As a soldier, I was completely unaccustomed to this laxity. From my training all I knew was a strict organisation, clear instructions and orders. Total obedience was the supreme duty, and independent thinking, even one's own decision-making, did not exist. Thinking, we were informed, was best left to horses, because they had bigger heads. It seemed that it was time for me to forget the barracks. Things here were different.

So I spent three days with my grandmother at Oppeln. She lived alone – my grandfather having died in 1936. After my return to Berlin, I found out in a roundabout way why I had been able to have this short holiday; Hitler was not in Berlin. Immediately after I met him, he had left for the Western Front,[14] where he would remain for two months.[15] During this period of the French campaign, another Blitzkrieg, I had the quietest period of my service.

Wilhelm-Strasse 77

One of Hitler's servants,[16] I cannot remember whether it was Bussmann or Hans Junge, used the absence of 'the boss' to show me the Führer-suite. What I eventually saw, after leaving the adjutants' wing and

and chaired by Soviet Marshal Ivan Konyev met at the Hotel Imperial.

14 The Wehrmacht invaded the Netherlands, Belgium and Luxembourg for the attack on the enemy France on 10 May 1940.

15 Hitler did not return until after Paris fell. He arrived there on 23 June 1940, the day after signing the armistice at Compiègne,

16 According to Heinz Linge, Bussmann was not a servant of Hitler and Linge's deputy until 1942: prior to that it had been Hans Junge. Heinz Linge, *With Hitler to the End,* London 2009, p.20.

going through the lobby, was something quite different from what one would have expected of a man in Hitler's position. I was disappointed by the dimensions of the suite. The four rooms and bathroom covered no more than a hundred square metres.

The private tour began in the living room, with its small library. I was impressed by the unbelievably comprehensive *Meyers Lexikon*, with its gigantic volumes. From there, one went to the study and, on the other side, to the bedroom, which was somewhat smaller. It had a brass bedstead and above it, exactly central, hung a picture of Hitler's mother. Left near the bed was a dumb waiter; there was additionally a round table with two cocktail chairs, a clothes cupboard and shoe cupboard – the whole room measured no more than five by six metres. Off the bedroom was a narrow, green-ceramic bath. It was all very simply furnished, almost spartan. The walls were painted an eggshell colour. When I saw the suite during Hitler's absence in May 1940, there were no private things around. All I noticed was all kinds of sketching material with ruled lines and numerous crayons, and an extensive Wagner score. It was Hitler's birthday the month before and a great pile of official presents awaited a decision on what should be done with them.

The guest room seemed smaller to me than the bedroom. This was where Eva Braun lived when she stayed in Berlin. I did not know her then, and at that point there had been no talk about her. There was a small stool in the guest room just before the corridor to the bedroom, on which we would leave the despatches at night. The bedroom windows faced onto the gardens.

If Hitler had a private guest, his half-sister for example, he would receive them in the so-called Stairs Room, which had four chairs and a round table. It was a little forward of the suite proper and was so called because two stairways led down from it. One led into the domestic offices, and the other to the adjutants' wing. The offices of Dietrich, Hewel and Lorenz were located on the same floor as Hitler's private rooms. Hitler had access directly from his study to the large conference room – the military officials entering it from the Wehrmacht wing on the other side.

The Old Campaigners

My anxiety at running across Hitler had evaporated. Soon I would be seeing him several times a day. During his two-month absence in the early summer of 1940 I had time to find my feet in peace.

One of the first things I did led me to Hitler's personal tailor in Tauentzien-Strasse. Here I got myself a new bespoke uniform not much different in form from the old one but of better material, closer to an officer's version. From a fine supplier on Friedrich-Strasse I changed my soldier's boots so unloved by Hitler for more carpet-friendly ones.

After a while, I had my first conversations with Hitler's servants and adjutants. The Alte Kämpfer (Old Campaigners) were those men who before Hitler's seizure of power, in the so-called period of struggle, had been in his service or were close supporters. They made it easy for me to find my way around. Adi Dirr,[17] Hitler's long-serving companion, initiated me into internal idiosyncrasies such as the widespread use of the word 'Wolf'. I learnt that the prefix or suffix in the names of the various Führer-HQs Wolfschanze, Wolfsschlucht, FHQ Fehrwolf – there were not many in which Wolf did not appear somewhere – went back to earlier election tours. Either the hotel in which Hitler lodged advertised his presence, and the local people would besiege it, or the reply would be, when attempting to reserve rooms, unfortunately we do not have a room vacant for Herr Hitler. Therefore, whether a hotel was well-disposed towards the Nazis or not, it was better to book under another name, and Hitler ordered that in future all rooms were to be reserved under the pseudonym Wolf.

Some people thought that the origin of its usage had something to do with one of his secretaries, Johanna Wolf, but the name was already

---

17   Adolf Dirr (1907–?) was one of the first eight members of the *SS-Begleitkommando des Führers* founded on 29 February 1932. See Peter Hoffmann, *Die Sicherheit des Diktators*, Munich/Zürich 1975, pp.64f.

in use before she joined Hitler's staff. It was probably the case, too, that Hitler's forename had a connection to the word Wolf. Whatever the reason, Hitler liked it. His sister Paula also used the surname Wolf on her brother's instructions.

The Old Campaigners in the bodyguard, Party members from the beginning, enjoyed relating their experiences about the early period of the Movement to interested newcomers. They were identified by a low Party membership number, and nearly all of them were of no great military rank: 'narrow-gauge soldiers', one might say. An exception was Max Amann:[18] he had fought alongside Hitler in the First World War. Amann had been present at the 1923 putsch[19] and had shared imprisonment with Hitler. On our first meeting, he reminisced about the old times with great pleasure, including when he piddled against a tree with Hitler.

I recall the story of the Kaiserhof. The hotel lay diagonally across from the Reich Chancellery, and Hitler had lived there temporarily while electioneering.[20] Later, he liked to go over there in the afternoon for tea. He had been told that a small band played there and that he should hear the bandsmen. After he had made a regular thing of this in the afternoons at the Kaiserhof, he had said in surprise: 'Those are the same ladies every day sitting opposite me.' It turned out that the waiters had been able to start a thriving business, thanks to their celebrated

18   Max Amann (1891–1957) was Hitler's sergeant in the First World War, later owner of the NSDAP publishing house Franz-Eher-Verlag.

19   The Munich Putsch, or Hitler-Ludendorff-Putsch, was an attempt by Hitler, Erich Ludendorff and other National Socialists to move the Bavarian state government to overthrow the Reich government. The putsch came to grief, thirteen National Socialists and one passer-by being killed. Hitler, who took flight in panic when the shooting began, was sentenced by the Munich People's Court to a minimum of five years for high treason, but on 20 December 1924 he was released from Landsberg after only eight months.

20   In the 1920s, the owners of the Kaiserhof sympathised with the Nationalist Right. The upper floor of the hotel was used temporarily as the provisional NSDAP Party HQ. Hitler was staying there on the day of his swearing-in as Reich chancellor on 30 January 1933.

guest. As soon as Hitler left, they sold the tableware, knife, fork and spoon he had used. Probably they bribed the staff to reserve the same places for them every day. When Hitler found out, he ordered that the waiters should not be punished, but from then on he abandoned these visits.

The Old Campaigners at the Reich Chancellery were anything but soldierly – the place being more like a public authority. Inside the building, one never saluted with outstretched arm if one came across a superior. After all the military drill, such social behaviour was difficult to get used to. Rituals of address were used only to Hitler. We juniors addressed him as '*Mein Führer*', the Old Campaigners said 'Boss' or merely 'Herr Hitler'. Among the household staff, he was 'the boss' for everyone; nobody used the word 'Führer'. In the street when opening the car door, the Hitler salute was obligatory. As he got out we had to offer him a helping hand, but he never accepted it. He never returned a salute when one met him in the morning, not even a nod or anything similar. I was told however that I should not think that he did not notice me. He always knew by sight and by name everybody who worked in the Reich Chancellery. He was renowned for his first-class memory; he never forgot a name. I discovered later that this was true.

I was quickly accepted into the group of close colleagues around Hitler. We were soon a sworn circle. Besides Dirr, who I have already mentioned, were also Otto Hansen, Helmuth Beermann, Karl Weichelt, Hermann Bornholdt and Paul Holtz, as well as Schlotmann and Rüss, whose forenames I no longer recall.

Otto Hansen was a fatherly type, one of the Old Campaigners, and deputy chief of the bodyguards at the Berghof. I got on very well with him. We juniors always addressed the Old Campaigners as 'Sie', the formal form of 'you', but among ourselves, at least of the same rank, we quickly used the informal and familiar 'Du'. Hermann Bornholdt had also belonged for ages to Hitler's personal bodyguard. He, Schlotmann and Rüss were fanatical Nazis. Schlotmann was a very calm, matter-of-fact type, while Rüss was a really nice guy who gratefully accepted the apples I gave him from my Aunt Sofia. We called Helmuth Beermann, our mail and courier service senior, the 'Supplier'; he got through to everybody. Karl Tenazek, who joined the bodyguard after me, was another loner like myself. We did not need to exchange many words, as we understood each other from the start. Karl Weichelt belonged neither among the Old Campaigners nor us youngsters. He was the only one of us who belonged to neither group, but was one of the few Party Gold Badge holders – 'narrow-gauge soldiers' – who could teach the others something about soldiering.

My position at the Reich Chancellery attracted an increase of fifty Reichsmarks, the so-called 'Führer-supplement', making my total pay 337 Reichsmarks. The Reich Chancellery also paid one's rent and telephone bill, and a free pass for the Reichsbahn railway network was another useful financial perk. The Reich Chancellery and the Ministry of the Interior were jointly responsible for the bodyguards' salary. We therefore had a hybrid status between military and civilian service.

Everyday Life in the Reich Chancellery

Hitler returned to Berlin at the beginning of July 1940, from France. At just about the time he arrived at the Anhalter station, I was coming off-duty. On the street, jubilant masses were preparing to give him a tumultuous welcome. I ran to the trams on Potsdamerplatz to get home as quickly as possible. I hate great crowds and have a horror of hysterical masses. To whoever of my generation who speaks to me in a reproachful undertone of my service with Hitler, I retort: 'You, all of you, rejoiced!' Yes, they did. Almost everyone of them.

In August 1940, after my probationary period, I received my final service identity document, an 'Open Sesame' as big as an envelope:

Herr Rochus Misch is a member of my personal bodyguard. I request all military, political and civilian authorities to provide him with all possible assistance in the execution of his duties. Herr

Misch is authorised to pass through all barriers and has access to the Führer apartment.

Adolf Hitler

I no longer remember the precise wording, but it was roughly along those lines. The ID was changed every year, and the new one had a different colour. The last one was yellow; an earlier one had been bright grey.

I know that, at least during my probationary period, I was under surveillance by the Reich Security Service RSD.[21] Whether it continued afterwards I cannot say. Certainly my mail was examined from time to time. An RSD man approached me once, brandished a letter addressed to me and wanted to know how I came to be receiving mail from the police president of Düsseldorf. Well, I could explain easily, but not without some embarrassment. I had a female penfriend whom I had got to know during my convalescence at Bayrischzell. Not far from the sanatorium was a police rest home, where she used to spend her holidays. I had had to accompany her a couple of times to cultural institutions; among other things, her chauffeur had driven us to the opera at Salzburg. I knew that she was the wife of a police commissioner in Düsseldorf. I was therefore very surprised to receive a letter from her written on the official notepaper of the police authority. I had a fit of the horrors when I saw the envelope with the office of the sender printed on the back until I grasped the connection. Since then,

---

21 The RSD had been grounded as the Führer protection squad, a protection service for the Chancellor alongside the SS bodyguard. On 1 August 1935, it formally became the RSD, with Himmler as its head and commanded by the later Gruppenführer Johann Rattenhuber. Instructions did not pass through Himmler, but to Rattenhuber from Hitler personally, his adjutants or later Bormann. The setting up of the various bodyguards involved all kinds of competence wrangling between the involved administrations, offices and persons. See Peter Hoffmann, *Die Sicherheit des Diktators*, Munich/Zürich 1975, pp.44ff. In Misch's accounts, a slightly deprecatory tone slips in when he talks of RSD members; control of weapons and the searching of guests was the prerogative of the RSD, but probably 'beneath the dignity' of the SS bodyguard.

we had continued writing to each other on and off, as I made clear to the RSD enquirer.

Shortly after the end of my probationary period I accompanied Hitler for the first time, on 4 September 1940. It was to a speech he was making at the Sportpalast. He only went inside with the Old Campaigners; we, the young men of the bodyguard, were left behind in the car. Applause swelled up now and again, which we heard from outside, but I never really regretted not being present at such occasions. Talks with generals – certainly, I would like to have had those frequently, the course of the war being a hot topic, which naturally interested my comrades-in-arms and myself. We would descend on the waiters who brought in table water from time to time, and question them as to what they had been able to pick up. Hitler's speeches however – no, I never thought I might be missing something. Mostly after a while people would begin to gather around us and the vehicles, and so it was never tedious.

On the whole, I found my duties exciting. My colleagues and I were constant fliers with Flugkapitän Baur and his courier planes. We handled all the courier services. It must be remembered that there was a daily exchange of reports from the current Führer-HQ to the presidential Chancellery under Otto Meissner, for the affairs of the Reich president were carried out separately, even though Hitler was Reich chancellor and head of state at the same time.[22] The bodyguard was also responsible for the many minor messenger runs and auxiliary services. Hitler would mostly express his wishes to his adjutants or servants, but often he would tell us directly. There was always something that had to be done. Maybe it would be the delivery of flowers and other courtesies, or footballs had to be arranged at short notice for a children's home that Hitler was due to open. I remember

---

22 By virtue of the *Gesetz über das Staatsoberhaupt des Deutschen Reiches* of 1 August 1934 the offices of Reich president and Reich chancellor were merged.

Hitler discovering the impending engagement of Wolfgang Wagner:[23] 'Misch – arrange the flowers.'

Blumen Rothe of Zehlendorf had a branch in Hotel Adlon, and I used to go there to place such orders. I myself brought the bouquet for the couple to the Wagners' house on the Kaiserdamm.

Naturally, Christmas was a very busy time with its gift deliveries. I would have to travel through Berlin and its environs, delivering presents, for example, to Wilhelm Furtwängler,[24] Josef von Manowarda,[25] Lida Baarová[26] and Olga Chekhova. A duty driver from the Reich Chancellery chauffeured me. I remember standing lost in the Great Hall of the Furtwängler villa, astonished that the room was totally bare – no paintings on the walls, no mirrors, nothing. In the centre was a magnificent grand piano – but otherwise emptiness reigned. I was so impressed that, when the conductor appeared, I almost spluttered my usual 'The Führer Adolf Hitler is pleased to . . .' opening line. As would almost all recipients of these gifts, Furtwängler enquired as to the Führer's health. Mostly no more than a couple of empty phrases would be exchanged, and then I would find myself outside again. On the other hand, when I called on the sisters Hedi and Margo Höpfner, the dancers known as the 'prancing jackdaws of the Reich',[27] their mother invited me to stay for tea and then we had a really long chat.

---

23 Wolfgang Wagner (b.1919) was operatic director, and grandson of the composer Richard Wagner. His mother Winifred was a close confidante of Hitler. The engagement mentioned by Misch took place with Ethel Drexel. Wagner was married to her from 1943 to 1976.

24 Wilhelm Furtwängler (1886–1954), conductor and composer, was appointed head of the Berlin State Opera and vice-president of the Reich Chamber of Music in 1933 by Goebbels.

25 Josef von Manowarda (1890–1942) was a bass baritone contracted to the Berlin State Opera from 1935.

26 Lida Baarová (1914–2000) was a Czech actress and mistress of Joseph Goebbels.

27 Hedi (1910–1988) and Margot (1912–2000) Höpfner were dancers and former child stars.

These excursions with my valuable freight of presents gave me great pleasure, but I did not always get to visit where I wanted: a colleague got a run to Max Schmeling and I did not ask him in time if he was willing to do a swap. The gifts from the highest level were almost never bought specially. Mostly Hitler would choose something from the stock of presents he had received himself. One can scarcely believe the small and large tokens of admiration people sent him, not only on the standard occasions but throughout the whole year from all corners of the Reich. I was specially impressed by a farmer's wife from Westphalia who sent a home-baked loaf every week. On one of his journeys, Hitler had happened to stay at her farm, tried her home-made bread and praised her highly for it. We had instructions to take the loaf down to the kitchen as soon as the mail van brought it. Only very close to the end of the war did the aromatic packages stop arriving.

Frequently, we would go over the guest list for a dinner. This would usually not take much time. It was important to apply some simple rules, but above all never to seat two guests from the same profession close to each other: two lawyers together, two medical men – that could only lead to friction. An invitation to dinner from Hitler was never turned down; even the short-notice 'stand-by candidates' would put in an appearance promptly. Should an empty place threaten, I would call the local Gau leader myself and ask if there were any visiting Gauleiters staying in Berlin. Then the answer might come back: 'Yes, so-and-so is in Hotel Excelsior.' Then I would telephone the Herr Gauleiter at Hotel Excelsior and give him my 'The Führer Adolf Hitler is pleased to . . .' line. The Gauleiter in question would generally be highly delighted to receive a personal invitation from Hitler, although the latter of course had not even been aware that the Gauleiter was in Berlin. Everything had been arranged by me. Until immediately before the reception of the guests, Hitler would as a rule not know who was going to come. He would be given the guest list on a slip of paper just beforehand. Only Dr Goebbels and Albert Speer[28] would dare to turn down an invitation. It was an unwritten rule at these dinners that the politics of the day should not be a topic of discussion. The conversation revolved mostly around the old days. Hitler's private guests were never subjected by us, his private bodyguards, to any kind of security control.

My colleagues and I, about twenty of us in Hitler's closest proximity, could go wherever we liked completely unchecked. Even on journeys, nobody from the RSD would go through our bags. I never saw Hitler carrying a weapon. I never saw the golden pistol he was said to possess, nor did any colleague ever say they had seen it. The inside pockets of his trousers were not of cloth but leather. His valets informed me of that. If he carried a weapon there was no sign of it – in contrast to Göring, whose revolver bulged in his coat pocket.

Once when Göring gave me his things in the foyer the revolver fell out of greatcoat pocket with a loud metallic thump on the cloakroom table. It looked like a Colt from the Wild West. Even Hitler used to make fun of Göring's love of gimmicks and showmanship. 'If it gives him pleasure . . .' he would then say, as if he were speaking about a child who wanted to wear odd socks.

It was an important part of our duties to receive Hitler's personal guests and their escort. If the gentlemen had to wait, then we would keep them company.

I remember a visit by Leni Riefenstahl.[29] She was a very attractive woman. When I reported her presence to Julius Schaub, the successor to Wilhelm Brückner as chief adjutant, he muttered in his native Bavarian dialect: 'She's probably come for more money – hmm.' I served Frau Riefenstahl tea, assuming that Hitler, sitting in the corner of his study, would invite her in after a short delay. After a while, he

---

28   Albert Speer (1905–1981) was Hitler's architect; from 1942 he was Reich minister for Armaments and War Production.

29   Berta Helene Amalie Riefenstahl (1902–2003) was a dancer, actress, film director and photographer; her idealised representations of the human body and filming of the masses for best effect were perfect for Nazi propaganda purposes.

let me know that he did not wish to receive Frau Riefenstahl today. She left again. I would strongly dispute any romance between Hitler and Leni Riefenstahl. She always got his approval to film in the Reich Chancellery. All day long her crew would turn every door handle and chair leg for this or that documentary. Occasionally I would stand by and watch.

At the beginning of the war, Hitler would frequently receive artists and film actors. Once, there was a well-known comedian among the guests who told me some of his best jokes, but I no longer remember his name.[30] He remarked that it was a good thing Hitler's surname was not Kräuter (meaning weeds), for then everybody would be shouting 'Heil Weeds!' He also told a joke about a man named Adolf Pflaumenmus, who was desperate to have a change of name. The man at the registry asked him what he preferred to be called. 'Alfred Pflaumenmus!' he replied. I do not know how Hitler would have reacted to this, but like everybody else he probably gave a smile of amusement.

I cannot state for a fact that Hitler had a sense of humour. I never heard him laugh out loud. That may be because I did not know him until after the war began. The Old Campaigners told me that the warlord Hitler was a quite different personality to the pre-war Hitler. 'The boss' himself had a small fund of jokes, which he liked to bring out from time to time. He was very fond of telling Blondi, his Alsatian bitch: 'Now Blondi, what do young women do?' Blondi would then lay on her back with her legs up.

When Field Marshal Erwin Rommel[31] had to wait twenty minutes for Hitler, he began to get impatient. His adjutant had come to see us in the service room after finding out that Hitler was still not ready to receive Rommel, and I was sent to placate him. I asked about

---

30 The joke related by Misch originated from the Bavarian comedian Karl Valentin (1882–1948).

31 Johannes Erwin Eugen Rommel (1891–1944), field marshal, committed suicide as an alternative to a prejudiced trial and the detention of his family (*Sippenhaft*) 'on Hitler's orders'.

North Africa and succeeded in distracting him. Rommel retrieved his greatcoat from the cloakroom, felt around in the pockets and drew out a stack of photos. He sat on the cloakroom table and told me to do the same. While sitting on the table, he spread out his North Africa photos, which he wanted to present to Hitler. We looked at them together. When I saw whisky bottles in the photos, I asked. 'Alcohol in the heat, Herr Generalfeldmarschall?'

He praised me with: 'A justified question,' and explained that alcohol is good for thinning the blood in high temperatures. A whisky and soda make the body feel much lighter. Naturally I tried it out later on a hot day in Munich with my colleagues and, well, I can confirm that the field marshal was right.

Hitler's guests, irrespective of whom they were, were mostly very friendly to us bodyguards, because of our proximity to Hitler. Nobody could ever know whether whatever was said beyond irrelevancies might not get to his ears. Although we youngsters would not have taken it upon ourselves to repeat to Hitler something we had picked up on such occasions, the Old Campaigners did it all the time. It was therefore thoroughly advisable to keep on the right side of them and not to do or say anything that it were better for Hitler not to know.

If the guests thought they ought to converse with us while we escorted them to his presence, mostly they would enquire after his health. Himmler,[32] a guest very rarely, used to joke: 'Is the Führer healthy? I hope he is well. Take good care of the Führer – you know what will happen otherwise.'

---

32 Heinrich Luitpold Himmler (1900–1945, suicide); as Reichsführer-SS and chief of police he had under his control the SS, the security service (SD) and the Gestapo.

Chapter 5

My Reich – The Telephone Switchboard

To avoid any dangers to our alertness caused by routine, we rotated our duties daily. Best of all I liked to be on telephone duty. The position required there to be two men always present, for each of the three eight-hour shifts. Telephoning all round the world was fun. I was also interested in telephone technology. I soon developed the urge to be an expert, and volunteered eagerly for every course. I was extraordinarily successful in this endeavour, which would much later win me the dubious 'advancement' to being Hitler's personal bunker telephonist.

The Reich Chancellery telephone switchboard on which we were trained was a very modern Siemens installations with push buttons, not plugs or cables. It was the engineers' pride and joy. I knew a girl at the Reichspost, and she just had to have a look at it. I agreed with Gruppenführer Albrecht, who was in charge of the Reich Chancellery staff, that I could invite her for a demonstration and initiate her into the mysteries of the button keyboard. There were buttons of various colours – white, green and yellow. One line was reserved for Hitler. If it was occupied, a red button lit up.

This particular button had its own story. It was first introduced after Hitler's number caused a number of problems. One night, a colleague on duty made a mistake with the internal dialling and reached the telephone in Hitler's private rooms. 'Hey, comrade, what's the time?' he asked unsuspectingly.

'What . . . what time is it?' the Führer responded.

'Well, what time *is* it? I've forgotten my watch!'

When only a few days later he was roused from bed for a similar type of incident, something had to be done. Subsequently, all calls for Hitler went exclusively through the telephone switchboard. The Führer's suite could only be called from there; dialling it directly was no longer possible.

Dialling Hitler's extension 120050[1] brought the caller through to me. Whoever wanted to speak to Hitler had to go through me. I would answer by saying 'Reich Chancellery' or merely 'Chancellery'. The telephone number in the Berlin public directory under Reich Chancellery was the telephone switchboard in the New Chancellery. Although the number of the Führer's suite was not listed, it was not by any means a secret. At least, I was never cautioned not to pass it on. That would later have its bitter consequence. Because the telephone lines in the Reich capital remained for the most part intact to the end of the war, during the battle for Berlin a host of outraged citizens were always ringing in.

I also had my own extension number. I could be reached in my service room under 120050–127. When it rang, it also did so in the house of my future parents-in-law at Rudow. Hermann Gretz, the Reich Chancellery telecommunications engineer, had installed it that way so that I could be reached when I was away.

Naturally, I did not want my female friend from the Reichspost, to whom I had shown the Siemens installation, to go without seeing more of the Holy of Holies. An RSD colleague, Michel Graf, said it would be no problem and accompanied us with his great ring of keys on a private tour of the New and Old Reich Chancelleries. Right at the end,

---

1 The RSHA, the chief of the security police and the security service SD at Prinz-Albrecht-Strasse 8 had the telephone number 120040; the Chancellery of the Führer of the NSDAP was listed in the official Berlin directory as 120054.

when we were in the area of the Führer-suite, a door opened suddenly, and my female friend literally fell into Hitler's arms. '*Mein Führer*, may I introduce you to Frau Lehmann of the Reichspost.' I hastened to explain: 'She is finding out about our telephone switchboard.' Hitler sized her up in a friendly manner and gave her his hand: 'Is that so? Very good. Yes, yes, show her everything here.'

I even took my Gerda into the Reich Chancellery once. We never came across Hitler, but Gerda did not mind at all. She had come only reluctantly anyway, when I invited her. With her, I walked along my usual everyday routes through the corridors of the building. Gerda was interested in me and my workplace, not in Hitler, and she never met him in person.

As a telephonist, I was responsible for the tone quality of the connection, so I controlled the volume at the switchboard. To do that, it was necessary to listen in to the conversation. After putting a call through, I would always put on the headphones and press the yellow button, which gave me access to that line. In this way I could reassure myself that everything was working free of interference. Whether the caller or recipient was aware acoustically of my listening in I cannot say. There was, additionally, an apparatus that secured against eavesdropping. I was seldom able to follow any part of these conversations, all I overheard was broken fragments. If it was any more, I never spoke a word of it.

Of course, a host of reports reached me long before the public was told of them, and even often before Hitler got them. He would joke about this: 'Why are you asking me? I am the last one here to find out anything!' This advantage in information as to war events, particularly as regards the later bombing raids on Berlin, was to prove extremely useful to me. Apart from that, I would never have dared to pass information outside.

All despatches came to us; we collected them together and then took them to Hitler. Those that I gave him personally he would mostly read at once. He would reach out for his reading glasses and take a step to one side – I would wait until he had chosen those reports to which he wanted to give more attention. The servants had to leave reading glasses scattered everywhere so that 'the boss' had a pair quickly to hand, to avoid having to carry them with him constantly. It was extremely rare that he would wear his reading glasses when strangers were around. Poor vision is a weakness – and he did not like it to be seen.

While reading through the paperwork, his face would be a mask. It was impossible to tell by his expression if the news was good or bad. If a file interested him, he would put it under his left armpit; on the others he would inflict a tear ten centimetres long and hand them back. These had to be taken directly to the paper shredder in the hallway and destroyed immediately. Initially, I was not entrusted with this job. Only after I had been there a while was I allowed to bring him the collected brief reports about all events considered important by the press staff.

My colleague Erich Kraut began one day to keep some of these despatches for a collection. I was not aware that anything had happened, but only wondered now and again why he was never around any more. When I mentioned it once to another colleague, he told me: 'He went away'. Whoever failed to perform his position adequately 'went away'. That meant either he went into a concentration camp or to the fighting front. I supposed that in Kraut's case it would be to the latter. In 1934, he had been a drummer at the cadet institution at Lichterfelde, when people had been shot to death there, in connection with the Röhm Putsch,[2] but he had never said anything about it to me. I first knew about it in connection with the hoarded despatches. I should like to have known more but dared not enquire. It interested me a lot, but

2 During the so-called Röhm Putsch Hitler had the SA leader Ernst Röhm and his followers shot and other SA leaders killed or held captive. In the wake of this putsch, on 30 June 1934 at the SS-Leibstandarte barracks, Berlin-Lichterfelde, there were numerous shootings. See Joachin Fest, *Hitler*, Frankfurt/Main, Berlin 1973, p.636: 'The SA-leaders mentioned in the "Reich List" were captured, brought to the cadet academy Lichterfelde and in contrast to their comrades at Munich lined up against a wall and shot without further ado.'

in these things one had to be cautious. Why he kept some of these despatches I could not explain. Espionage? I have no idea. Officially we were not informed about such events and their consequences. Now and again, one would become aware that such-and-such was seen no more. Few words were spoken on how we of the bodyguard were to behave, and what was in store for us in the event of a lapse. 'You all know where you are,' we were told. That had to suffice, and in general it did. As regards myself, it most certainly did.

Never would it have occurred to me to steal official papers. Back to the slush and filth of the battlefield? Not on your life. I admit to having risked a peep at a despatch in order to find out what was happening in the world. For example, I remember seeing a report about the development of the atom bomb. It stated that the American research was at least nine months behind the German. I knew Hitler's attitude to the atom bomb: 'Nobody will win a war with it.' Of that he was convinced. The Western Allies had threatened that, if Germany used the atom bomb, they would assemble 15,000 aircraft in North Africa and use them to drench all Germany with poison gas. Hitler had experienced gas attacks in the First World War, and he panicked at the thought of them. He would never be able to justify taking the responsibility on himself, he emphasised, and therefore he had no interest in using an atom bomb.

Even when, occasionally, I glanced through the highly important reports I brought to Hitler, every scrap of paper that passed through my hands went to the paper shredder without a detour. Every slip that I received from 'the boss' for destruction went there immediately. Had I left it lying around only briefly, any of the office girls might have found it.

Neither this way nor through my service at the telephone switchboard did I ever learn anything about what went on later in the concentration camps. I can only explain it by there being a flow of signals and orders only in one direction. I was only confronted by what came in and what was intended for Hitler. As in every undertaking or administration, not everything makes its way through to the highest level: 'Should we show that to the boss?' 'Ought the boss to be burdened with that?' 'Is this really for the eyes of the boss only?' A great deal was sifted out beforehand. I often noticed that the pile in the in-box was considerably greater than what the Reich press chief finally put together for Hitler. Often when I was on the way to Hitler, somebody would come up to me and take away some papers. On the other hand, much of what Hitler ordered will have made its way in personal conversations down the chain of command. None of us would then have been an intermediary to it.

I only ever noticed one single report regarding concentration camps. This was a report by the Swedish newspaper *Svenska Dagbladet* about an inspection of a German concentration camp by a party from the International Red Cross. The newspaper had printed a report by Graf Bernadotte[3] containing the results of the inspection; the despatch had the translation. I brought this report to Lorenz at Dietrich's press office. Before I handed it over, contrary to the rules, I read it. It contained nothing disturbing. There had been no 'Complaints', and points such as 'Rations' and 'Accommodation' were listed individually and assessed. I remember very clearly the sentence: 'A report was not necessary'. I am unaware if the report ever reached Hitler.[4]

---

3 Folke Bernadotte Graf von Wisborg (1895–1948 murdered) was a Swedish officer, from 1943 vice-president and later president of the Swedish Red Cross. After a meeting with Himmler on 19 February 1945, Bernadotte organised the rescue of about 15,000 concentration camp inmates from more than twenty countries. The inmates, mainly women, were evacuated to Sweden in white buses.

4 The German Red Cross (DRK) states that it has no record of this firm report. Delegates of the International Committee of the Red Cross (IKRK) often inspected German concentration camps. In 1935, an IKRK delegation led by Carl Jakob Burckhardt received approval to inspect the concentration camps at Lichtenburg, Esterwegen and Dachau. After Burckhardt had drawn up a list of deficiencies, he was invited by the Gestapo to make a later visit to inspect the improvements. In August 1938, an inspection at Dachau by an IKRK delegation with SS escort took place. The delegate, Colonel Guillaume Favre, wrote a positive report. The DRK assessed the visit as a complete success. A Danish Red Cross delegation and the IKRK delegate Maurice Rossel were shown over the Theresienstadt camp on 23 June 1944, which

When, later, I learnt of the dreadful occurrences in the eastern occupied territories, it struck me that Hitler, whenever he met Himmler, would always have talked to him in private. Whatever it was that they discussed behind closed doors I never discovered, neither directly or indirectly, unlike other times when one could ask the table waiters or adjutants for snippets of what they had heard. Never once with colleagues did I ever discuss concentration camps. That it was best to steer clear of this topic with whomsoever one spoke, even one's best friend, was absolutely clear. 'You never spoke about it with your closest colleagues?' I have been asked over and again, and then they answer their own question: 'Did you fear to speak about it?' One always felt a little bit of fear.

had been expressly made 'showable' for the visit. Rossel was deceived, and in his report later spoke of 'finding in the ghetto a town living an almost normal life.'

Chapter 6

The Berghof, Hitler's Special Train and Rudolf Hess

AT THE BEGINNING OF 1940 Hitler returned to Berlin, though only for a few days. Then we were told to get everything ready, as we were going to Berchtesgaden.

Hitler was driven to Gatow airport for the flight. His Grosser Mercedes Type 770K with valet and two adjutants set off first, then came the SS bodyguard, also in a Mercedes; at the rear was a vehicle occupied by members of the RSD. We did not give the impression of being a convoy, as there were no motorcycle outriders or sirens. It was only when we stopped at a red light that somebody might recognise Hitler.

Gatow airport at Berlin-Spandau was used only by government members. Hitler preferred the seclusion of the small airport and avoided flying out from bustling Tempelhof.[1] Generally there would be two Ju 52s standing ready: one for Hitler and his entourage, and the other for us and the RSD. After three or four hours we landed at a small airport near Salzburg, from where it was only about forty kilometres to Berchtesgaden. A car fetched us; I saw nothing more of Hitler's aircraft, nor did I see him again that day.[2]

---

1 In the 1930s, Tempelhof airport had more European passenger traffic than Paris, Amsterdam and London airports.

2 Hitler had flown first to Munich. See Nicolaus von Below, *At Hitler's Side*, London 2004.

From my period under training with the *SS-Leibstandarte*, the countryside around the Berghof was well known to me. The Berghof was an expansion of the former Haus Wachenfeld, which Hitler's half-sister Angela had once rented for him. In 1934, he bought the small house and then had it converted. Not until 1939 was the addition of the service/domestic wing completed.

A wide flight of steps led up to the main floor. To the right was the Great Hall with its gigantic window, which could be lowered for effect. The view towards the mountains was overwhelming. In front of this panoramic window was a marble table several metres long, while on the floor were valuable Persian carpets. The room had wood panelling up to waist height and a coffered ceiling. There were two areas of seating: one arranged before the great hearth; the other with red easy chairs about a round wooden table near the window. An enormous cupboard about five metres long and three metres high stored Hitler's record collection and other private possessions.

Although this room was really the finest at Berchtesgaden, the official house guests preferred the rustic, simply furnished living room of the former Haus Wachenfeld. This cosy room was separated from the Hall by a heavy curtain. A green glazed stove warmed in winter – and cooled in summer – those on the surrounding seating.

The restrooms for Hitler's personal staff and adjutants were on the ground floor. Further on were located laundry rooms and a large kitchen, near the dining room. Hitler's small private area was on the first floor. The rooms for guests, the staff, the adjutants and the housekeepers were also there. One of the guest rooms with bathroom was separated from Hitler's suite only by a space between doors. Inside this wing, one could therefore pass from room to room without having to go into the corridor. Eva Braun lived in this particular guest room. Why would the female housekeeper at the Berghof, Eva, having been introduced to us as such, have this special access to Hitler's sleeping quarters? One soon had one's own ideas about this.

On the second floor were more guest rooms. The female secretaries and some women of the house staff also lodged there. Below, in the cellar, Hitler had had a bowling alley built. The fact that he liked to bowl he kept to himself. This passion did not seem to him to be fitting for a great statesman, and he was concerned that all the bowling clubs of the Reich, should they discover his predilection, would make him honorary chairman. To these nether regions of the house Eva would often resort with female friends or the secretaries to watch films, if Hitler had an official visit and her presence was therefore not required.

A large number of valuable paintings were scattered about the walls of the whole house. They belonged to Hitler, and I heard that he wanted to exhibit them one day at Linz in a specially designed museum – the Führer-museum.[3]

We of the SS bodyguard were not given quarters in the main house but in a wooden annexe about twenty metres long. We reached our service rooms by an open balcony on the valley side, which was always beautifully arranged with tubs of flowers. The commandant of the bodyguard had his room in this annexe, and the secretaries worked there too. The washing facilities were located hereabouts. Close to us was the dental surgery. Professor Hugo Blaschke, an elderly-looking gentleman, was not only Hitler's private dental surgeon but he also treated many other people in the closer circle of 'the boss'.

From our veranda we could see in the distance the Hohensalzburg fortress on a hilltop. Below in the valley was Berchtesgaden. The annexe balcony also gave an unfettered view of the Berghof terrace, on which the numerous get-togethers and receptions were played out. Here I had a grandstand view of world history or of Eva lounging on a sunbed.

The mood on the Obersalzberg was always unforced. The war would not be passing by this way. Even many high-ranking representatives of non-allied states seemed to forget the war completely when at the

---

3 Adolf Hitler lived from 1899 with his family at Leonding near Linz, and from 1905 to 1908 in Linz.

Berghof. I remember the visit of a US envoy with whom Hitler was chatting in the best of moods. It even continued when Hitler casually handed him a note, which the envoy equally casually tucked into a pocket. My colleague was of the opinion that the note had something to do with the entry of the United States into the war. In any case the two of them went on with their free and easy conversation, Hitler describing the region with alluring gestures.

Built onto our wooden annexe was another small, two-storey building. The upper floor was occupied for most of the time by Hitler's Luftwaffe adjutant Colonel Nicolaus von Below, whom I remember as a very pleasant man.

Additional to the Berghof plot of land, which belonged to Hitler personally and for which he had paid with the royalties from *Mein Kampf*, Martin Bormann had bought in trust for the NSDAP other parcels on which he had erected new structures or torn down the existing ones.[4] Over the course of time nearly everybody in the leadership had a domicile on the Obersalzberg: Göring,[5] Speer, Hitler's deputy in the Party Rudolf Hess[6] and many others. By 1943, almost the whole of the Obersalzberg was the property of the NSDAP.

In 1933, Bormann had bought the inn Zum Türken, which was situated above Haus Wachenfeld. Even the Platterhof, a former farm, belonged to the NSDAP and was converted into a hotel. It had a multi-purpose hall with about two thousand seats and was used by Hitler from time to time to deliver a speech. Generally on these occasions, contrary to the practice in Berlin or Munich, I would be in the hall. In any case, Obersalzberg was a long-term building site.

---

4 The owner and occupant was given the choice of compulsory purchase or concentration camp. Bormann had whole houses bulldozed down to provide an unobstructed view.

5 Hermann Göring (1893–1946, suicide elected by him as an alternative to execution), Reichsmarschall, was C-in-C Luftwaffe.

6 Rudolf Hess (1894–1987) was until 1941 Hitler's deputy as Party leader.

Duty in a Holiday Camp Atmosphere

I enjoyed the time at the Berghof very much, because my colleagues and I had very little to do. There was a permanent telephonist, who only seldom needed assistance. There were only six of us of the SS bodyguard present – more beds than that stood empty. On the Obersalzberg, therefore, I spent much more of my time as a bodyguard.

State receptions were held in the small baroque palace Klessheim, near Salzburg. From 1942, the castle served as a guest house, and I remember it particularly for a special outbreak of rage by Hitler. Apart from one other instance, this was actually the only time that I saw him infuriated. Otherwise, I never witnessed him shouting wildly. When consorting with the generals he could not let himself go in that way, and he would pull himself together. It was at Schloss Klessheim that I saw him almost raging. He had a meeting with the Hungarian envoy Admiral Nikolaus von Horthy,[7] and I could hear from outside the door of the room in which the conversation took place the loud tones in which it was being conducted. Suddenly they both emerged, not so much as looking at each other, Horthy going one way, Hitler the other.[8]

At the Berghof there was at least one military situation conference daily and there were also numerous receptions. Many guests were present almost constantly: Eva Braun; personal physician Theo Morell and his wife Hannelore; Sepp Dietrich; Margarete and Albert Speer; photographer Heinrich Hoffmann[9] and his second wife Erna; state secretary Hermann Esser;[10] medical officers Hans-Karl von Hasselbach and Karl Brandt; and others. It was almost a family environment, with

---

7 Admiral Nikolaus von Horthy von Nagybanya (1869–1957) was Hungarian regent 1920–44.

8 On 18 March 1944, there was an altercation between Hitler and Horthy, in the course of which Horthy attempted to leave precipitately. Hitler prevented this by making him believe that there was an air-raid alarm. See Ian Kershaw, *Hitler 1936–1945*, Stuttgart 2000, p.830. Misch does not remember this circumstance.

9 Heinrich Hoffmann (1885–1957) was Hitler's personal photographer.

10 Hermann Esser (1900–1981) was State Secretary in the Reich Propaganda Ministry.

grown-ups sunning themselves, children running around madly, and between them yapping dogs.

My time at the Berghof was for me the finest. The daily programme was laid down a day beforehand, but which colleague did what was of little interest to our commander. The splitting up of the work was more or less left to ourselves. The main thing was to have somebody responsible for each task. Thus, one could change jobs at will with a colleague to suit some objective one had in mind, or work a longer shift so as to have a shorter one owed for another occasion.

Even on duty, however, the Berghof was like a hotel to us. It was just like being on holiday – we could even take what photos we liked with our own cameras. To capture Hitler and his guests through the lens of my Retina[11] was possible. Only during official visits to the Berghof would the photographs taken that day have to be submitted to Heinrich Hoffmann. This was just a formality, however. At the time I did not understand the significance of it. I took a photo of Hitler with his hands in his trouser pockets – that it was somehow unusual never occurred to me. So I just clicked the shutter whenever I wanted without really considering what might be of interest to 'the world afterwards'.

Hoffmann also gave me the prototype of a technically improved colour film for testing. I used it to take the first colour pictures of my later wife wearing a colourful summer dress in a meadow. It has always been my favourite photo of her.

When I was off duty, usually I would walk down into Berchtesgaden. Long rambles were another way of spending time. Occasionally on Sundays I would go to mass with a colleague. I would like to have made a regular thing of it but going alone never appealed. Therefore, my presence at mass depended on whether the colleague with whom I was sharing duty at the Berghof was a churchgoer or not. Incidentally, Eva often went to mass.[12]

---

11 The Retina was a very popular Kodak camera.

12 According to Per Uwe Bahnsen and James P. O'Donnell, *Die Katakombe – Das*

During the stays at the Berghof between 1940 and 1944, I repeatedly accompanied Hitler as his bodyguard on his many short rambles on the Obersalzberg. Almost every day after lunch he would go alone or with guests to the Tea House, which he had had built in 1936 and 1937. It was only a twenty-minute walk there, but even on fine days he would often have himself driven, mostly choosing to go in a black Volkswagen Cabriolet.

On my first day at the Berghof, I was somewhat put out to have a pair of leather shorts pressed into my hands. Apparently, I was obliged to wear them if Hitler appeared for a ramble similarly dressed. I was very grateful that he never wore leather shorts during wartime, and so the time never came when I had to turn out in this traditional Austrian garb.

In good weather Blondi, Hitler's Alsatian bitch, would accompany her master, but only on the leash, because the countryside surrounding the Berghof was a paradise for wild animals. Blondi by the way had been an idea originating from within the SS bodyguard. Before Blondi, Hitler had had an almost black sheepdog called Muck. When this dog died, Hitler did not get a replacement until the Old Campaigners in the bodyguard decided that he had to have another. The old dog had always had a positive effect on Hitler, providing him with diversion and cheering him up. An RSD man had heard that the Alsatian bitch of Gerdy Troost,[13] architect and wife of Speer's predecessor Paul Ludwig Troost, had had puppies, in Munich. The female puppy from this brood, Blondi, so-named for her very light coat, was thus visually the opposite of Muck.

Hitler did not like only Alsatians. One day, the small dog owned by the cook Helene Marie ('Marlene') von Exner ran across his path. She had received it as a gift from her former employer, the Romanian president Ion Antonescu.[14] Hitler kneeled beside the dog and said:

Ende in der Reichskanzlei (Stuttgart 1975, p.480), the local Berchtesgaden priest stated that the only people in Hitler's closer circle at the Berghof who attended mass regularly were Sepp Dietrich, Eva Braun and Rochus Misch.

13 Gerhardine 'Gerdy' Troost (1904–2003).

14 In her memoir *Until the Final Hour: Hitler's Last Secretary,* London 2003,

'Where have you come from, you little rascal?' He then played with the joyful little animal. Eva also loved dogs. She had two Scotch terriers called Negus and Stasi. They were always around, yapping.

The Tea House was built on a small rocky plateau, which provided a glorious view over the valley. Coffee was prepared there in the tiny kitchen for guests and a fire would be lit in the hearth in winter. Hitler never drank anything but apple or caraway tea. Indulging his passion for cakes and pastry, he never needed a coffee break; he nibbled all day long on pastries and chocolates. After stuffing himself full, he would sometimes nod off in his chair, but on days when many guests arrived he would always be on top form, in high spirits and talkative. For the SS bodyguard there was a special duty room at the Tea House.

In the late evenings, the cinema show would begin, presented by Erich Stein or his colleague Ellerbeck. Hitler was a great film fan. Often he would sit watching one film after another. Stein had to organise a constant supply from the Propaganda Ministry or the Reich film archive. Mostly they were US productions. Stein was also responsible for providing the films Hitler watched in the music room at the Reich Chancellery. I watched these films from the perspective of Stein or Ellerbeck more out of boredom than anything. As the presentation took place in the large Hall at the Berghof, the SS bodyguard made up the viewing public. The projector was near the external staircase, and I usually sat on the steps. Hitler loved Charlie Chaplin films. Unfortunately, I cannot remember which ones he ordered, nor if the anti-Hitler satire *Der grosse Diktator* (The Great Dictator) was among them.[15]

I recall especially that we watched *Vom Winde verweht* (Gone with the Wind) at least three times. After seeing this epic for the first time, Hitler sent for Goebbels at once, and they sat watching

---

p.111, Traudl Junge stated: 'Hitler found this gift by a statesman unworthy. He hastened to make Frau von Exner a gift of a dog... the best, noblest and most expensive fox terrier.' Misch does not recall this.

15 It is thought there are files that indicate that Hitler did order this film.

the whole film over again. 'Something like that,' he said afterwards to Goebbels emphatically, 'something like that might bring our people round again!'

Eva

I noticed the presence of Eva Braun more frequently in the summer of 1940. My first personal contact with her was in the Munich house on Wasserburger-Strasse.[16] I had to bring her something and she detained me in conversation – pleasantries obviously, but she was not supposed to go even that far. We of the SS bodyguard never began a conversation. If we were asked something, we answered; otherwise we said only what was absolutely necessary.

Officially, Eva had been introduced as the female housekeeper. The arrangement of the rooms in the Reich Chancellery and at the Berghof told another story. We were supposed to address Eva Braun as Gnädiges Fräulein (Madam), but nobody ever did; she was simply Fräulein Braun. And she thoroughly approved. Eva did not correspond to the ideal of a German maiden, as one might perhaps have expected. A natural girl, a girl rooted to the soil, this was not her thing. She changed her attire several times a day, was always carefully made up and wore expensive jewellery. I never saw any intimacies between Hitler and Eva, and neither did my colleagues, or at least nobody spoke of them if they did. I would also have kept silent had I seen anything of that kind. As far as I could make out, they certainly never rang each other daily when Eva was at the Berghof and Hitler was in Berlin. If Eva rang to speak to Hitler, the telephonist at the far end putting her through would merely say: 'The Berghof for the suite'. Then one would know.

Fairly soon after my new duties began I had an unusual encounter with Eva. One morning, still quite early, just after beginning duty I

---

16 The house in the Bogenhausen district, at Wasserburger-Strasse 12, today Delp-Strasse, had been bought for Eva Braun by Hitler's personal photographer Heinrich Hoffmann in 1936 at Hitler's instigation.

went into Hitler's suite in the Old Chancellery as I did so often, in order to leave reports on the small stool outside his bedroom.

The flow of reports obviously did not come to a stop at night, and so our duties continued all around the clock. If the servants and adjutants were still asleep, we brought the despatches immediately from the bodyguard quarter and directly to Hitler without the usual detours. One could reach his bedroom from the study or the guest room; both, therefore, always had a small 'stool for despatches'. From the stairs the route through the guest room was somewhat shorter than through the study, so it was my custom to deposit the despatches on the stool in the guest area. Therefore, I opened the door, took a couple of steps inside and just as I was putting the batch of papers down I noticed that the guest bed was occupied. In shock I recognised Eva Braun, wearing only a very flimsy nightie. I went hot and cold.

Eva had already seen me; therefore, our eyes met. She said nothing, but merely raised her right forefinger to her closed lips. I turned away at once and crept off to the nearby study, heart beating furiously, deposited the paperwork on the stool there and made myself scarce. Well, that's the end of my service with the Führer, I thought immediately. But why hadn't she shut the damned door? I was also furious with my colleagues. None of them had warned me when I began my shift that Eva had arrived. Over the next few weeks I expected every day to have to face the consequences. Nothing ever came of it.

In the autumn of 1940, Hitler began shuttling between Berlin and Berchtesgaden. That October, after a fleeting stay at my fiancée's house, I was at the Berghof again. At the end of that month, Hitler left the Obersalzberg for a meeting with General Franco on the Franco-Spanish border.[17]

Scarcely had Hitler driven off than Eva took control. She was a woman of two quite distinct personalities. In Hitler's presence she was reserved; at state functions she retired to her room or went down to

---

17 The meeting was held on 23 October 1940 at the railway station at Hendaye, a French Basque town on the border with Spain.

the bowling alley in the cellar. She would make small talk, maintaining a good atmosphere and trying to please everybody. Once Hitler left the Berghof, Eva changed at once. While one could still see the limousines driving down the serpentine road below, the first preparations for much entertainment would already have been taken in hand. Still as virtuous as a governess, she turned everything on its head, and then she would be gay and carefree, almost child-like.

On that October day when Hitler set off for southwest France, only Karl Tenazek and I of the bodyguard had remained behind. Soon afterwards, Eva appeared and invited us to join the others in the great living room. The girls needed dancing partners. Hesitant and uncertain, Karl and I followed her. In a flash she had organised a party – foxtrot music and a small buffet. We nibbled on the sly and talked.

'You have to enjoy yourselves,' Eva urged us both continually. 'You have to dance.' Eva was aiming to fix me up with one of the house employees called Gretl. 'You would be a lovely couple,' she giggled like a silly teenage girl. Relationships between the female employees at the Berghof and the SS bodyguard were common. Sometime or other, the last housemaid had netted herself a bodyguard, it appeared. Among those who – like myself – were already attached, not all could resist a flirtation with one of the girls from the Berghof or Berchtesgaden. Many of the men had been away from home for a long time. I was lucky enough to be able to see Gerda regularly during my stays in Berlin. This Gretl whom Eva continually manoeuvred into my proximity was the 'bar girl' at the Berghof. At receptions and festivities she supplied the alcohol, mixed wonderful cocktails and supervised the drinks. That made her interesting of course.

Even when Hitler was there, Eva would often invite her friends Herta Schneider[18] or the Austrian girl Marion Schönmann[19] to visit.

---

18 Herta Schneider, née Ostermeyer, was a friend from Eva Braun's youth.

19 Marianne 'Marion' Schönmann, née Petzl, was a friend of Hoffmann and Eva Braun. Hitler attended her wedding in 1937.

Because of Eva, the atmosphere at the Berghof was above all unforced, almost cheerful. One thing was taboo for me, however – I never danced with Eva. That really was not done. She was the Führer's girl. Eva had a zest for living almost until the end. I liked her.

Molotov's Bunker

After the meeting with Franco, and contrary to expectations, Hitler did not return to the Berghof.[20] Karl and I were therefore flown back to Berlin, where we awaited the visit of the Soviet foreign minister Molotov[21] in mid-November.[22] I was on duty when Hitler and Molotov dined at the Reich Chancellery. The Soviet foreign minister decided to return to the Schloss Bellevue guest house afterwards, and I brought a blanket to the limousine, which he had requested for his legs. It was a bitterly cold night.

Back at the Reich Chancellery, I went to the smoking room in which the other diners had gathered. My duty post was the telephone. Everybody was talking about Molotov, but I heard none of it because telephone reports were coming in constantly. Finally I was told: an Allied aircraft had been identified over Lüneburg heading on a southeasterly course – and therefore towards Berlin. I reported it at once to the chief of protocol, Alexander Freiherr von Dörnberg,[23] who was standing close by me. Hitler was not far away and asked at once what the problem was. When Dörnberg explained the situation, the Foreign Ministry liaison officer to Hitler, Hewel, asked: 'What should

---

20　On 24 October 1940, the day following the talk with Franco, Hitler met the French head of state Marshal Pétain and his deputy Pierre Laval at Montoire, and on 28 October Mussolini in Florence. These meetings were all arranged at short notice. Nicolaus von Below, *At Hitler's Side*, London 2004, pp.75–6. Von Below accompanied Hitler throughout the period.

21　Vyacheslav Mikhailovitch Molotov (1890–1986) was from 1939 People's Commissar for External Affairs of the Soviet Union.

22　The visit took place on 12 November 1940.

23　Alexander Freiherr von Dörnberg (1901–1983) was chief of protocol at the Foreign Ministry and member of the Reichsführer-SS staff, 1938–1945.

we do about Molotov, if that aircraft is actually heading for Berlin? We should bring him at once to Hotel Adlon!'

'Why there?' Hitler asked in irritation.

'Because Hotel Adlon has a bombproof bunker.'

This kindled a discussion about secure bunker installations below the Reich Chancellery. It had an air-raid cellar, which many called a bunker, but it would not survive a direct hit. Accordingly, that same evening Hitler decided to build a bunker there: 'It is high time that the head of state of the German Reich is also in a position to offer his guests at least as safe a place to shelter as Hotel Adlon.'

Construction work on the bunker was held back, however, and not until 1943 was it begun. In the centre of the Reich Chancellery garden a giant hole was suddenly dug. 'Wonderful, now we're going to have a swimming pool,' my colleagues joked. The bunker was never fully finished. To the very end, which would concentrate my duties, the Third Reich and Hitler precisely into that very place, the subterranean labyrinth never really dried out.

The Ban on Hess Flying

Shortly after the visit of the Soviet foreign minister, in November 1940, I was again with Hitler on the Obersalzberg – this time only for a few days.[24] One evening, one of the adjutants asked us to prepare a place for another guest at dinner. Hitler liked to eat in company at the Berghof and, as often happened, he gave us very little notice of his dinner guests. A colleague knew that Hess was staying in his house on the Obersalzberg, and I reached him by telephone. He was free that evening and set off for the Berghof straight away.

Towards the end of the meal a courier arrived and handed a despatch to Reich press chief Otto Dietrich. He ran his eye over it quickly and then passed it to Hitler, who read it standing up and then

---

24 In the second half of November 1940, Hitler spent some time on the Obersalzberg, and on 19 November received King Boris of Bulgaria. See Nicolaus von Below, *At Hitler's Side*, London 2004, p.78.

exclaimed: 'My God, what am I supposed to do? I can't fly there and beg on my knees.'

I didn't know the background, but as the talk subsequently increased in volume I picked up a few scraps. I understood that the discussion was all about a meeting in Portugal between the military attaché Enno Emil von Rintelen, whom we called 'Hitler's postman', and his Swedish colleague Graf Bernadotte. The exact purpose or the aim of the whole thing was not revealed to me. Only later did I hear the rumours of secret negotiations with the British. What I do remember, however, was that Hess, answering Hitler's earlier observation, not to him but to his adjutant, uttered something like: 'Perhaps he can't. But I – I can!'

Hess excused himself relatively soon after this incident and took his leave. I was on very good terms with Josef 'Sepp' Platzer, Hess's servant, and when we were in Soviet captivity together much later he took the opportunity to give me a full report on what happened next during that evening and how things panned out. Sepp drove back with Hess to his house, and in the car he repeated that sentence: 'Hitler cannot. But I can!' Then he let Sepp into his plan. He had decided to fly to Britain on his own account. Nobody else was to know – at first, not even his own adjutants. First of all, Sepp had to obtain two British history books. Above all, however, Hess had to have knowledge about the flight safety zones, especially the code words, which were changed daily, so as to find the 'dead zones' and avoid coming under friendly flak fire. Sepp mentioned to Flugkapitän Baur the map with the safety zones marked out on it. At first, Baur declined the request. Sepp insisted: 'You know my boss, he wants to be informed about everything.' Baur then personally obtained a copy from Göring, commander-in-chief of the Luftwaffe, on the pretext that the map was needed by his deputy, Hitler's second pilot, Georg Betz.

After this had been achieved, Hess needed a place to which he could withdraw and prepare for his operation. He got his servant to ask a Gauleiter to put a farmstead in Austria at his disposal. At that point, Hess had never made a parachute jump. Sepp got him some special beginners' boots and bandages used by paratroopers at the start of their training. Hess stuck the map on the wall of his hut in the Austrian mountains and studied it lying in bed. Sepp had seen that for himself.

Hess incessantly flew an Me 110 fighter bomber. He even made some courier flights. One day when he met Hitler in Berlin – I was on duty – Hitler looked at him in surprise: 'What are you doing here?' Hess requested to familiarise himself officially with courier flights, but Hitler refused, and forbade Hess as well as Göring as his deputies – Hess as deputy Party chairman, Göring as Reich chancellor – from flying altogether. Obviously neither took any notice.

In February 1941, Hess took off on his first 'British flight' attempt. Sepp advised him that, at all costs, he must wear uniform. As a civilian, the British would put him before a firing squad; they were very strict about it. Shortly before getting into the Messerschmitt aircraft, Hess gave to his adjutants Karl-Heinz Pintsch and Alfred Leitgen an envelope, with strict instructions that it was only to be opened if he did not return within twenty minutes. Hess had hardly gone off to the aircraft when the two adjutants became anxious and tore open the envelope. Inside the outer envelope was another addressed to Hitler; it was marked 'Very Urgent'. Before the adjutants could decide what to do next, Hess came back after only seven minutes. He had in fact taken off, but landed again immediately. He spoke briefly with the flight engineer Neumaier, who – also under the greatest secrecy regarding the mission – had placed explosives and additional fuel tanks in the aircraft and then got back in the car with Sepp, the adjutants and the driver Rudi,[25] and drove back to Munich. Nobody knows whether there was really a technical problem with the aircraft or if Hess suddenly lost courage. Sepp and I thought the latter, because Hess had trained incessantly on the plane, and a defect at this stage was unlikely.

---

25 The driver was Rudi Lippert.

The adjutants finally found their tongues and admitted to Hess that they had opened the letter prematurely. They therefore knew that their boss was planning something that made it urgent for them to inform Hitler of the fact once Hess had flown off. At first, Hess was silent. Sepp tried to clarify the situation and give his superior the opportunity to decide on how to proceed. As they drove through a stretch of woodland, Sepp therefore suggested that Hess might like to take a walk since he liked walking through woods so much. 'Platzer thinks I should take a little walk. Good, I'll walk!'

Hess told Rudi to stop the car, and he spent half an hour walking round. Back in the limousine, he then addressed his adjutants. They now knew something that they had to keep secret under all circumstances. The events to which they had just been witness had never taken place. Everybody held firm to that.

In February 1941, Hess made another attempt, but abandoned it without having taken off this time. It would be May before the third attempt was made, and this time he went.

Amerika

In the spring of 1941, Hitler made many trips. I did not always accompany him. It was the time of the Balkans campaign.

In the Reich Chancellery there were often very important visitors. Above all, the Japanese foreign minister Yosuke Matsuoka was received with special honours.[26] The Japanese always brought the strangest gifts with them. I remember a very old sea chart according to which one could walk to Great Britain from the European continent without ever getting one's feet wet.

If there was a state banquet, then Herr Lange, the kitchen chef of the Führer-suite, did not cook; instead, the chief chef of the Kaiserhof hotel was used. He was called Weigert or Weigelt – I do not remember exactly. Even the waiters came from the Kaiserhof. They were men

---

26　The Japanese foreign minister Yosuke Matsuoka stayed in Berlin from 27 February to 19 March 1941.

Left: Rochus Misch (born 29 July 1917) shown here at the age of four. His father was also named Rochus.

Below: Soldiers in the family: the father was a soldier, the son was a soldier; Rochus Misch senior is standing behind his seated comrade.

Above: Rochus Misch was born in this house at Alt-Schalkowitz near Oppeln (Upper Silesia). *The grandparents lived in the left wing, the parents (until their deaths) in the right wing. The children's room was at the rear overlooking the garden. (This photo was taken around 1958. A cousin of Rochus Misch with her family is in front of the house.)*

Below: Father, mother, brother dead – the orphan Rochus Misch (back row, last right) was cared for by his grandparents Franz and Ottilie Fronia from the age of five, seen here around 1930 celebrating their golden anniversary with relatives. Aunt Sofia Fronia, who later brought up the boy, is in the second row, on the right.

Above: Free ticket to see Hitler. On 1 August 1936 Rochus Misch and his Aunt Sofia saw his later 'boss' for the first time (they claimed to have stood on the roundabout). This photo shows the South Gate to the Olympic stadium by which Hitler entered.

Below: Already the tallest man as a young footballer: Rochus Misch (second right) with his Hoyerswerda Club, 1934.

Above left: *Wilhelm Mohnke, one of the first SS men in Hitler's 'SS Stabswache Berlin' and commander, 5th Company, SS-Leibstandarte: he brought Rochus Misch to Hitler.*

Above right: *Hitler's sister Paula. Early in his service in May 1940 Rochus Misch travelled to Vienna to give her a letter and a parcel from her brother.*

Below: *Without knowing what significance the area would have for him later, Rochus Misch spent six weeks at the Berghof during military training with 5th Company,* SS-Leibstandarte; *photo by Rochus Misch, 1941.*

Above: This may have been Rochus Misch's first impression of Wilhelm-Strasse 77: at the beginning of May 1940 he began his duties for Hitler in the Reich Chancellery; behind it is the Reich president's palace in which he had his room (approximately under the central flag pole).

Above: *The lobby outside Hitler's apartment in the Old Reich Chancellery with the connection to the New Reich Chancellery.*

Opposite below: *Innsbruck main railway station, 30 July 1940: a stop off on the way to see Mussolini. Behind Hitler is the Gauleiter of Tyrol, Franz Hofer, while the SS officer without headwear is Hitler's valet Heinz Linge.*

Below: *Hitler's study in the Old Reich Chancellery.*

Above left: Hitler's private living room before the conversion. The door leads into the bedroom in the Old Reich Chancellery.

Below: Hitler's suite in the Old Reich Chancellery – Rochus Misch was disappointed by its small dimensions and the furnishings of the individual rooms.

Above: Life as a courier, 1941: Rochus Misch photographed his colleagues on a flight from FHQ Wolfsschanze to Berlin.

Opposite above right: The 'new boys' – here the Austrian Joseph 'Joschi' Graf, a colleague of Rochus Misch, had to be initiated into the internal idiosyncrasies of the Reich Chancellery; photo taken by Misch.

Below: Rochus Misch (right), with Joseph Graf, in a Ju 52, around 1941.

Left: *To the Berghof in two Ju 52s: Hitler would board the first plane with his close entourage, while the second was reserved for all his bodyguards (SS-Begleitkommando) and the members of the RSD. The photo is dated 1 June 1943.*

Below: *Field Marshal Erwin Rommel and Hitler, 1942. Rommel showed Rochus Misch his North Africa photos at the Reich Chancellery. Later Hitler gave Rommel the choice of suicide as the result of his belief that Rommel had links to the military resistance plot of 20 July 1944.*

Above: Hitler's study on the Obersalzberg (Berghof).

Below: One of the many soirées in the Great Hall at the Berghof. Eva Braun and Hitler are seated on the sofa in front of the standing officer: the photograph is dated 1 May 1944.

Left: *The 20-metre long, wooden annexe to the Berghof, with its various service rooms. On the left was the secretaries' workroom, Dr Blaschke's dental surgery, the sanitary installation and the SS bodyguard duty room. The corner office was occupied by the bodyguard's commander (mostly Otto Hansen or Fritz Schädle), while the bedrooms were at the rear. Until 1943, Luftwaffe adjutant Nicolaus von Below lived in the first storey, reached from the outside stairway.*

Below: *Guests on the Berghof terrace, as photographed by Rochus Misch in 1942. From left to right; Walther Hewel, liaison officer to the Foreign Ministry and Reich press chief Otto Dietrich (both sitting on the parapet); Eva Braun (filming); Adjutant Fritz Darges (bent over the table); Captain Gerhard Engel, Hitler's army adjutant, back to camera; Frau Morell feet up on the sunbed nearest Eva Braun; Commandant Sepp Dietrich (crouching with one of the Speer children, another nearby); secretary Gerda Christian; Theodor Morell, Hitler's personal physician (seated reading); secretary Christa Schroeder; and (far right) Margarethe Speer.*

Left: This photo Rochus Misch took of his fiancée Gerda remained his favourite all his life.

Below right: The dog Blondi at play – she owed her name to her bright coat.

Below: Hitler liked to put Eva Braun's dog in the pen with the rabbits. He would then amuse himself: 'What race of animal would come from it?' From the left: Hitler, in the background his personal physician Theodor Morell and adjutant Hans Pfeiffer. On the sunbed (far right) Rochus Misch recognised Margarete Speer; standing near her is State Secretary Hermann Esser. With her back to the camera beside the rabbit pen is Eva Braun's sister Margarethe. Photo taken in 1942 by Rochus Misch.

Below: Rochus Misch at the Berghof, behind the main entrance gate, 1941.

Above: Rochus Misch on the Berghof terrace in the summer of 1941.

Below: Eva Braun on the Berghof terrace looking at photographer Rochus Misch. Kneeling is Sepp Dietrich with two of the Speer children and Hitler's secretary Christa Schroeder; about 1942.

Above: The Tea House on the Berghof. Hitler drank apple or caraway tea here. Photo by Rochus Misch in 1942.

Below: Obersalzberg, spring 1944; Hitler returning from the Tea House to the Berghof; in the back seat is Heinrich Himmler and an adjutant is driving. On foot the journey took twenty minutes.

Above left: Warlord and
bodyguard: a photo-montage
of Hitler and Rochus Misch.

Above right: In front of the special train Amerika; from left to right: Foreign
Minister Joachim von Ribbentrop; Theodor Morell, Hitler's private physician;
Hitler; army adjutant Gerhard Engel; and, without cap, Karl Brandt, Hitler's
accompanying physician.

Below: Rochus Misch in the dining car of the special train Amerika; it was
renamed Brandenburg during the Russian campaign in 1941.

of long service who had once been employed by Kaiser Wilhelm, all imposing figures, tall and well turned out, not Nazis but German Nationalists.[27] These waiters had wardrobes in the cellar of the Reich Chancellery in which their extremely elegant work attire was hung, including strap shoes. Before festivities, they changed there. These waiters were also employed at Schloss Klessheim.

At the beginning of April, I accompanied Hitler for the first time in his special train, named *Amerika*. Later, from 1 February 1943, it was renamed *Brandenburg*, but none of us could get used to the change and we continued to refer to it as *Amerika* among ourselves. The special train was a fully functioning Führer-HQ on wheels. It was kept at the ready at the Berlin Anhalter station, in a shed near Bautzener-Strasse and Yorck-Strasse, and was taken from there to the best positioned railway station for where Hitler wanted to travel in it. Later, it stood at FHQ Wolfsschanze in East Prussia.

The special train was drawn by two locomotives and consisted of a flak wagon, luggage wagon, work coach and domestic coach for Hitler, then came our coach with the bodyguard and a dining car mostly used as an officers' mess. Coupled up behind these was the Wehrmacht coach as well as others for the female secretaries, which I never entered. The windows were, for the most part, darkened. The refurbished train was luxurious throughout – the individual coaches having washrooms with hot and cold water and a telephone connection between coaches.

I had a compartment to myself alone. Situation conferences were held in the conference coach, which had a large wooden table in the centre. The Führer-coach, which incidentally I never visited, was used occasionally for small-scale conferences. Once, when I was leaning casually at a window, somebody tapped me on the shoulder. I turned round – it was Hitler, who wanted to get by. In such situations, it was not necessary to say anything.

---

27 The German National Volks Party (DNVP), which advocated the return of the monarchy, was in coalition with Hitler's NSDAP for a time, but in June 1933 disbanded itself under pressure.

The train was a very sociable place. Now and again, Hitler would sit diagonally facing me in the officers' mess coach drinking his Holzkirchner beer. The firm Mitropa ran the dining car. Mitropa offered the most carefully selected culinary specialities, a land of milk and honey. It was here on the train that I saw Hitler eat meat for the only time in the five years I was with him.

The Mitropa also provided other riches – those to make the heart of a lady beat faster: perfume, stockings, handkerchiefs from Paris and other such things. Once, directly after a night shift, I had to take a train from Berlin to Berchtesgaden. On the way I fell into conversation with a young lady who lent me a book called *Gedanken nach zwei Uhr nachts* (Thoughts after Two in the Morning) by Aribert Wäscher, for the long journey. When she was preparing to alight I attempted to return the book to her, but she told me to hold onto it until I had finished it. I insisted that, at least, she give me an address to where I could send the book. She fished out a scrap of paper and wrote her name and address on it. I did not look at it until she had left the train – and was irritated to find that both the name and address were almost illegible. I thought that might have been because of the motion of the train. Ursula Lüben, Rüben, Roben? Well, I thought, my RSD colleagues could help out here, and I gave them the task of 'finding the lady', which they did and where she lived. This turned out to be at Lübben in Brandenburg, just where she had got out. I bought her a gift from Mitropa and also sent a telegram worded: 'Thoughts after two in the morning to follow'. The man in the telegraph office smirked when he read this ambiguous greeting.

In April 1941, the special train brought us to near Vienna, in a more or less improvised Führer-HQ train christened *Frühlingssturm* (Spring storm). It was stationed at a tunnel entrance near Mönichkirchen. If there was an aircraft alarm, the train pulled back into the tunnel. Train travel was not the quickest way of moving around the country. In order not to interfere with the regular Reichsbahn timetables and to avoid being noticed, the journey would be interrupted frequently.

The Reichbahn had priority. We often went down lesser-used tracks. Sometimes, we would be stuck for ages in some siding, such as on the way to Mönichkirchen, when we had a very long wait near Hof. On 20 April 1941, Hitler celebrated his fifty-second birthday in FHQ Frühlingssturm. As it happened, I had taken the plane back to Berlin shortly before this. Hitler did not then arrive back in the Reich capital until the end of April.

A Mad Flight and its Consequences

After Hitler had addressed the Reichstag at the beginning of May 1941, he returned to the Berghof. At that time there now occurred the 'flight to Britain' by Hess, for which he had been preparing for so long.[28]

On the evening of 10 May 1941, his plane left the runway at the Messerschmitt Works, Augsburg. This time everything aboard the Me 110 was in order, and probably he had worked up the necessary courage. The twenty minutes' deadline, during which period he had told his adjutants to stand by and wait before they did anything else, passed without any sign of his returning. Karl-Heinz Pintsch – as arranged – presented himself at the Berghof next morning to hand the prepared letter to Hitler. Hitler was outraged.* 'Hess?! Hess?! Hess of all people did that? Hess of all people? Why did he do that to me?' Hitler did not tire of repeating himself.

---

28 Hess flew to Scotland and parachuted down near Glasgow. His intention was to visit Douglas, Duke of Hamilton on his landed estate so as to use Hamilton's connections to Winston Churchill to negotiate peace. The project came to grief. Hess stated later that he had acted alone, on his own initiative and Hitler did not know. This is still debated by historians.

* According to Hitler's valet Heinz Linge, adjutant Pintsch arrived at 0930 hrs. Linge said that Hitler had been awake until the early hours and was not to be disturbed until noon. When Linge knocked on his door, however, Hitler appeared dressed and shaved, leading Linge to believe that Hitler already knew. Heinz Linge, *With Hitler to the End*, London 2009, p.97. (TN)

For the next three days, 11–13 May, Hitler absented himself from the military situation conferences, and confined himself to his room on the first floor. The generals came to the situation conferences and withdrew without being able to report anything. Even Goebbels was only received upstairs in Hitler's room, when he arrived on 12 May.

The official line later was that Hess had acted as the result of mental derangement. A communiqué to that effect was worked on with Dietrich. Hess wanted to see the Duke of Hamilton in order to conduct his own private peace talks with the British. The duke was apparently close to Churchill. We of the SS bodyguard got quickly to the crux of the matter. Had Hess really acted off his own bat? We were agreed that Hitler would have needed to be a good actor to fake the indignation and upset he had displayed when reading Hess's letter. At any rate, after what I saw in November 1940, there must have been complete accord between Hess and Hitler at least with regard to the aim of his undertaking. We were well aware, of course, that one of Hitler's utopian ideas was of fighting shoulder to shoulder with the highly esteemed British against Bolshevism.

The Party leadership had to be passed to somebody else, and Hitler then appointed Martin Bormann as chief of the Party chancellery.[29] In this, Hitler chose the wrong man, in our opinion. 'Goebbels in, Bormann out,' we said. We might have admitted that Martin Bormann's contacts with us were conciliatory to some extent, but nobody had a soft spot for him. Even his own brother did not exist for him, after Albert Bormann had married a woman completely unacceptable in Martin's eyes. Goebbels we liked. He was usually cheerful and was man enough to contradict Hitler even if only to turn down a dinner invitation. That impressed us. Meanwhile Bormann always fawned on Hitler. Certainly almost everyone did, but Bormann was the champion

29 On 11 May 1941, Hitler framed an edict that the office of 'The Führer's Representative' would be known henceforth as 'The Party chancellery' and headed by Martin Bormann. NB Original footnote says 10 May, Hitler did not know of Hess's defection until the morning of 11 May, hence my correction. (TN)

at it. He was always scheming how to improve his position. Most of the time he was involved in intrigues and power play. This won him no friends. Only Hitler's old Party comrades would dare to say something about it openly, particularly August Körber. Later, Körber even tried to describe to Hitler the true situation at the front after he had been there himself. Hitler did not take his criticisms the wrong way, but they didn't count for anything with him: 'That may seem to be the case for you . . .' What his old comrade had told him was worth no more than that.

At Bormann's insistence, everybody who had had knowledge of Hess's flight to Britain was arrested and taken to Sachsenhausen concentration camp. This included Hess's two adjutants, the mechanic Neumaier and also my friend Sepp Platzer. Afterwards, Sepp served at the front and, as previously described, was made a POW by the Soviets.

After the uproar caused by Hess, towards the end of May another piece of bad news was received at the Berghof. The *Bismarck*, the most powerful battleship in the world, had been sunk by British naval forces while aiming to reach the occupied port of Saint-Nazaire.[30] This was the first major loss on the German side. We still had no suspicion that the invasion of the Soviet Union was now imminent.

---

30 Saint-Nazaire had the only dry dock on the French coast large enough to accommodate the *Bismarck* for repairs. NB Original footnote only mentions the bunkers for German U-boats, which had not been built in May 1941, and it was obviously not in the hope of reaching these that the *Bismarck* was heading for Saint-Nazaire, hence my replacement footnote above. (TN)

Chapter 7

FHQ Wolfsschanze: 1941

O N THE AFTERNOON OF 22 June 1941, as Operation Barbarossa[1] began, Hitler left Berlin. Initially he went into the newly built FHQ Wolfsschanze about ten kilometres east of the East Prussian town of Rastenburg.[2] The barrack camp had been built by the Organisation Todt.[3] It had bombproof bunkers, and the whole installation was covered with camouflage netting, so that the bunkers, paths and structures could not be seen from the air. Meanwhile, work continued on other security measures and extensions. FHQ Wolfsschanze was equipped with fully functioning logistics. Hitler could direct the state, Party and war from there. There was a daily courier service from there to the presidential Chancellery in Berlin.

OKH (Army High Command) was located near Angerburg, about twenty-five kilometres from FHQ Wolfsschanze. OKH representatives came twice daily for the military situation conferences, mostly by train, in an old railway coach, which stopped at the purpose-

---

1 The attack on the Soviet Union was planned under the cover name Barbarossa.

2 Today Kętrzyn (Poland).

3 Organisation Todt (OT), named after its founder and leader, was created in 1938 as a building firm for military works. After the death of Fritz Todt in 1942, Speer headed the OT. A large number of its workers were forced labourers, POWs and concentration camp inmates.

built Bahnhof Görlitz within the security confines of the Führer-HQ. FHQ Wolfsschanze had its own railway track and an enormous platform to receive official state visits.

FHQ Wolfsschanze was within two Sperrkreise (protected areas). All kinds of special passes existed, which gave limited entry here or there. The password was changed daily. The pass with the most extensive permission had a red diagonal stripe and allowed access to Sperrkreis 1, the Führer-Sperrkreis. None of this applied to us of the bodyguard. We had our 'Open Sesame', which I have mentioned before, and it lived up to its name, even in the FHQ Wolfsschanze.

Whereas the OKH headquarters – known as Mauerwald because of its location on the Mauer Lake – offered 1,500 generals, officers and men a bed and shelter, and was accordingly the size of a small town, FHQ Wolfsschanze was extremely modest both in size and its accommodation. We in the bodyguard were given quarters in wooden barracks within the inner Sperrkreis. As time went on, the wooden walls were reinforced with concrete. Our barrack hut was the only place where one could enter the Führer-Sperrkreis uncontrolled. The barrack hut straddled Sperrkreis 2 and Sperrkreis 1.

Hitler's bunker was basically built around his 'office'. There was a bedroom and washroom, and a very small living room equipped with a table and some chairs.

Bormann, after his appointment as chief of the Party chancellery, and naturally as befitted his more important status, had his quarters opposite those of Hitler. Göring lived near the railway line, while Himmler's own field-command post was about half an hour away and was called Hochwald (high woodland) corresponding to the scenery.

We spent the longest period of the war with Hitler at FHQ Wolfsschanze. The first days in that summer of 1941 were almost perfect, the reports from the Eastern Front were excellent, and everybody was in the best of spirits. At first, I had nothing to do. The Wehrmacht handled the telephone service, my colleague Helmuth Beermann was given responsibility for the mail and courier services, and the RSD escorted the guests. My work was limited to being within range of Hitler for possible assignments.

Nothing exciting happened, and the mood became generally more informal. To put it another way, we lazed around. Soon we sought to overcome our boredom by swimming in the nearby Moysee lake. Civilians came there from the nearby villages to bathe. They had no worries about being disturbed by us. We took the car for trips ever further afield, into the glorious countryside. The lakes of the Masurian plateau and the beauty of the scenery enchanted me.

In the evenings we sat in our barrack hut and played cards, mostly Tarock – the room hazy with the cigarette smoke of my colleagues. During my lifetime I was never a smoker, but, when off duty, nearly all my colleagues would puff away for all they were worth. Much to my distress, Helmuth Beermann organised a never-ending supply of tobacco wares of all kinds from Mitropa. Obviously, it was forbidden for the bodyguards to obtain luxury goods from the Mitropa stocks, but Helmuth had a good friend among the Mitropa people, who supplied him under the counter.

Besides Hitler, we also had time to look after a young roe fawn, which came to us one day. We fed it peanuts, and the crafty animal soon knew exactly where we kept these and was soon helping itself. It would also come up the steps to the hut, push open the door with its snout and lick up the peanuts from the floor. We would leave the door open intentionally, and often the fawn would come up to our beds for assistance if it failed to find what it was looking for.

Less pleasant experiences were had with the mosquitoes. They plagued us, and bothered us endlessly. Without the nets which covered our heads, we would have been eaten alive. For one of our colleagues, the mosquitoes provided another quite unexpected consequence. Adjutant Fritz Darges,[4] previously adjutant to Martin Bormann, was standing one day with his hands in his trouser pockets close to Hitler awaiting

---

4 Friedrich Darges (b.1913) had the final rank of lieutenant colonel.

his orders. I was not far away and saw Hitler leafing through a batch of papers. Suddenly a mosquito began buzzing stubbornly about Hitler's head. Heavy-handed and angry, Hitler hit out at the mosquito with the paperwork but without the desired result. The accursed thing appeared quite unimpressed, and after the wild gesticulations had ended would always settle again on exactly the same spot from where Hitler had attempted to shoo it away. Fritz could hardly conceal his laughter at the Führer being second best in an aerial dogfight with a mosquito. Fritz had not moved a centimetre from where he was; his hands were still in his pockets, and he was grinning. This was not overlooked by Hitler, even in his excitement. He looked at Fritz sharply: 'If you are not even able to keep a thing like that off my body, then you have no business being here!' Fritz understood at once and went to pack his trunk. The same evening he was already on his way to the front. In the autumn of 2007 when we conversed by telephone we discussed this incident. Fritz is older than me, but he still remembered it very clearly.

The daily routine in the FHQ Wolfsschanze soon followed the same well-rehearsed ritual as at the Berghof. Towards midday, Hitler would receive generals Keitel and Jodl for the first situation conference. After tea, towards 1800 hrs, the second one would take place, and towards midnight a third lasting around half an hour. Between these meetings, lunch would be taken at 1400 hrs and the evening meal at 1930 hrs. After the late night conference, Hitler would meet the adjutants and female secretaries. There would then be a rather festive spirit abroad and to touch on any political or military theme was strictly taboo. At this, we colleagues would usually withdraw to the mess in order to discuss the latest developments on the fronts.

Hitler dined in officers' mess 1, we in officers' mess 2. When the special train was at FHQ Wolfsschanze, Mitropa would keep us supplied with delicacies. Armed with these, Krümel (Crumb) the cook[5] got to work. He was a very small man who looked even smaller

---

5   See also Christa Schroeder, *He Was My Chief*, London 2009, pp.94–5. According to her, Krümel was the former Mitropa cook Otto Günther.

alongside us giants of the SS bodyguard. In his kitchen empire he had hung a motto: '*Wer den Krümel nicht ehrt, ist des Kuchens nicht wert!*' (Whoever does not honour Crumb, does not deserve a slice of the cake!) What came first, the slogan or his nickname I cannot remember. In any case, a better nickname could not have been found for him.

We used to amuse ourselves a lot over our colleague Jörg, whose surname I forget. Through injury, he had lost his sense of taste. While enjoying a Fernet-Branca, with straight faces we would pour him a similar-looking preparation made with Maggi seasoning and spices, and then smirk behind his back like schoolboys.

Models and Miniature Buildings

The good mood fell away a little when in late summer 1941 the stream of reported successes began to trail off. I was shuttling meanwhile between Rastenburg and Berlin. Two weeks here, three weeks there; it went on for quite a while. Mostly I went by courier aircraft, a Ju 52. Meanwhile, I missed the visit of Mussolini to the FHQ Wolfsschanze.[6]

At the Reich Chancellery, I had been allocated another service room. I had been asking for this for some time, because I was really put out at being so far from my colleagues and near to 'the boss'. When I heard that the two nieces of house administrator Kannenberg were giving up their room, I enquired at once if I might not take it over – and I succeeded. My new service room was on the ground floor and also much nicer than my old one. It did not matter to me that I had to share it with the films controller Stein. Stein also lived at a private address in Berlin and usually drove there after duty. Our paths never crossed. Hans Junge, Hitler's servant and later the husband of Hitler's secretary Traudl Humps, had the adjoining room until his death – he fell at the front after being transferred there at his own request. Dr Blaschke[7] also had his dental surgery in this sector. Once a week he

---

6 Mussolini arrived at FHQ Wolfsschanze on 25 August 1941.

7 In May 1945, Dr Blaschke's assistant, Käthe Heusermann, provided the Russians with fragments of a denture which she identified as fitting the profile of Hitler's

left his practice on the Kurfürstendamm for the Reich Chancellery. Thus, I would often escort patients to his consulting room for their appointment. There were rare occasions when some of the clientele, perhaps Frau Goebbels, might exchange a few words with me beyond pleasantries. Perhaps fear of the drill loosened their tongues. None of this chatter has remained in my memory.

I was relieved at no longer having to pass Hitler's suite any more when returning to my own room. I was told that he was very sensitive to noises and heard everything. My duty brought me there at all hours of the day and night, and always having to creep by silently had been a nuisance. I had also been easily reachable there, and I did not like the idea of being the next best thing should the valet or other servant not be around. That happened often enough if I had drawn the sentry post at the small table near the trademen's entrance, Hitler wanted his valet, and the valet had gone off early to the restroom. If Hitler saw that the servant did not answer his summons and bell ringing, he would lean over the stairway banisters and call down, 'Sentry!' to which I would reply: '*Jawohl, mein Führer*?!' Then he would send me in search of the valet or tell me what he wanted. At night, it would often be for his hot-water bottle. When that happened the first time, I thought it might be about the stomach trouble which plagued him, but he wanted it to warm his feet. This extraordinarily important bed companion, always wrapped in a snow-white cotton bag, would have to be organised by me very promptly.

In order not to disturb Hitler with unnecessary noise if at all possible, we of the bodyguard could move about everywhere with absolute freedom. Because of this, we were not informed expressly if unusual guests were announced. In November 1941, I was particularly impressed by one visitor – the Grand Mufti of Jerusalem. I came across Hitler in the corridor just as he was about to disappear into his study with Mohammed Amin al-Husseini. I stared after the gentleman with

dentition to the best of her memory.

the monstrous headgear in amazement – it was the first time I had seen somebody with such an attire in the flesh. As to the reason for the visit or what was talked about, I had no clue.[8]

I was often in the Balcony Room, so-called because from there one could enter a loggia, which Hitler had had built looking out onto the Wilhelm-Strasse. There was a billiards table in the Balcony Room, and on quiet days I would play against myself.

I also used to visit the Models Hall in the New Reich Chancellery a lot. I could easily find out if there was anything new exhibited there if told to bring a relief for one of the female secretaries. Hitler liked to dictate in the Models Hall. The secretary would type his oration directly into a stenographic machine. This could last for hours. Every half hour, the secretary would be relieved by another. I would wander around happily between the wood and plaster models, technical prototypes and structures in miniature. I reflected for a long time on a model of Tempelhof airport. According to the plans, the airport boundaries would extend much further out to Neukölln than people realised. Hitler said that the airport was 'not being thought of for eternity'. He considered that air passenger traffic would increase so much that a city airport would no longer have the capacity for it. Sooner or later, Tempelhof would be turned into a great sports arena: racetracks, tennis courts, a swimming bath, one could make it into a health resort, he said, or an amusement park.

Much more than for many of Speer's architectural fantasies, I was interested in anything to do with technology. I was very taken by the design for a tidal power station. Like Hitler, the idea of using the tide's ebb and flow for energy production fascinated me. I was present in the Models Hall when two engineers delivered a long and complicated discourse on the use of tidal forces. 'One can only regulate a thing like that on the European level,' Hitler pointed out.

---

8 The Grand Mufti of Jerusalem visited Hitler on 28 November 1941. He supported the National Socialists, and from 1943 recruited a Muslim SS-division named *Handschar* – 13th Waffengebirgs division of SS-*Handschar*.

Hitler would come to regret the accessibility of the Models Hall. One day, he wanted to look at the model prototypes of the new Tiger tank[9] again, but they could not be found. Suspicion fell on two members of the RSD, whose own colleagues searched their houses. This brought to light – apart from the missing panzer models, which now served as toys for their sons – other items missing from the Reich Chancellery: porcelain, hand towels and cutlery. The two men, Wiebezick and Sander, had performed their duties irreproachably. I never saw either again.[10]

I was totally unable to understand this conduct. I would never have risked my position for a few trinkets from the Reich Chancellery. I was very happy in my rank, and I never attained a higher rank than Oberscharführer (sergeant). At some time or another, there was an agreement between Reichsleiter Martin Bormann and Reichsführer-SS Heinrich Himmler that there were to be no more promotions for the SS bodyguard. This decision meant that the ranks currently held were sufficient for the work done.

As I understood it, the bodyguard was paid for by the Reich Interior Ministry, for which Hans Lammers was the relevant administrator. Repeatedly, men would volunteer for the front in order to obtain promotions. Otto Günsche did this because he needed a higher rank for a career in the Foreign Ministry after the war. Of five colleagues who took this course of action, three fell at the front. Wild horses would not have dragged me back there. No, I was not desperate for a higher rank. What for? I was already 'with the Führer'.

---

9 The heavy Panzerkampfwagen VI, Tiger, was developed by the Henschel Works at Kassel. Hitler had the prototypes in service at the front during the construction phase.

10 Files of the Party chancellery reveal that, at the end of November 1940, Hitler declined to release the two from Dachau concentration camp. He added that, in future, theft and disloyalty, including stealing from SS comrades, would be dealt with (the death penalty was threatened). Payments to the wives of the inmates were to be stopped. See Institut für Zeitgeschichte, *Akten der Parteikanzlei der NSDAP*, Munich 1992, p.596.

Chapter 8

FHQ Wolfsschanze, FHQ Wehrwolf, *
Stalingrad, My Honeymoon: 1942

A T FIRST, THE DAILY routine at FHQ Wolfsschanze did not change much in the new year from the last months of the old. On the Eastern Front, the situation seemed to have stabilised, but no longer were the reports from the fronts all about successes. That we understood. I heard nothing of the Wannsee Conference on 20 January 1942 in Berlin, which was to organise in detail the extermination of the Jews which had already begun. As already mentioned, the subject of Jews and concentration camps never came up among us. Neither did anything ever filter through to us which might have led to a discussion, nor did we have any motive to talk about these things. We knew of the existence of concentration camps as work camps, but we knew nothing of what had been decided and brought into effect for the inmates of the concentration camps in the eastern territories. If Hitler had ever gone to one of those places, then we would have known, because the bodyguard was at his side around the clock. Wherever he went, we went too: from where he came, we came from there too. Our colleagues might have told me had I not

---

* Although often written 'Werwolf' (werewolf) as Misch does throughout the book, the correct spelling is Wehrwolf (play on the word 'Wehr' military). It was Hitler himself who gave this FHQ its name and spelling. See Franz Seidler & Dieter Zeigert, *Die Führerhauptquartiere*, Herbig 2001 p.222; see also Otto Wien, *Ein Leben und Viermal Deutschland*, Düsseldorf 1978, p.283. (TN)

been there myself. How could crimes of such enormity have remained such a well-kept secret?

In February and March 1942, Hitler made frequent short trips to Berlin, and we were there for a few days at the end of April before going via Munich to the Berghof, after Hitler had met Mussolini at Schloss Klessheim. Morale was exceptionally good. Hitler was openly delighted to see Mussolini again. He was quite in his element, talkative and in high spirits. After the banquets, we went back to the Berghof, where the Duce visited us the next day. At the beginning of May 1942, we were back at FHQ Wolfsschanze.

At that time, I was not in the best of health. I had stomach trouble, intermittent attacks, which caused me painful spasms. Apparently, people were aware of this, and to my great surprise even Hitler had noticed. One morning he spoke to me. He had gone past me into his barrack hut, but then returned into the open and, after giving me a critical look, said: 'Misch – you do not look well.' Rather hesitantly, I explained my medical problem, and he nodded with a sigh when I finished speaking: 'I have the same thing. Go and see Morell, he will give you something for it.' So Professor Morell, Hitler's personal physician, had the job of getting me fit again. That was not actually said. If Hitler was of the opinion that I did not look good, then Morell had to do something and I had to follow his decision. The doctor sent me at once to recover in the world-famous spa resort at Karlsbad.[1]

In the train on my way there I got to know a young lady, with whom I had an animated conversation. When a totally bald elderly gentleman got into the fully occupied compartment, I stood up to offer him my seat. He waved it aside: 'I would not want to disturb your pleasant conversation.' Still in elated mood from the train journey, not so boring as I thought it was going to be, I reported to the Karlsbad Sanatorium. I had been ordered to take a paid-for cure – and, far from the gloomy mood at FHQ Wolfsschanze, I gradually began to enjoy

---

1 Today Karlovy Vary (Czech Republic).

my stay at the spa. My happy mood soon dampened when I discovered what awaited me, however.

At a small welcoming ceremony for new arrivals we were informed with great emphasis about what the cure involved. Dietary preparations were the most important part of the treatment. The ban on salt was intended to be taken very seriously. Whoever was seen with a salt pot would be sent packing immediately, irrespective of person, rank or decorations. Then almost ceremoniously, the senior physician was introduced, and as he entered the room, everybody rose. In surprise, I recognised him as the bald-headed man from the train. The new arrivals lined up to greet him. When he saw me he showed by a brief friendly nod that he remembered me and that therefore I need not step forward to take part in the official greeting ceremony. It was in any case an advantage to be in the good books of the leading physician. I knew how to use that. I spent many delightful hours with a female fellow sufferer, a harmless admirer. Charlie Rivel made a guest appearance nearby, with his show *Akrobat schön*, and we had an unforgettable evening.

FHQ Wehrwolf

After my return to Berlin at the end of 1942 I was flown directly to FHQ Wehrwolf by one of the daily courier services. FHQ Wehrwolf was the largest of three installations in the conquered areas of the Soviet Union to be built as temporary headquarters. It was located in the Ukraine in birch woodland along the road between Zhitomir and the town of Vinniza on the Bug river. Nearby was a village called Kalinovka. FHQ Wehrwolf consisted of two bunkers and a large number of blockhouses and barrack huts.

My duties at FHQ Wehrwolf were mainly to be near Hitler, awaiting his orders. There was no telephone duty for me here either. Most of the day I was the man to ask about anti-mosquito measures. Unbelievable as it may be, this place had even more mosquitoes than FHQ Wolfsschanze.

On duty, therefore, I had not much to do, and off duty – well, it was pure country life. I found it no problem, I came from the land. My colleagues and I often hired a car and drove into the village near the headquarters to engage in trade. The locals produced a wonderful vegetable oil, which I sent to Gerda. I paid for it with women's clothing, sewing needles and stockings organised from Mitropa, but also with salt. Gerda would fetch the packet at the Reich Chancellery after receiving my telegram 'Today at R.Ch. – packet.' After we were married, she was given an identity card, which gave her unfettered entry, even into Hitler's suite.

While serving at FHQ Wehrwolf I obtained for the first time a deeper insight into the up-to-date war situation. In September, a violent exchange flared up among the participants of the daily Führer's situation conference. General Franz Halder, chief of staff at OKH, dared to tell Hitler that his field objectives asked too much of the soldiers at the front. Hitler bellowed at Halder, asking how he knew what a soldier was capable of. He himself could look back on four years' experience at the front in the First World War. Halder was immediately replaced by Kurt Zeitzler, recently promoted to General der Infanterie.[2]

After the altercation between Hitler and the Wehrmacht command staff, none of which I overheard, I noticed loud music coming from Hitler's study: *'Dein ist mein ganzes Herz, wo du nicht bist, kann ich nicht sein . . .'* – Joseph Schmidt[3] was a very well-known Jewish chamber music singer of the time. As I heard this beautiful song, from outside I looked in disbelief through the open window into Hitler's

---

2 Ian Kershaw reported two loud altercations: one on 24 August 1942, between Hitler and General Franz Halder, who was relieved of his post that day; and another on 5 September 1942, between Hitler and General Jodl, head of the Wehrmacht command staff at OKW. See Kershaw, *Hitler 1936–1945*, Stuttgart 2000, pp.698ff.

3 Joseph Schmidt (1904–1942) died, after fleeing the Nazis, in the Swiss internment camp at Girenbad, where he was awaiting a decision on his application for political asylum.

room. He was slumped in his chair, immersed in thought, the loneliest man in the world. Here I saw Hitler at his saddest.

The increasing disputes with the Wehrmacht command staff led to Hitler's order that, from now on, all situation conferences had to be recorded by shorthand writers. He himself had a wonderful memory. If ever there was an argument about what had been said, ordered or uttered in opinion – ultimately, if evidence existed – he would be proved right. It might be years later, but he remembered everything. If there were any disputes, he would have old papers brought from the archives and presented in triumph to his flabbergasted opposite number.

Hitler had a photographic memory – he would master reading material in a flash. If there were no files, Hitler could not prove that he had remembered accurately. By having stenographers take down everything verbatim, he would put a stop to people twisting his words and put an end once and for all to the tiresome and endless discussions about who had said what and when and in what connection. We were ordered: 'If Grenadier Arse arrives from the front, whatever he says must be recorded!' Indirectly, Hitler's decision to employ stenographers was to cost one his life[4] at FHQ Wolfsschanze on 20 July 1944.

Stalingrad

Towards the end of October 1942, the headquarters was pulled back to FHQ Wolfsschanze. All discussions revolved around the fighting at Stalingrad.

One morning after beginning duty I passed Hitler's rooms. He was at the breakfast table alone. Bussmann, his servant, approached me. He said I was to fetch General Friedrich Paulus.[5] 'He must come to Hitler at once.' I thought he would be with Keitel, but found there only one of his junior adjutants. 'He will probably be in the officers' mess,' the latter said. Paulus was indeed there, and I spoke first to one of his senior adjutants, who led me to him: 'Herr Generaloberst,

---

4 This stenographer was Heinrich Berger.
5 Field Marshal Friedrich Paulus (1890–1957).

96

will you please follow me, the Führer is waiting for you.' Outside it had been below zero for some time, and Paulus therefore put on his very long greatcoat. Then I brought him to Hitler's study. During the conversation Bussmann had things to do in the room, and there was no stenographer present. Hitler's servant and I had a good relationship. He came out from time to time to keep me informed.

It appears that Paulus had tried to convince Hitler to allow him to extract his forces to unite with the army of Field Marshal Ewald von Kleist, which was reforming in the Caucasus. At first, Hitler was against it, but then seemed to be in favour, because Bussmann came out and whispered: 'Paulus is drawing back to the Caucasus!'

Because the talk was drawn out, the midday situation conference that day began towards half past twelve. Beside Keitel, Jodl and Paulus, also present were Göring, Admiral Raeder, commander-in-chief of the Kriegsmarine and I think also Karl Dönitz, commander-in-chief of the U-boat arm,* Walter Warlimont, a Jodl representative and Zeitzler.

I remained on duty in front of the conference barrack hut until two that afternoon, went off for two hours, and when I returned at 1600 hrs the conference was still going on. Now and again, one of the participants would request a glass of water or a snack. I soon discovered what was being discussed. It was all about Paulus's withdrawal to join Kleist's forces, and there were two opposing camps – Göring being of the opinion that the Volga must not be abandoned under any circumstances. The river had to be blocked to cut off the Russian supply lines. If the Volga was closed down, not a drop of oil would get from the Caspian Sea to the north, and that would cut Stalin's artery. Paulus, on the other hand, wanted permission to abandon the positions held by Sixth Army at Stalingrad, in order to make a tactical withdrawal as soon as possible. He considered his position to be exposed and had major problems of supply. Göring's argument about cutting off Stalin's oil reserves from the Caspian Sea and pressing forward with the war

---

* Misch gets this wrong, Dönitz did not replace Raeder as commander-in-chief of the German Kriegsmarine until the beginning of 1943. (TN)

held the day, however. Accepting Göring's opinion, Hitler ruled: 'Paulus, you stay in Stalingrad.' This judgement ended hours of debate and sealed the fate of the Sixth Army.

Paulus took his defeat calmly. He made a serious but by no means downcast impression when passing me to climb into his car immediately after the conference, to drive back to the Wehrmacht-HQ Mauerwald. It was the last time I saw him.

On 7 November 1942, we travelled aboard the Führer's special train to Munich, so that Hitler could deliver on the following day his annual speech at the Löwenbräukeller, commemorating the 1923 attempted putsch. Afterwards, we spent a few days at the Berghof. We were there when news arrived of the encirclement of the Sixth Army.[6] Hitler planned to supply it from the air. He forbade any attempt to break out; the city had to be held at all costs. This bad news about the situation at Stalingrad forced Hitler to return to FHQ Wolfsschanze.

I know that many people perceived Hitler to be changed after Stalingrad. I did not find that to be so. I saw nothing about him outwardly that struck me as a different person. He seemed to me to be still absolutely convinced that what he was doing and what he intended was right; he was self-confident and decisive. Also, I did not notice any sudden physical decay. The trembling left hand, the ageing of his features – those I associate with the last few weeks in the Berlin bunker. But even then I could not identify an exact point when these changes were perceptible from one day to another. If one is in contact daily with a person, developments like that did not make much of an impression. Certainly, after Stalingrad there were increasingly periods of loneliness, in which Hitler would withdraw to his study, to be alone and introspective, but for me he continued to give the impression that he was the same man he had always been. Only the trips to Berlin became rarer, and he did away with the evening film shows.

---

6 As a result of a Soviet offensive begun on 19 November 1942, the Sixth Army was encircled on 22 November 1942.

My Honeymoon

I spent Christmas 1942 in Berlin. On New Year's Eve, I married Gerda. At that time she was an employee in the foreign trade department of the Reich Economy Ministry and learning English and Spanish. Later, she became secretary to a professor of medicine at the Humboldt University in Berlin. Gerda was ambitious and successful, and always had excellent assessments and references. We had not been able to spend much time together before our marriage, and we only saw each other regularly when I was in Berlin.

For our marriage we received from the Reich Chancellery two cases of wine, twenty bottles each of red and white. Herr Fechner, the cellarman at the Chancellery, was sixty-six years of age by then, and he had serviced the wine cellars of Kaiser Wilhelm II. He went in person to the wine warehouses at Potsdam, to make the selection. According to their labels, some of the wines were 1921 vintage – a very special year, as Fechner told me. There was also a special payment of 1,500 Reichsmark and a greetings card on which Hitler had written: 'My warmest best wishes – Adolf Hitler.' Fechner let me into the secret that Albert Bormann had informed 'the boss' of my impending marriage. My witnesses were my colleagues Karl Tenazek and Helmuth Beermann. Helmuth had proven himself once more as the 'supplier', and through Mitropa had obtained the wedding rings and the bride's veil, both from Paris. The wedding feast, of saddle of venison, was prepared for us by a female cook at the Reich Chancellery.

At the small celebration in the garden of my parents-in-law we drank only two bottles of the wine; the rest we buried later. When we changed out of our wedding apparel, we repeated the proceedings and then buried the wine in the new garden so as to make Hitler's present bombproof in the truest sense of the word. Whether it remained intact to the end, I do not know. We never dug up the chest, which also contained my decorations and the certificate from the rifle competition of 1936. Today, the spot lies under concrete with garages built over it.

After our marriage we were entitled to larger quarters, so we moved into a new place at Karlshorst. The rent of around eighty-seven Reichsmarks was paid by the Reich Chancellery. We really wanted to move to Lankwitz near the house of my Aunt Sofia, but shortly before there had been heavy air raids there, and no brick had been left standing on another.

Near the Reich Chancellery there was a police sector, and I knew quite well one of the officials who used to patrol past our dwelling. One day after the air raids I asked this man, who was called Herr Friedrich, where one could still find a nice place to live in Berlin. His own home was in Karlshorst, and he mentioned some addresses in the area. Thus, we selected a home in that district of Berlin where in May 1945 Field Marshal Wilhelm Keitel would sign the instrument of surrender.

My wedding had freed me of the gloomy mood at the year's end at FHQ Wolfsschanze, for which I was very glad. While the catastrophe at Stalingrad dominated everything there, Gerda and I went on honeymoon in a Reichsbahn couchette. We went to the Black Forest, to the hotel Zur Sonne at Bad Herrenalb. The sister of my colleague Bussmann was a cook there. Shortly after my marriage, I was promoted to Oberscharführer (sergeant) and my wife then received an identity card from the Reich Chancellery.

Chapter 9

The Eastern Front Begins to Turn West: 1943

I N MID-JANUARY 1943 I had to return to FHQ Wolfsschanze. At the end of January, Paulus held in the siege at Stalingrad surrendered. As the war situation began to look more serious, a mood of disquiet began to affect my colleagues in the bodyguard. It drew some to the front. They simply could not stand by and do nothing while others faced the foe. They wanted to fight.

Hitler was not at all happy about it. He complained to the commander of the *SS-Leibstandarte*, Sepp Dietrich: 'They are taking my best men!' One evening, when he was sitting with his female secretaries, Hitler asked everyone: 'What's the reason for it? What am I doing wrong? All my staff are running away from me!' Dara, as we called secretary Gerda Daranowski,[1] said: 'You are not doing anything wrong, *mein Führer*. They come to you as a reward. Only the young ones are soldiers! They do not want to run around in patent leather shoes. They want to be soldiers. Take people out of the bodyguard as adjutants.' She then went on – quite openly – to recommend Otto Günsche, after he had returned from fighting at the front in January 1943. He was actually appointed as Hitler's personal SS adjutant.[2]

---

1 Gerda Christian, née Daranowski (1913–1997), was from 1937 one of Hitler's secretaries.

2 Otto Günsche (1917–2003) did not become Hitler's personal adjutant until February 1944; from January 1943 he acted in a deputy capacity but

Günsche and Dara were very close, but she went onto marry Luftwaffe Major Eckhard Christian.

Apart from a few short breaks in Berlin, on the Berghof or in the Ukraine, Hitler was at FHQ Wolfsschanze. In February 1943, we left there to visit the Eastern Front in the sector of Army Group South. This was commanded by General Erich von Manstein, his headquarters being at Zaporozhye in the Donets Basin.[3] Five aircraft escorted us. As soon as we arrived, I felt the violent drop in temperature. It was bitterly cold, and I began to understand what it must have been like at Stalingrad.

Hitler had come to meet Manstein on account of the violent fighting for Kharkov in which first one and then the other side gained the upper hand.[4] Originally, Hitler had scheduled five days for the visit. On the third day, however, the Soviet artillery surprised us by advancing threateningly close to reach the airfield at Zaporozhye. Hitler had to be rushed to an airstrip about forty kilometres away in order to be flown to the secure FHQ Wehrwolf. My colleague Paul Holtz and I had to hold out one day more. We had been left behind to ensure that, in the haste of his departure, nothing had been forgotten. Fortunately, the Soviet tanks had pulled back to their positions without ever having suspected whom they had got within visual range of capturing.

---

between September 1943 and January 1944 he commanded a company of the *SS-Leibstandarte* Panzer Division at the front.

3 From 17 to 19 February 1943, Hitler stayed at the headquarters of Army Group South (previously Army Group Don). Nicolaus von Below, *At Hitler's Side*, London, 2004, p.165. Hitler had changed his plans at short notice after having intended to fly to Poltava; in this way, he avoided his assassination planned by General Hubert Lanz and Brigadier Hans Speidel. Peter Hoffmann, *Die Sicherheit des Diktators*, Munich/Zürich 1975, p.161.

4 The city of Kharkov was captured on 24 October 1941 by units of the Sixth Army and evacuated on 16 February 1943 by SS-General Paul Hausser to avoid his troops being encircled. This evacuation, which was contrary to his orders, lay behind Hitler's meeting with Manstein. Under Manstein's command, the city was regained in March 1943, but finally abandoned to the Soviets in August 1943.

Paul Holtz and I discovered nothing to bring back with us. Next day, we were not sure what was worse: to remain in close contact with Soviet tanks or fly out. There was a fearsome blizzard blowing. I was already queasy when, alone, I boarded the aircraft that was to fly to FHQ Wehrwolf. The men of Manstein's squad had given us more than enough to drink the previous evening. The flight was a horror. Turbulence gave us a roller-coaster of a ride. Only with a giant portion of luck did we come out of it alive.

In March we returned to East Prussia and FHQ Wolfsschanze.

Hitler's Treasure Chamber

I was pleased when, soon afterwards, my service schedule gave me the opportunity for a few days' stay in Berlin. In my private flat at Karlshorst I had two paintings that belonged to Hitler. They were on loan from the Treasure Chamber. When Gerda and I had moved in after our marriage, I had remarked to Albert Bormann that our new flat was very pleasant but the white walls were very bare. 'Well, why not look for something nice,' he replied and led me straight away to the so-called Treasure Chamber of the Old Reich Chancellery. This was where all manner of valuables were kept, particularly gifts made to Hitler. Among the many valuables – some glorious, some appalling – was a handwritten letter from Wilhelm, Prince of Prussia, son of the late German Kaiser Wilhelm II, who had died in 1940. In the most beautiful Sütterlin script, he notified the Reich chancellor of his father's death and made it known that he was now the head of the House of Hohenzollern. The Reich chancellor could rest assured that the House of Hohenzollern under his leadership would continue to support the government. It struck me that the letter was addressed expressly to 'Herr Reich chancellor', and that 'the Führer' was never mentioned, nor had the writer ended the letter with 'Heil Hitler!' Probably for these reasons the document had been consigned to the Treasure Chamber, instead of being exhibited somewhere for information.

Now, Albert Bormann really encouraged me to pick out two paintings on loan, with which I could decorate my home. I selected one large and one smaller picture. The larger one was of a rough sea with pounding waves; the other had three prancing horses and was a very valuable work of art by an artist whose name I have unfortunately forgotten, some professor or other in any case. Albert Bormann cautioned me that I must return the paintings at once, should they be required. He observed from other things that he could trust me. Thus, one day he showed me some proceedings he was working on right then in Hitler's private Chancellery, about maintenance for three children of a soldier who had got three women – mother, daughter and aunt – pregnant during a single stay at private quarters in Westphalia. The question of who was responsible for the support of a child of incest in the family of a cabinet member (whose name Bormann allowed me to see) was a tricky one. Hitler had to decide that kind of thing. Albert Bormann knew he could rely on my discretion. My commanding officer and Hitler's chief adjutant Schaub also valued my reliability. Thus, once I was sent as a courier alone all the way across Berlin to the postal cheque office with a travelling bag. Schaub laughed at my shocked expression when he told me what it had contained: 100,000 Reichsmarks – an enormous sum at that time.

From then on, the two paintings adorned our living room. Hitler never got them back. When my wife returned to her parents at Rudow towards the end of the war, she left them in our Karlshorst flat. Either the neighbours appropriated them or the Russians did so.

The paintings were not the only pieces that found their way to my flat from the Reich Chancellery. A ceiling lamp from the staff restroom dangled – and still does – above my kitchen table. When I saw the house technician Johannes Hentschel unscrewing it one day I asked what he was going to do with it. 'Throw it away,' he replied with a shrug of the shoulders. It was still working and outwardly whole, and so I claimed it. Another lamp from Hitler's reception room, which I liked very much, I had copied by the Berlin-Neukölln manufacturers.

Uncle Paul in a Concentration Camp

The relationship with my parents-in-law was, as I have said, very good. My father-in-law, with his SPD past, left me in no doubt as to what he thought of the regime, but that did not cloud our relationship. Before I met my wife I had never had contact with people, such as Gerda's father, of the extreme left. In my circle they were know as proletarians. In the intimate family circle, we often spoke about earlier SPD times. 'Uncle' Paul,[5] the often-mentioned close friend of my parents-in-law, had been a leading light with the Social Democrats for some time.

By chance, Paul's difficulties began when I was staying in Berlin. Excited fellow travellers of his hurried to Gerda to let her know that the Gestapo had come for him and taken him to Sachsenhausen concentration camp in Oranienburg. Gerda rang me at the Reich Chancellery at once. She sounded distressed. It was clear that people were hoping I could help. I knew to whom I should turn – and lost no time. Immediately, I went to Lieutenant General Karl Wolff[6] at his offices in Prinz-Albrecht Palace. It was not far to the SS RSHA[7] from the Reich Chancellery. Wolff was head of Himmler's personal staff, and from time to time acted as Waffen-SS liaison officer at FHQ. He did not seem to me to be an unpleasant type. He was also very calm and objective.[8]

---

5 Paul Volkmann was arrested frequently during the Nazi period as a Social Democrat and trade unionist. In December 1945, after making a speech at Königs Wusterhausen, he was arrested by the Soviets and tried for 'anti-state activities'. Sentenced to fifteen years' imprisonment, he died at Waldheim Prison in 1951.

6 Karl Friedrich Otto Wolff (1900–1984) was head of Reichsführer-SS Himmler's personal staff, Himmler's right-hand man.

7 Himmler's edict of 27 September 1939 had merged the Security Police (SiPo) and Security Service (SD). The new Reichssicherheitshauptamt RSHA (Reich security head Office) unified the state and Party organisations. The most important section of the RSHA was Abt.IV (combating opponents of regime) headed by Heinrich 'Gestapo' Müller. See Frank Gutermuth and Arno Netzband, *Die Gestapo*, Berlin 2005, p.117.

8 On 30 September 1964, Wolff was sentenced by a court in Munich to fifteen years' imprisonment for complicity in the murders of at least 300,000 people (deportations

Wolff received me at once, and I explained to him that a relative of my family had been wrongly arrested. I admitted that 'Uncle' Paul had once been a member of the SPD and active in trade unionism. But all that was long behind him. I swore that he no longer had any contact with prohibited opposition groups. The lie slipped easily off my tongue. On one thing I was certain: I would put my hand into the fire for 'Uncle' Paul. My feathers being ruffled, I added, I would not leave the room until I could be sure that he, Wolff, would look into the case. Wolff promised to do so without much fuss, took down the name, and three days later 'Uncle' Paul was back home. He and his wife called by my flat to thank me. I asked him about his experiences at the concentration camp, but he avoided the question, saying only that the worst thing had been the paper shirts the inmates were made to wear. Despite all my enquiries, I could get nothing out of him. Never in my presence did he ever say anything about what befell him there. Neither shortly after his release, nor later.

A Handshake with Mussolini

I was at the Berghof from April to July 1943. It was not such a carefree time as it has been the previous year. Hitler surrounded himself only with his intimate circle and met the most important Axis statesmen primarily at Schloss Klessheim. Besides Mussolini and Horthy, he received representatives from Norway, Slovakia, King Boris of Bulgaria, Ion Antonescu of Romania and the French politician Pierre Laval. The times when the Berghof would be filled with a large number of guests, including those from Eva's circle of friends, were past. Visits by the Speers were still very well received. Hitler continued to enjoy his conversations with Albert Speer on questions of architecture and city planning. One might suspect that the Allied air raids were nothing more than welcome demolition work for all the wonderful new city buildings that the pair were developing. Hitler found in

---

to the extermination camp at Treblinka).

Speer his ideal counterpart, a man capable of embracing his visions and turning them into what he had in mind in this area. Whenever Hitler and the buildings inspector-general were engrossed in their plans and drawings, Hitler was usually in a good mood. For his ability to cheer Hitler up, we of the bodyguard valued Speer, but otherwise he seemed to us to be a really queer fish, even a little crazy as artists tend to be.

At the beginning of July, Hitler returned to FHQ Wolfsschanze. At the same time, the major summer offensive in the east, code-named Zitadelle,[9] began – and I got some leave.

The choice of where to go I had made some time previously: Niedersee in Masuria. I met my wife in Berlin, and we took the night train to Rastenburg. Earlier, I had informed my colleagues about our arrival, so somebody from the FHQ Wolfsschanze motor pool fetched us from the railway station and took us to Niedersee. The driver returned to FHQ Wolfsschanze, leaving Gerda and myself to spend two weeks holidaying in the region, which I had reconnoitred for that purpose on my many car excursions with my colleagues. We took boat trips, went swimming a lot and enjoyed the amenities of our hotel, in which, incidentally, a troupe of well-known German actors were resting, among them the great René Deltgen. As we discovered, a UFA film was being shot in the area.[10]

At the end of the two weeks, our holiday was at an end, and the summer offensive had come to grief. The Soviet breach of the German southern front, the Kursk Elbow, had not been repulsed. Now, on all fronts on Soviet territory, the retreat began. I went back with Gerda to Berlin, spent the last week of my leave there and celebrated my twenty-sixth birthday. Then I returned to FHQ Wolfsschanze and caught up with what had happened during my leave. Without exception, it was bad news. Allied troops had landed in Sicily (Operation Husky).

---

9 Operation Zitadelle was the code name for an attack on the bend in the Soviet front near the town of Kursk ('the Kursk Elbow'). This operation between 5 and 13 July 1943 was the last major German offensive in the east.

10 This was the UFA production *Sommernächte* (Summer Nights).

Mussolini had been deposed and arrested on the order of King Victor Emanuel III. There had been a coup in Italy, and a devastating thousand-bomber air raid[11] on Hamburg, which had reduced the city to rubble and ashes. The mood was edgy. Hitler railed endlessly against the Luftwaffe, calling for an immediate strengthening of the flak and air defences.

At the beginning of September, Italy capitulated.[12] Hitler did not have a good word to say about Italian soldiers. They were a mixture of the best and the worst. He considered German and French soldiers to be the most capable. He allowed that Britain was the only nation that could run colonies successfully. In passing, I picked up that Hitler had had Prince Philipp of Hesse, the son-in-law of the king of Italy, arrested.[13]

Mussolini was finally freed by an SS special squad,[14] and later he was installed by Hitler as leader of the Italian Social Republic.[15] On 14 September 1943, Hitler received the freed Mussolini at FHQ Wolfsschanze. Everybody paraded on the airfield at Rastenburg to greet him, and the Duce was apparently very touched by the entire event. He shook the hand of every man of the bodyguard very heartily, as if we were old acquaintances from whom he had been long parted. The atmosphere was, in any case, always special when Mussolini visited Hitler. There was

---

11 Between 24 and 30 July 1943 there were a series of air raids over Hamburg, which claimed the lives of more than 30,000 inhabitants (Operation Gomorrah).

12 It was made known on 8 September that, on 3 September, Italy had signed an armistice with the Western Allies.

13 'Partly from spite, partly because he might know too much and prove dangerous, Hitler had Prince Philip of Hesse, the King of Italy's son-in-law, who had been at FHQ for some weeks, promptly arrested and deposited in Gestapo Headquarters in Königsberg.' See Ian Kershaw, *Hitler 1936–1945*, London 2000, p.60.

14 Mussolini was freed from an alpine hotel on the Gran Sasso in the Abruzzen by paratroopers and an SS squad led by Austrian SS-Hauptsturmführer (captain) Otto Skorzeny, using troop gliders.

15 Republica Sociale Italiana (RSI) was a Fascist state in northern Italy under German protection from September 1943 to April 1945. Mussolini was its head of state.

no other meeting with a politician that compared to it. The two of them would actually have an almost friendly conversation. Otto Skorzeny, the SS officer who had been behind the liberation of Mussolini, was also at FHQ Wolfsschanze that autumn day. He celebrated amply. I met him as he left the officers' mess, making his way through many handshakes by colleagues. He even shook my hand in elation.

The liberation of Mussolini provided only a brief excuse to celebrate. Along the whole Eastern Front, the Soviets had taken the initiative and did not let it up again. The situation became ever more threatening. My colleagues had intense discussions about every report from the front.

From November 1943, the population of Berlin began to experience heavy air raids.[16] Through my duties at Führer-HQ, I was often able to give my family early warning of impending air raids. At FHQ Wolfsschanze, we were obviously informed first by Göring's staff about incoming bomber formations. Often we knew they would be coming before the aircraft in England had even taken off. We told each other at once, and I would ring Gerda in Berlin to warn her. This advance information was naturally of great value. Above all, however, it gave one a feeling of being underhand, but in the anxiety one had for one's family also provided a comforting feeling of safety.

Many incidents would have seemed trifling in peacetime. On the way to lunch in the officers' mess, I could hardly believe my eyes – wasn't that Heinz Rühmann coming towards me? Quax, the pilot who always crashed?[17] Yes, it definitely was him. I had no idea what he was doing at FHQ Wolfsschanze, and neither did my colleagues. It was not the case that we of the SS bodyguard would be informed especially of such visitors. Not until later did I discover that Rühmann

---

16 Air Marshal Harris ordered the 'Air Battle of Berlin'. The RAF attacks began on the night of 18 November 1943; in the next four months, sixteen major air raids were flown. www.raf.uk/bombercommand/nov43.html

17 In the first film of the series *Quax der Bruchpilot* (1941), Heinz Rühmann played the role of the trainee pilot Otto Groschenbügel, named Quax.

had shown his new film *Die Feuerzangenbowle* here, because the Ministry of Propaganda had a problem with it, and the matter had to be decided at the highest level. Whether Rühmann showed the film to Hitler personally I do not know; anyway, I never saw the two of them together.[18]

At the beginning of November 1943, we boarded the special train at Rastenburg for Munich, where on 8 November Hitler made his annual speech in the Bürgerbräukeller, in remembrance of the martyrs of the movement. This would be the last speech on the anniversary of the 1923 attempted putsch.

Belief in 'Final Victory' was no longer unshakeable. 'The war is lost' – in the autumn of 1943, the phrase escaped from even Hitler's mouth. I did not hear it myself, but it spread like wildfire. The colleague who told me said that Hitler had not uttered it in conversation, but more to himself, as if he were telling himself.

New strategies and technical developments were always coming to the forefront, with great hopes attached. I was especially impressed by a display of new aircraft on the airfield at Insterburg (today Chernyakhovsk, near FHQ Wolfsschanze). The pilots were introduced to Hitler in the presence of General Jodl[19] and manufacturer Ernst Heinkel.[20] Then the trio stationed themselves up on the hangar, while

---

18 Heinz Rühmann stated in his memoirs that the film was shown not to Hitler, but to Göring among others. 'At midday came the report, Göring had reported to Hitler at the early conference and told him that the film had been forbidden for release. Why he had no idea but in any case yesterday everybody had been laughing their heads off.' Hitler had then decided that the film should be released, but he had not been able to receive him, Rühmann, personally because of the bad situation on the Eastern Front. See Heinz Rühmann, *Das war's*, Frankfurt/Main, Berlin 1987 (first edn 1982) p.154.

19 On 26 November 1943 at the Insterburg airfield, Göring organised exhibition flights by aircraft including the Ju 390 and Me 262. According to the memoirs of Hitler's Luftwaffe adjutant Nicolaus von Below, neither Jodl nor Heinkel were present, but among others Göring, Speer and aircraft manufacturer Messerschmitt were. See Nicolaus von Below, *At Hitler's Side*, London 2004, pp.186–7.

20 Ernst Heinkel (1888–1958) was a German engineer and aircraft manufacturer.

I stood with two colleagues near the apron. The display began with the six-engined Ju 390 and some four-engined Blohm & Voss machines. The Ju 390 had a range of more than 10,000 kilometres without refuelling.[21] The aircraft played their war games in the sky and were replaced by a couple of night-fighters. After that, two jet aircraft took off. Their flight path could only be followed briefly before the clouds swallowed them up.

Finally came the high point of the display – a rocket-fighter.[22] A major took his leave of Hitler and climbed into a capsule on a firing ramp. Hinged cockpit lid up, lid closed. My colleagues and I stared at the capsule fascinated and expectant. Suddenly, we heard an explosion, a deafening noise and the capsule was on its way. For some time, nothing happened. Somewhere, there was a sound like thunder, but nothing could be seen in the direction from which it came. Long before the thunder, a large triangular object had swept past us slowly losing height. It rocked left and right like a gigantic bat. Not fifty metres from us, it set down on its skid and inclined slightly to one side. The capsule was not opened at once, but a tractor arrived to tow the machine with its occupant still inside into the hangar. I was impressed. Special warnings about secrecy were not issued, even on occasions like this.

Heilig Abend and Two Rendezvous

Around Christmas 1943, it was relatively quiet. Hitler was at FHQ Wehrwolf, while my duties kept me at the Reich Chancellery. On Heilig Abend (Christmas Eve) there were three of us on the telephone, and we were bored. There was little work, and we had received information

---

21 Two prototypes (models V1 and V2) of the Ju 390 were built. It does not appear that their range was ever quoted at 'more than 10,000 kilometres'.

22 Misch is describing here a Messerschmitt 163 Komet. This rocket-driven, short-range interceptor fighter was the fastest aircraft of the Second World War, and an Me 163A-0 broke the world speed record at 1003 km/h in a flight on 2 October 1941. According to the Air and Space Travel section of the Deutscher Museum, this aircraft would have been a prototype in autumn 1943.

that no Allied air raids were expected for the coming hours. We began to joke and fool around with the switchboard. Suddenly, Karl Weichelt seized the telephone directory: 'I have a suitably festive idea.' The directory sailed over my head and landed on the table beyond me. 'Just look for Heilig.'

'What for?'

'Look!'

Eagerly he flicked through another directory. There were lots of subscribers called 'Heilig'. Karl tapped his finger on another surname: 'Abend'. We grinned. We needed to make a number of calls before the people rung announced their surnames together and we obtained the desired 'Heilig Abend'. A man's voice first: 'Here is Heilig.' Then a woman: 'Abend'.

Herr Heilig reacted gruffly: 'What do you want then?'

'But you called me.'

'Don't talk nonsense, you called me!'

At first the pair of them were quite indignant, but then the man began to suspect a prank. We listened in to the conversation discreetly and became the witnesses to a small telephone flirtation. Karl could not believe it: 'Man, they're still talking.' The conversation went on for half an hour, and at the end of it they arranged to meet. Herr Heilig said he would bring along the provisions intended for his brother in France, and Frau Abend promised to bake a cake. Who had brought them together they had no idea. We decided we had done our good deed for the day. That it was strictly forbidden to set up private conversations was something overlooked by us that Christmas Eve.

Chapter 10

The Philanderer: 1944

THE MOOD OF CHRISTMAS cheer was soon gone. Incessant bad reports followed. The situation on the Eastern Front was more worrying every day. Hitler's order of 'Hold out at all costs' could not be complied with; in the south, the Soviets had broken through to the Bug. And now troops were being withdrawn from there, in order to stop the Allied invasion in Italy. Hitler wanted to use all available forces to prevent the advance of the Allies from their landing point at Anzio.

In mid-February, we moved to the Berghof. FHQ Wolfsschanze was meanwhile being expanded and made safer against possible air raids. This work was again done by Organisation Todt. New bunkers were built and the roof thickness of the Führerbunker was increased to seven metres.

Before we reached the Berghof, Hitler stopped off in Munich to meet Gerdy Troost. We went to the Führerbau,[1] where Frau Troost led Hitler through an exhibition. She handled questions on the inner architecture of many government buildings. Hitler had once lived at a house in Prinzregent-Strasse 16, where a Frau Winter still kept two of the six bedrooms, which he had rented long ago, available for him.

---

1 The Führerbau in Arcis-Strasse was built between 1933 and 1937 by Paul Ludwig Troost and served as Adolf Hitler's reception building. Among other things, the 1938 Munich Agreement was signed there. Today, it is a music school.

The rooms were on the second floor. We of the bodyguard were two staircases higher up.

Apart from her exhibition of panzers, aircraft and automobiles, I had little interest in Frau Troost's field of activity, and I made no attempt to follow her and Hitler into the exhibition room, but remained in the reception hall. I passed the time in conversation with the female cloakroom attendant. She mentioned that she would like to meet me after duty for a glass of wine, but I had to decline regretfully, because I would still be on duty and have to accompany the Führer when he left that evening.

Finally, Hitler reappeared and, just as he was passing her, to my horror she said: 'I would like to go out with him this evening.' Here, she pointed at me: 'but he says he will be on duty.' Hitler looked around for our commander: 'Gesche, Gesche – Misch has the evening free.' After 'the boss' had therefore forced me, I did take the girl out for dinner and then returned to my colleagues. I was naturally surprised by Hitler's reaction – even more by the fact that he remembered my name. Since entering his service in 1940, he had perhaps called me 'Misch' only twice, but he had never forgotten my name, for his famously good memory served him well.

Philanderer Bormann

The following day we arrived at the Berghof. To protect against Allied air raids, something special had been dreamed up. If there was an air raid over Bavaria, the entire Berchtesgaden Valley was to be concealed in artificial smoke. Smoke barrels had been set up, which would envelope the whole area in a thick soup within minutes.

Over the next few weeks, the usual clique assembled at the Berghof. Among them were SS-General Sepp Dietrich, Professor Morell, diplomat Hewel, the Speers and, of course, Martin Bormann. Of all these people, I only really liked Hewel. He was always in a good mood and had excellent social manners.

Hitler was 'zabel-ing' again. We invented the verb for the local Zabel Sanatorium named after Professor Werner Zabel and which prepared Hitler's diet. He stuck to his regimen with an iron will. Nothing and nobody could deflect him from his oatmeal gruel and the repellent rest, which he himself decreed for his stomach problems. I myself – no stranger to such problems – did not have this discipline. I just needed a proper diet.

Apart from the special Zabel cures, Hitler's dietary plan was not very varied. He employed his own diet-cook. In 1944, there was a lot of interest in Marlene von Exner, a rather austere-looking but attractive young woman of my age. Hitler had got her from Antonescu after he told Hitler on a visit that only this Viennese woman had been able control his own stomach problems. Frau von Exner then replaced Hitler's former female cook, Scharfitzel, whom house administrator Kannenberg had dismissed one day on suspicion of misappropriating food supplies. Because food had long been on ration, Scharfitzel's target had been the butter. Well yes, even I helped myself now and again from the large tub with iced water in which many small lumps of butter floated, but it equalled itself out, because I supplied Hitler with apples. One day I had received a basket of apples from my Aunt Sofia, but had to go back to the Reich Chancellery. Aunt Sofia was working at that time in a tree-improvement business. When I left the apples briefly in the kitchen, the cook Herr Lange came running up delighted: 'Just leave them here.' From then until late in the war, I was therefore Hitler's apple supplier. At the end of the war there was no fresh fruit to be had anywhere.

Shortly after the dismissal of Frau Scharfitzel, Hitler ordered that at every meal only two pats of butter were to be distributed at each place. Herr Lange later ran his own restaurant – the Kurfürstendamm in Berlin. When I visited him long after the war with my wife, he remembered immediately: 'Liver with onions!' Yes, that was my favourite dish, and Lange prepared it for me that evening in celebration of our reunion.

The diet-cook Frau von Exner was, as mentioned, a very beautiful woman. That had not escaped Martin Bormann. The nickname 'The Buck Bormann' had not come about by chance. Anyway, Bormann went all out for Frau von Exner, but failed utterly. When she left in 1944, we of the bodyguard thought it must have had something to do with these attempts to woo her. It was said that Frau von Exner had requested permission to leave and that could only have been caused by the pressure. She did not have proof of Aryan ancestry, but her departure had nothing to do with that.[2] In any case, after the termination of her employment as cook, she lived for several months at the Reich Chancellery. I often reflected later on whether I had ever noticed that Hitler hated Jews. Then I remembered Frau von Exner – and did not know the right answer.

---

2 According to Traudl Junge, the racial origin of Frau von Exner's grandmother could not be established because she had been a foundling. Hitler knew this when he employed her. Finally, it had come to light that she had Jewish ancestry. Traudl Junge remembered that Hitler had then had a talk with Marlene von Exner in which he expressed his regret at having to release her, and in which he promised to Aryanise her whole family. Junge went onto say that Martin Bormann received instructions to deal with it and he accepted this only reluctantly 'for he had had no luck in his attempts to win the charming Viennese girl and could never forgive her for it.' See Traudl Junge, *Bis zur letzten Stunde – Hitlers Sekretärin erzählt ihr Leben*, Munich 2002, p.132. Misch interpreted the resignation of Frau von Exner in May 1944 as being a reaction to the stalking by Bormann. Misch is certain that Frau von Exner lived for some time at the Reich Chancellery without being in Hitler's employment.

Chapter 11

Weddings and Treason: 1944

On 3 June 1944, Eva Braun's sister Gretl married Major General Hermann Fegelein. The festivities were held on the Obersalzberg. Fegelein had been the Waffen-SS liaison officer to Hitler since the beginning of the year and had, as one heard, distinguished himself in the field.[1] Above all, however, Fegelein was a dare-devil, braggart, pretentious boorish ape, for whom women fell one after another. Eva, herself not without tangible feelings for the heart-breaker, coupled him up to her younger sister Gretl.

On the night of 5 June 1944, the Allied invasion of Normandy began. Hitler was not informed until midday on 6 June. He believed for quite some time that it could be halted. When it quickly became clear that the coastal sectors could not be held, he became absolutely convinced that the whole operation was connected to treason.

He saw himself confirmed in this opinion when, some weeks later, photos were released in Sweden in which a German colonel commanding an Abwehr fortified bunker installation was seen clinking glasses with two British officers – obviously, without a shot having been fired. Damn – how could they have given up without a fight? They had guns there, which could have hit Plymouth, so we were told. Nothing,

---

1 By this time, Hermann Fegelein was the holder of the Knights Cross with Oak Leaves. It was claimed that units of his division, 8.SS-Kavallerie-division *Florian Geyer*, had committed several war crimes.

absolutely nothing had gone right on the German side in connection with the invasion. There was, therefore, only one explanation – treason and sabotage. Hitler imagined it behind almost every action that failed. In fact, from the information coming in to us, it actually was possible to perceive that something of that kind was often the case. Now we began to receive reports more frequently of sabotage in sectors of armaments production. There were constant altercations with the Wehrmacht command staff, and Hitler did not exclude even Jodl and Keitel from his suspicions of manipulation. I knew many of Hitler's moods, but he always remained friendly towards me. As the war situation deteriorated, however, I also no longer believed in Final Victory.

Under the pressure of this mood impregnated with distrust, on 22 June 1944 Hitler addressed 280 high-ranking officers and generals on the Platterhof. It was very moving. Hitler implored them to show their unity and their loyalty as German officers. If they left him in the lurch, no longer believed in victory, no longer gave their all, then Germany was lost. Victory or defeat, that lay in their hands, not in his. If they wanted to give it up, how would he operate the rudder alone? Hitler was several times close to tears. The speech moved me very much, I really felt sorry for Hitler. On the evening of that June day I saw the popular General Eduard Dietl at the Berghof, who gave Hitler the up-to-date picture of the situation in Norway and Finland. The following day I learnt that Dietl's aircraft had crashed at Semmering near Vienna, and all aboard had been killed. I was very upset at the news.

Because of the situation on the Eastern Front, Hitler wanted to return to Rastenburg but kept putting it off for some conversion work or other to his barrack hut at FHQ Wolfsschanze. Thus, on 7 July 1944, we were still at Berchtesgaden, and Hitler went to Schloss Klessheim to see a display of new uniforms. Not until much later did I discover that Brigadier Helmuth Stieff had planned an assassination attempt on Hitler that day.[2]

---

2 Helmuth Stieff (1901–1944) did not carry out the attempt. He was sentenced to death on 8 August 1944, in connection with the attempted coup of 20 July 1944 and

These were to be Hitler's last days at the Berghof. As a result of a stupid incident, I had to leave the Obersalzberg much earlier. While out walking with Karl Tenazek we met a young lady who, after strolling with us awhile, invited us to the Berchtesgadener Hof for the afternoon. Karl did not go along. I went alone but had an uneasy feeling about it, not only for that reason but also because of the presence of some generals there. Two or three tables further on, Hitler's chauffeur Erich Hitler's chauffeur Erich Kempka was seated with his wife, the widow of our former colleague now fallen at the front, Rudi Mumme. She was an attractive woman, and my female companion made a comment about it. 'Yes, yes, she's beautiful all right, but not for marrying', slipped from my lips. I knew a thing or two about the former Frau Mumme and made the mistake of telling my table companion.

My companion then revealed herself to be a secretary at OKH, later the wife of Alfred Jodl.[3] She rang the Berghof from the Berchtesgadener Hof to gossip, and when I got back there Albert Bormann came up to me at once. 'Misch – what's this shit you've stirred up?' he shouted at me. 'Kempka is going to speak to the boss tomorrow. See that you're gone.' Albert Bormann liked me. I was always resolving this or that private matter he asked me to attend to. He was very grateful to me for taking a gift to his mother. He wanted me to work for him after the war – that was his wish. In this particular case, Albert Bormann had already arranged for me to leave the Berghof the next morning on the regular courier flight at nine, to allow the storm to die down a little.

In Berlin I waited anxiously for the aftermath. Anticipating this, my colleague Beermann rang me the next day from the Berghof: 'Don't shit your pants. The marriage is going to be dissolved.' On Hitler's instructions, Kempka was already separated from his wife because her past did not conform to the required moral standard.[4]

---

executed the same day at Berlin-Plötzensee.

3 On 7 March 1945, Alfred Jodl, head of the Wehrmacht command staff at OKW, married his secretary Luise Katharina von Benda.

4 The marriage was apparently annulled on 2 October 1944. See Christa Schroeder,

I think Hitler was forced to intervene, because it was unlike him to want to get involved in these affairs of passion. Thus, he took into his close staff men whom Admiral Raeder had forced out of the Kriegsmarine for conduct unbecoming an officer. A colleague of Bormann, Alwin-Broder Albrecht, had been relieved of his post in the navy after marrying a woman whose morals did not meet the approval of Admiral Raeder.

Only a few days after my rushed departure, on 14 July 1944, Hitler also left the Berghof. Shortly afterwards at FHQ Wolfsschanze I had to go to his car to open the passenger door. This brought me into contact with Kempka. He gave me a nod. Forgiven, forgotten. Despite the official enforced separation, he remained in touch with his ex-wife. After the war, she helped him through her contacts with the American occupiers. Then they remarried.

With my inglorious retreat from the Obersalzberg, my carefree days at the Berghof ended for ever. Not until later did that become clear.

20 July 1944

The RSD and the Führer's bodyguard, the *SS-Begleitkommando*, were responsible for the protection of Hitler, the RSD additionally for ministers. The RSD colleagues were almost without exception from Munich, the RSD having been drawn from the Munich detective force. Since 1933, it had been under the command of Johann Rattenhuber, lieutenant of the Bavarian state police, and by 1944 had a complement of 250 men.[5] Hitler tolerated only one bodyguard in his immediate presence, and this man would be from the *SS-Begleitkommando*. The RSD man appointed for Führer protection had to take up a position some distance away from Hitler and the *SS-Begleitkommando* bodyguard. This resulted ultimately in there being only one 'pure' bodyguard, and he was a rather weak guardian as far as

---

He Was My Chief, London 2009, pp.196–7.

5 By the end of the war there were about 400 RSD men. See Peter Hoffmann, *Die Sicherheit des Diktators*, Munich/Zürich 1975, p.56.

our weapons were concerned. In contrast to my better equipped RSD colleagues, we carried only the standard small Walther Polizei pistol ('PP') of 7.65 calibre, and nothing else. This handgun would be our constant companion, and we never gave it in, not even in the area of the Führer suite.

We were not searched, and neither did we conduct searches for weapons. The RSD carried out all necessary controls. The whole arrangement was rather slack. The more important people had their own armed bodyguard, and we would know these individuals as time went on.

To all intents and purposes, the Führer-suite in the Old Reich Chancellery had long been unguarded – the doors at the tradesmen's entrance to the Reich Chancellery having only one sentry. I often did duty there myself. Frequently, people one did not know would come in, wanting to speak or visit one of the house staff. In that instance, I would have the staff member telephoned from the front door, and advised. It was not unknown for strangers to call by. It would probably not have been difficult to visit one of the staff, disable him with a spray of some kind and then run up the twenty-two steps leading from the tradesmen's entrance to the Holy of Holies. An intruder would have had a free run, for there was no other sentry.

I pointed out to Johann Rattenhuber another possibility once: 'Do you bet that somebody couldn't make it from the street to Hitler's bedroom in two minutes?' I challenged him. I was thinking of the tradesmen's entrance, but also of the situation at the Foreign Ministry; from some of the windows, it was less than three metres to the flat of house administrator Kannenberg in the Old Reich Chancellery. All it needed from there was a plank between the buildings and an acrobat could have made it to the balcony and Hitler's bedroom. One might not believe it, but it was so – the Führer-suite was not guarded expressly.

I was also very surprised at the security precautions when Hitler drove through Berlin. Some time after the war began, he and his bodyguard would cross the Reich capital in two Volkswagens, to dine with Magda Goebbels or Inga Ley.[6] In the first Beetle would be his valet, adjutant and the driver Kempka; in the other, the driver Martin Schmiedel and two of my colleagues. That was the total protection. I have personally seen how a crowd would immediately gather around our cars if for some reason we had to stop for a moment. Then we would have a job to keep people at a distance. On several occasions, Hitler was very annoyed with us for forcing people back too briskly in his opinion. His security men were always working to introduce functioning security structures. It was down to Hitler himself that there were glaring holes in his personal protection measures, but whenever he was addressed on the matter he would reply in the most relaxed manner: 'Nothing will happen to me.'

On the late evening of 19 July 1944, I was seated in the courier compartment of the night train from Insterburg to Berlin. I was bringing the daily mailbag from FHQ Wolfsschanze to the Reich Chancellery. In the train I ate my rations. I had grabbed the specially selected rolls from a nicely built pyramid of bread rolls intended for the participants at the situation conference. At first, I did not know how I was going to smuggle them out. By chance, Bussmann was removing a tray from Hitler's study. One of his serviettes was on the tray. Bussmann made a gesture in agreement when I asked him if I could have the serviette: 'Sure, we have enough of them.' They bore Hitler's initials and were meant for his personal use only. The other serviettes were embroidered with the initials 'RK' for Reichskanzlei (Reich Chancellery). When the Russians arrived, my wife burnt everything that could have been dangerous for us – she forgot the serviette.

After I had delivered the mail to Otto Meissner at the presidential Chancellery in the early morning of 20 July, I drove home. In the

---

6 The Volkswagen of KdF car (KdF= Kraft durch Freude, Strength through Joy, a National Socialist holidays organisation) had the typical look of a beetle, but the name VW Beetle comes from the 1950s. Inga Spilker, actress, was the second wife of Robert Ley (1890–1945), leader of the single German 'trade union', the Arbeitsfront.

evening I had to take the night train back to Rastenburg, and I wanted to rest and see my family.

A few months previously, on 11 April 1944, our daughter Brigitta had been born. Eva Braun had given us a large pile of baby clothes and a pram. 'From the stock,' she said, playing down her nice gesture when I protested that I could not accept it all.

Brigitta's first car ride had been in an official car from the Reich Chancellery motor pool. Gerda had been confined in a mothers' home just outside Berlin, and when she was ready to go home with the baby I heard that one of Albert Bormann's colleagues was driving to a state property north of Berlin. 'You will pass the home where my wife is,' I told him. The colleague asked Bormann for permission, who had no objections to his picking up my wife and the newborn child. Thus, Brigitta was driven in the black Mercedes from the Führer-car-fleet.

The birth of my daughter was a joyful event, but it was around this date, from the spring of 1944, that I began to have a permanent unpleasant feeling. At midday on 20 July, I was lying on the living room settee at the house of my parents-in-law, resting after the night train journey. Since Gitta's birth my wife had been living in Rudow again, to avoid being alone at Karlshorst and so that her own mother could help with the baby. I had just fallen asleep when the phone rang. Gerda shook me awake. 'RK!'

'*Ach*, they should leave me in peace,' I murmured, still drunk with sleep.

'Take it, it's urgent!'

With a deep sigh I seized the receiver. I was to go at once to the Reich Chancellery, a car was already on the way to fetch me. What was up, I wanted to know. 'This is no time for questions. Get here at once!' I got a move on, but had not finished dressing when the car arrived.

The Reich Chancellery, the whole government quarter, was surrounded by troops of the Berlin Wachbataillon under Major Otto Ernst Remer. There were about seventy men in the Reich Chancellery courtyard. Nobody was entering or leaving. Despite the host of people around, a deathly silence reigned. Somebody arranged for me to be admitted to the telephone switchboard in the Old Reich Chancellery – my workplace. Two colleagues were seated at the switchboard and looked very busy. Remer's people were here and there; some had even penetrated into the Führer-suite. An attitude of helplessness prevailed everywhere.

I was informed briefly that an attempt had been made to assassinate Hitler. Initially, I could not find out any more. Remer was in Goebbels's service villa,[7] and there was no certainty about who was in command. I felt very uneasy about all this. What the hell was going on here? Were they going to start shooting soon? Who was friend, who foe? I looked around me. Remer's people looked no less anxious. They stood around indecisively, and let my two colleagues get on with it. They were phoning round incessantly and needed my help. There was something wrong with the telephone connections to FHQ Wolfsschanze.

Goebbels insisted several times on being connected to Hitler, and both at the Propaganda Ministry and Reich Chancellery all possible lines had to be checked over to ensure they were working and free of interference. Officially, I was not on duty, being a courier, but my colleagues would not be able to solve the problems quickly, and I knew the telephone switchboard best.

'Let me take over,' I said as I relieved one of my two despairing colleagues. The very modern switchboard did not let us down, and it was possible, partly by circuitous routing, to restore all required lines to FHQ Wolfsschanze for Goebbels.[8] Not until later did I learn that the conspirators had blocked off some of the telephone lines.

---

7 Goebbels resided south of the Brandenburg Gate, on Hermann-Göring-Strasse (since 1999 Friedrich Ebert Platz) in a palace adjoining the ministerial gardens and the Reich Chancellery park: today, parts of the bunker of the former service villa lie below the monument to the murdered Jews of Europe.

8 Albert Speer, who was present with Hitler during the telephone conversations with Remer and Goebbels, wrote of it: 'Goebbels had himself connected to Führer-HQ over a special line in the telephone switchboard of his Ministry . . . a single intact telephone line finally frustrated the coup attempt.' See Albert Speer, *Erinnerungen*,

Hitler was alive. He spoke to Goebbels, then Remer. 'Do you recognise my voice?' he asked the major. Remer agreed that he did. Hitler ordered Remer to place himself and his battalion under his, therefore Hitler's, and Goebbels's personal orders. 'You will have to work things out with Goebbels. I cannot undertake anything from here.' Thus the phantom was gone. Only minutes later, I saw Remer in the Reich Chancellery courtyard. Suddenly it grew hectic, and I heard excited shouting: '*Schnell*! *Schnell*!' Quicker than it takes to tell, Remer took his troops out. The Reich Chancellery was back in our hands. My tension fell away, and I was soon overcome by exhaustion, having been torn from sleep on account of the assassination attempt.

In all I spent only about half an hour at my workplace, and there was time to go to my service quarters and the kitchen to prepare my rations for the journey back. As planned, I was at Berlin Anhalter station at 2100 hrs to return to FHQ Wolfsschanze. That same night, Hitler made a radio broadcast to the people, in which he said that a quite small clique of ambitious, unscrupulous, criminal and stupid officers had wanted to get rid of him. He considered that the failure of the attempted assassination was a sign that he should continue with his life's work, as he had done hitherto.

I heard about the speech later. I slept most of the time on the night train to Rastenburg. Being so tired, I had hardly given thought to what the location of the attempted assassination of Hitler was going to look like. I reached FHQ Wolfsschanze in the early morning hours of 21 July. My colleagues gave me an excited report on the previous day's events.

The situation conference barrack hut was a wreck. An RSD colleague let me through the barriers and led me to the incident

---

Frankfurt/Main, Berlin 1996 reprint, p.395. Misch was not able to describe the manner in which the line was restored so that the technical procedure could be replicated. According to his statement, the connection between Goebbels's service villa and FHQ Wolfsschanze came about as a result of the efforts at the switchboard of the Führer-suite, Old Reich Chancellery. 'It went through us,' he said.

scene. The bomb would have killed Hitler had Major General Rudolf Schmundt, the Wehrmacht chief adjutant to Hitler, not lifted Stauffenberg's briefcase, which the latter had placed below the table, and placed it behind himself because his feet kept coming into contact with it. Otto Günsche, who had been hurled through the window by the blast, had observed that and told my colleague Arthur Adam, who repeated it to me. Schmundt had therefore taken most of the blast.

Adam had been duty telephonist at the time of the attempt, and it was he who had first identified Stauffenberg as the perpetrator. Adam made his report to Hitler personally that Stauffenberg had left the conference without retrieving his belt and cap from the cloakroom. The telephonist remembered that Stauffenberg had impressed upon him to have a car ready from the motor pool, but it had not arrived at the required time. As a result of his jitters, which Adam had not observed however, Stauffenberg must then have forgotten his cap and belt. Once the bomb had gone off, Stauffenberg had succeeded in leaving the Führer-Sperrkreis without any problems, but then he had been stopped at the outer Sperrkreis exit. The colleague who drove him to the airfield told me that, when they were stopped at the control post, he had turned off the engine. Stauffenberg had then barked at him to leave the engine running. Stauffenberg wanted to speak to the responsible lieutenant colonel about being stopped, but he was not present, and so he had himself connected to his deputy. Rittmeister Leonhard von Möllendorff finally gave permission for him to proceed.

I knew who Stauffenberg was. In the latter days at the Berghof, he had frequently attended situation conferences. Nothing else about him had struck me, apart from his outer disfigurement.[9] We colleagues did not think of him as a would-be assassin of Hitler. An assassin he certainly was. But his assassination attempt was levelled at everybody

---

9 As a result of wounds received with the Afrika Korps in Tunisia, Claus Schenk Graf von Stauffenberg had lost his left eye, right hand and two fingers of the left hand.

present in that room in which he had placed the bomb. Four men[10] had ultimately died because of it, but not Hitler. At the time of the explosion, Stauffenberg would not have been in the conference room, but might have had himself called out to take a telephone call, as often happened.

It could have been the way in which things would end for me. I had often imagined it: I report that I have a telephone call for the Führer, and bang! – it is over for me. That something could happen to me in the bodyguard – that was obvious. Not for nothing were our lives each assured in the sum of 100,000 Reichsmarks. But that an assassination attempt would be planned in such a way as to make short work of our own men too, that was something we had never thought of. That made Stauffenberg a murderer of his colleagues for us. There was really nothing worse. I had known Rudolf Schmundt since he had been a captain, and I thought a lot of him. I was much affected when he died as a result of his injuries in the military hospital at Rastenburg at the beginning of October.

Hitler showed himself to be particularly bitter that Stauffenberg had not shot himself after his plan failed. That was cowardly and unworthy of an officer. With the failure of this assassination attempt, it got through to Hitler's opponents that once more he had proved unconquerable. He felt himself as a person confirmed in his incomparably outstanding importance and believed in Providence. His standard retort 'Nothing will happen to me' now had a completely different meaning. In any case, behind the events of 20 July there stood a clear exclamation mark.

As arranged, Hitler received Mussolini on the day of the assassination attempt. His work had to go on. When I arrived on 21 July, everything was proceeding as usual. No especial excitement. I

---

10 The victims were: General Günther Korten, chief of the Luftwaffe general staff; Colonel Heinz Brandt, 1a Army general staff officer; Major General Rudolf Schmundt, Wehrmacht chief adjutant to Hitler; and the stenographer Heinrich Berger.

watched the repairs to the barrack hut and talked to the men of the building squad. I briefly befriended one of the workers and established that he came from Silesia. Later, I sent him all the photos that I had taken of him at work repairing the barrack hut. How could I have anticipated that one day a Hollywood film producer would ask me about them.[11] The photographs are now all in Poland with the man's heirs, I kept none back; I did not appear in any of them.

Dreadful revenge was taken against the conspirators. After Stauffenberg and some of his co-conspirators had been sentenced to death and executed that same night, Hitler ordered that the remainder should be tried by the People's Court. In the bodyguard we never spoke about these trials. They were things never talked of. It is alleged occasionally nowadays that Hitler asked to see photos of the executions of convicted conspirators. I do not believe that. It was not like him – that was not his concern. To the best of my knowledge, he never looked at pictures of gruesome events, nor could he bring himself to confront human suffering by looking at it directly. If he could avoid it, he would not address such things. Visits to military hospitals and such like were anathema to him.

Outstanding Generals

I did not find the situation after the assassination attempt to be particularly changed or tense. We received no new instructions on security precautions, nor were we of the *SS-Begleitkommando* more anxious afterwards – Hitler himself least of all. Nevertheless, more often than before, he would smell conspiracy and treason whenever we had bad news. On one occasion I heard him and Keitel arguing loudly near an open window. I found it difficult to identify which of the two was talking – their voice tone was very similar.

---

11 In the summer of 2007, during the filming of the Hollywood film about the Stauffenberg plot (*Valkyrie*), Misch was interviewed in Berlin by the director Bryan Singer as an eyewitness to the events.

The cause had been an operation in Finland[12] in which heavy losses had been sustained. This had resulted from wrong information being supplied by the Wehrmacht command staff. Accordingly, Hitler had given the order to advance without the necessary military equipment being to hand. Three hundred urgently needed field guns were in the harbour at Tallinn and had not been unloaded. Hitler was beside himself: 'How can something like that happen? How can I give orders if I have not been correctly informed about the situation? I – I am ultimately responsible for everything!'

Finally, Hitler fell seriously ill with jaundice, which kept him bedridden for a fortnight. He could not make the daily situation conferences. He still looked quite weak when he resumed at these conferences in early October. Shortly afterwards, he dismissed the doctors who had treated him – Karl Brandt and Hans-Karl von Hasselbach. He continued to trust only Professor Morell.

In October, we heard of Rommel's death, and of the circumstances of his forced suicide. That he had been given the choice of poison or a pistol. I did not want to think about it and pushed it from my mind. Much later, in Soviet captivity, I met Alfred Gause, Rommel's former chief of the general staff, who had been replaced later by Hans Speidel.[13] Gause had not understood why he had been replaced.* He told me how he had tried to convince Rommel to stay clear of the plot. Gause had noticed that plans for a coup were circulating. Rommel was involved in so far as feelers had been put out to see if he would

---

12 On 19 September 1944, Finland signed a treaty of armistice with the Soviet Union.

13 This exchange occurred during the the preparatory stage of Operation Valkyrie, the plot to overthrow the Hitler government. The German Resistance of 20 July used the same name as the Wehrmacht plan to confront an insurrection. Speidel, who supported the coup plan, had the job of winning Rommel over.

* Major General Alfred Gause was replaced as Rommel's chief of general staff on 15 April 1944. Rommel was implicated in talks to assassinate Hitler around then. In the conversation with Karl Strölin in the spring of 1944 at Herrlingen there had been talk of the possibility and justification for the assassination. See Manfred Rommel, *1944- Das Jahr der Entscheidung*, Hohenheim Verlag 2010, p.203. (TN)

be prepared to accept the post of Reich president in the event of a successful coup. Gause confided that the best he had been able to come up with was to request leave to visit his wife for her birthday, then he went not to his own wife, but to see Rommel's wife Lucie. He had visited her out of consideration for her safety and also to make her understand as clearly as possible that her husband was in great danger. He had almost pleaded: 'Frau Rommel, save your husband! He must go to Hitler.' His only way out of the trap was to report at the higher level that something was afoot. The field marshal did not actually need to go into details. 'Your husband has access to the Führer at any time, but he just has to tip him off, and then he is free of the thing,' Gause recalled having attempted to convince Frau Rommel. Well, later Rommel could not be saved.

I took an increasing interest in the course of the war and weighed up whether I should take a chance and visit my native province of Silesia. I talked to Albert Bormann about having a couple of days' leave. We were standing in front of the situation conference barrack hut. The conference had just ended and Hitler was coming out. Bormann was carrying a signature blotting book, and I had some despatches to deliver. Hitler saw that and came over to us directly. Bormann told him: 'This young man wants to visit his home in Upper Silesia. What do you think of that? Can we let him?'

'Yes, yes,' Hitler said, nodded and added impishly, 'but if you fall into Schörner's hands, even I will not be able to do anything for you. Then even my own signature will not be of any use to you.'

He probably meant that General Ferdinand Schörner would press-gang me into his ranks, as he needed every man he could lay hands on. Hitler had a very high opinion of the general, recently awarded the Swords to his Knights Cross with Oak Leaves,[14] and he was not the

---

14 Ferdinand Schörner (1892–1972) was awarded the Diamonds to his Knights Cross with Oak Leaves and Swords in January 1945. He was also known as 'The greatest knacker of comrades of all times'.

only one. After the war, a Russian said to me: 'If Hitler had had a dozen Schörners, then you would have had a chance!'

In the end I did not go to Silesia – my enquiry having originated basically from my curiosity to hear from Hitler how things really were on the Eastern Front. I would have liked to have brought some papers and photos to safety from there, but my Aunt Sofia did that later. She spent the end of the war not in Berlin but with her mother at Alt-Schalkowitz. I never saw my grandmother Ottilie again. I discovered years later that she had died at the age of eighty-seven. Her last word to my aunt was 'sugar'. I believed that this was because my grandmother always had a very sweet tooth.

On 20 November 1944, we left FHQ Wolfsschanze for ever. Hitler transferred his headquarters to the vicinity of Bad Nauheim, from where he would direct the impending Ardennes offensive. We had a short stay in Berlin before going on. I was shocked at the scene that greeted me. Since I had left the capital on 20 July, it had received some devastating bombing raids.

We took the special train to FHQ Adlerhorst, so-named by Hitler at Ziegenberg. The opening days of the offensive from 16 December 1944 were very successful, but when the weather changed the Allies regained air superiority and the offensive came to a standstill. I remember only constant military conferences, and a coming and going of generals. My memory of it was overshadowed by what followed. At Ziegenberg it became certain – we were heading for the end.

Chapter 12

Preparing the Berlin Bunker:
February–April 1945

IN MID-FEBRUARY 1945, WE finally returned from the Western
Front to Berlin. The drive from Silesian Station, nowadays Berlin
Ostbahnhof, to the Reich Chancellery was quiet. The capital had
not expected us, and evidently people had other things to do. To the
right and left of the streets, many of which were totally impassable,
stood row upon row of houses reduced to skeletons – mere walls
lacking a façade and roof timbering. During the journey, nobody
said a word.

Now all were gathered in the capital: we of the SS bodyguard, the
female secretaries, doctors, adjutants, servants and, naturally, house
administrator Kannenberg with all his staff. The intimate circle around
Hitler had taken up its position: Reich press chief Otto Dietrich, the
Bormann brothers, diplomat Hewel. Keitel and Jodl went to their
villas at Zehlendorf, while Göring had withdrawn to his country seat
Carinhall, near Berlin.

An experience, which had nothing to do with the war, upset me
greatly. It happened shortly after we arrived in Berlin. I had noticed
previously at Ziegenberg that Karl Tenazek was acting strangely. We
had a close friendship, and I had made several attempts to find out
what was bothering him. 'Something not right with you?' I asked him
bluntly. 'Debts? Something else eating you up?'

'No, no, everything's OK,' he replied unconvincingly. I did not press the matter.

Now, in Berlin, he asked me to to take over his shift one afternoon. He wanted to leave early – tomorrow his leave began. I had no objection to double shifts. They were no problem for me, and I had a much longer off-duty period afterwards. Accordingly, I released Karl from duty as he wanted and asked, as usual, if there had been anything special to report. 'Nothing new,' he assured me and handed me the register into which all telephone calls had to be entered. I wished him a good journey home, a nice holiday and enquired after his wife, whom I knew to be pregnant.

'Would you prefer a boy or a girl?' I asked him.

'No idea.' He shrugged his shoulders sadly. 'It makes no difference.'

It made no sense to me. Why didn't he confide in me?

Karl disappeared into his service room, where our cleaner, Frau Herrmann, was at work. She told me later it had surprised her to see Karl putting on his best new uniform. He said 'No' to her question asking if he were going out. Scarcely had she left the room when she heard a round fired. She ran back inside immediately. Karl had sat down on the bed and shot himself dead.

The initial suspicion was that he might have got himself involved in some cloak-and-dagger activity. Obviously, we were all exposed to being recruited by foreign secret services. After some enquiries, the real reason soon came to light. The child that his wife was expecting was not Karl's. It could not be his. My friend had consulted Hitler's personal physician Professor Morell, and an urologist at Berchtesgaden. Both came to the same conclusion – Karl was sterile. He had not been able to handle the situation. The incident was rough on all of us in the bodyguard. His loss came as a great shock.

After being apprised of the details, Hitler decided to treat the matter as an accident. When Hitler decided that a thing was an accident, then it must have been one. Every member of the SS bodyguard had 100,000 Reichmarks life assurance, and this was what Karl's wife received.

Bunker Telephonist

At that time I became what the post-war world knows me as – Hitler's bunker telephonist. Our commanding officer Franz Schädle – he had relieved Bruno Gesche in January – let me know that he had selected me for the switchboard in the now technically fully equipped deep bunker: 'Make yourself familiar with the installation and make sure everything works.' I must have looked at him in surprise a little, for he added: 'You have always done a good job, Misch.' However, I was not really surprised. I was not really thinking anything at that moment. If I had asked why I had been selected for this undoubtedly responsible position, then he would have told me. I had been there already for years, had always taken an interest in my work and taught it to a large number of people. Recently, I was the only one to attend a two-week advanced telex training and scrambler course.

That the new job was a special distinction for me, that I would be closer to Hitler in those days than any other person, that I had got myself a cosy number in the best protected place in Berlin – I had no time for such ideas. I was to man the bunker telephone switchboard, that was an order like any other. Therefore, I had to familiarise myself with it as quickly as possible. After Schädle had made me bunker telephonist, I rang Hermann Gretz at once, the Reichspost technician. He was ready to show me everything straight away. With him, I descended into the catacomb for the first time.

Not far from my room on the ground floor of the adjutants' wing, we descended some red-carpeted steps into the cellars of the Old Reich Chancellery. Gretz hurried past the staff kitchen, the festival hall cloakroom and the toilets, and indicated the door to a narrow corridor leading into the New Reich Chancellery. This narrow, endless tunnel was about eighty metres long, and we called it Kannenberg-Allee after the house administrator. Its actual purpose was for bringing food from the supply rooms in the New Reich Chancellery to the dining hall in the Old Reich Chancellery. We did not go along it on this occasion, although often enough in the future I would use it to reach the cellars of the New Reich Chancellery. Gretz took me back a little, and after leaving a gas-proof steel door behind us we entered a sluice room equipped with two similar doors. Both were open. The door straight ahead led into the ministerial gardens. The Reichspost technician went through the other one, however, and stepped up the pace, which told me we still had far to go. Then we found ourselves in the ante-bunker before the deep bunker.

This ante-bunker lay below the festival hall of the Old Reich Chancellery. Because of the explosive force of British and American bombs, the sounding boards of the festival hall had been reinforced with concrete between 1943 and 1944, during building work on the deep bunker. The garden of the neighbouring Foreign Ministry could be reached through an emergency exit. The large cellar below the festival hall and the winter garden, only separated from the bunker walls by about three metres, led to the area in the west where the ante-bunker adjoined the deep bunker around a concrete block. The ante-bunker had its own 40kW generator, which provided lighting and heating and also operated the water pumps and fresh air supply. Several WCs and washrooms were available there, as well as a kitchen with a pantry and storage room. There were also two more storage rooms, in one of which bedframes and mattresses were stacked; shortly afterwards, the other storage room was filled to just under the ceiling with provisions. There were also restrooms. Later, one side of the corridor was the lived-in side; the other, the unoccupied side. In all, not counting the central corridor and technical rooms, there were sixteen small rooms in the ante-bunker, none larger than four by four metres.

The first time I went down there with Gretz I didn't take in all the detail. Hurriedly, we cut through the ante-bunker by the narrow central corridor with its long wooden tables, and never met a living soul. Everything swam before my eyes. It was a true labyrinth.

The Führerbunker

At the end of the ante-bunker corridor were more heavy steel doors, which served as gas-proof sluices. In front of them, one of the SS bodyguard would do sentry duty, while sitting at a small table – the last guardian before the bridge into the subterranean abode and refuge of the Führer. Gretz led the way forward. Down a couple of steps and finally we were in the deep bunker, Hitler's bunker suite. Construction work on the Führerbunker had begun far too late, and it was not ready – having not yet dried out. Because of the remaining damp in the ground and walls, it smelt stale. The main contractors, ARGE Hochtief AG, had to improvise.

'No time remained to air it properly,' Gretz explained. Because the bunker was below the water table in a kind of concrete trough, ground water had to be continuously pumped out. I looked around and screwed up my eyes, getting accustomed only slowly to the harsh lighting of the naked lamp bulbs, reflected off the naked white walls. How minute everything was – how sad, unready, unworthy. Standing in the corridor, the Reichspost technician explained to me the division of the rooms. They were no more than cells, as in the ante-bunker. The corridor was only about fifteen metres long and divided into two halves by a concrete bulkhead with a door. On the left wall in the rear section were lockers with firefighting equipment, while on the opposite wall was a longish, narrow table with chairs. Right at the end was another bulkhead, behind which was the emergency exit into the garden of the Reich Chancellery. Additionally, a room had been allocated for the RSD, which had a rear area for the dogs at the back – Blondi the Alastian dog had had some pups.

In the first room right of the corridor, chief technician Johannes Hentschel worked at his machinery and installations; these were all supplied with the necessary electricity. I had known Hentschel for many years. He had been employed at the Reich Chancellery since 1933 and had a four-room flat there. He had had an important role in the building of the Führerbunker and was now responsible for the technical installations in the machinery room. Hannes, as I called him, knew the whole technology inside out. In the machinery room near the door was an emergency diesel generator with various pumps, which among other things kept the dressing station below the Reich Chancellery supplied with fresh water from a deep spring bored for the purpose.

Ten to twelve barrels of diesel oil were stacked near the air-conditioning plant. This could run for about a thousand hours and might also absorb battlefield gases sucked in. Once there was great alarm during a situation conference, when a kind of acrid burning smell was noticed, and the installation had to be shut down immediately. It turned out that Göring's car had been parked below an air intake, and the car, which used wood for fuel, had produced gases and vapours sucked in by the intake. During the last days in the bunker, the exhaust gases of the machinery created a kind of gymnasium fug, so that it fairly stank below.

Opposite the machinery room, on the left side, was the so-called wet room (a bathroom with toilets) and immediately adjoining Hentschel's machinery room was 'my' room in which the telephone switchboard was installed. Instead of the fine telephone switchboard above, I now had this cell. I had not previously operated this kind of switchboard, which was now occupying the deep bunker. I saw at once that it had plug connections. I sighed. Gone was the time with the modern Siemens unit and its many colourful buttons. Now it was plug and drop-flap again. The junction box on the wall was the size of a shoe box. No suspicion whose bright idea this pitiful fitment was. It might have been all right for a small boarding house, but not for the Führerbunker at the Reich Chancellery. Obviously, nobody had thought that the underground telephone switchboard here might become the most important switching centre for reports. Calls rerouted from the main switchboard in the New Reich Chancellery to the Führerbunker telephone switchboard reached only five extensions.

One telephone was in Hitler's private rooms, another in Professor Morell's room abutting the switchboard, and other extensions were with the valet Linge in his restroom and the guard. The fifth telephone was in the corridor.

The room containing the telephone exchange was open to the whole floor, therefore without door, curtain or other screening. Apart from the junction box, there was a telex machine, a scrambler and two Silenta typewriters, extra quiet and used by Hitler's secretaries. Additionally, on the stool in front of the distributor box, there was another place to sit. Once down here, this room was the only contact with the outside world. One could no longer see or hear what was happening above – no matter what.

As well as the telephone room, there were four others. The corridor to them could be closed by a door, but this mostly stood open. First one came into an anteroom with a table and four chairs on the left-hand side. From this anteroom it was possible to access another room, occupied by Dr Morell, and later Goebbels. To the right the corridor went down to Linge's room and a rather larger surgery and dressing station, where the most important medical utensils, instruments and medication were kept.

One reached Hitler's rooms from the second floor. The first door on the left led immediately into a lobby. Linge held himself in readiness there for assignments; he also used it for writing and serving meals. From there, one went left into a room intended as Hitler's dressing room but which was taken by Eva Braun. The lobby led into Hitler's study and living rooms. Even these rooms were only 3.5 by 3.2 metres in size. In the living room, a sofa and three chairs were squashed together. The big furniture pieces made the room look more cramped than it actually was. From this part of the suite, one turned right into Hitler's bedroom, with the bed in the far corner. There was a bell above the night table to summon Linge whenever he was needed, and near the bed was an oxygen bottle.

The first time I was below with Gretz I did not take a great deal of notice of Hitler's rooms. Everything looked very unreal to me. Later, after Hitler had moved in, I never went into his private rooms again.*

On the other side of the lobby, one crossed a small floor with a narrow clothing compartment into a wetroom with toilet and shower, then reached Eva's room. Here too tortoiseshell lamps hung from the ceiling. The bright glare nipped in the bud any hint of snugness which the furniture introduced from the Führer-suite should have provided. It made everything look only more repulsive.

From the central corridor, the second door left led into the map room in which, in the final weeks, military situation conferences were held despite its tightness. The room was hardly larger than the others, maybe 4 by 3.6 metres. In the middle was a large table, and narrow benches were fitted along the walls. If the overall situation was being discussed, so many people entered that the participants had to stand to deliver their reports to Hitler, who would be seated. Often the table would be carried out into the central corridor, and the situation conference continued there.

After the first tour with Gretz I was greatly relieved to step out into the garden through the emergency exit. Strewn around were all kinds of equipment, including shovels and spades stuck in the ground. The bunker was still being worked on – an observation tower at its centre. Then I looked up at the clouds. Fresh air, daylight. I began to sense what it meant to have to endure this over a long period of time, and I also realised that for me such a time was dawning.

Up and Down

At first, the bunker was uninhabited. Not even Hitler lived there. Until a direct hit by a heavy bomb made it impossible, he ate and slept in his flat on the first floor of the Old Chancellery. When the air-raid

---

* Misch must mean here 'in Hitler's lifetime', since he went into the study – the death room – immediately after the suicide. (TN)

warning went off, Hitler would not go down into the deep bunker, but only to the air-raid shelter and even then he would leave the shelter as soon as they gave the 'All-clear'. Often when there was a warning he would go to the upper rooms 'for a better picture of the attack', as he would say. Once he even took my colleague Joseph 'Joschi' Graf into the open air during an air raid. Poor Joschi was appalled and tried desperately to make Hitler seek shelter, '*Ach was*, nothing can happen to me', was his stock reply. Even in the heart of the inferno, always the same old reply. Joschi pointed to the rain of flak splinters falling over the Reich Chancellery, but it made no impression on Hitler.

We would wait in suspense for the incoming reports on the military situation, but increasingly without any great hope. On 11 March, Hitler made a surprise visit to Ninth Army HQ at Saarow, between Frankfurt on the Oder and Berlin. It was his last visit to the troops at the front.

The daily situation conferences would now begin towards three in the afternoon. They were usually held in Hitler's study in the New Chancellery – the conference room in the Old Chancellery having been badly damaged in air raids. The first conference of the day would last two or three hours. Towards midnight or one, Hitler would hold a night situation conference.

Hitler was constantly preparing new strategies to turn the tide at the last hour. Nobody within the bodyguard believed in such a miracle any longer. It was just a question of 'how' defeat would come about. What fate was in store for us the vanquished, and especially those of us in Hitler's closest circle?

Around mid-March, Eva Braun arrived at the Reich Chancellery. She stayed only a short while, but then resurfaced a second time to everybody's surprise a few days later. It appeared that nobody had been informed – Hitler included. He was anything but delighted when she turned up again, and he did everything he could to convince her to return to Munich. Everybody else prevailed upon to go did so, but all his efforts here were in vain. Eva Braun made it clear to him that her place was at his side, and nobody would make her change her mind. She seemed absolutely determined on the matter. My colleagues sighed, but I was really quite pleased she was there. Her almost perpetual cheerful mood would do much to brighten up the gloomy atmosphere. All the same, I did wonder about her decision. It had not been long, perhaps a month ago, when she had first arrived and I had been instructed to take her with all her baggage back to the station. '*Ach*, what would I do in Berlin anyway,' she had said. 'There are only bomb craters here.'

Soon after her second appearance she came to me in the lobby and handed me her watch: '*Ach*, please, it doesn't work.'

'I'll have it seen to,' I promised. She handed it to me, a small watch of white gold, the face enclosed by diamonds. I took it to a jeweller in the Friedrichs-Strasse and collected it the next afternoon. The jeweller Wiese was still going, and so now was Eva's watch. I had a servant take it to her, and I was happy to have been of small service to her.

On the night of 12 April 1945, after the late situation conference I met press secretary Heinz Lorenz. He was very excited and brandished a telex in front of my nose. After he came back from seeing the Führer, he told me that Franklin Roosevelt was dead. Lorenz said that, upon receiving the news, Hitler had jumped up, but then commented soberly: 'A half year too late.' Nevertheless, he mentioned having had a presentiment about it. Goebbels seemed to find new hope in Roosevelt's death. Once again, the talk was of 'a turn' in events.

Of course, there was nothing at all in the days that followed which pointed to such a turn. I took ever less interest in my service instructions, which required me to eavesdrop telephone conversations infrequently to check the tone quality, and now I listened into everything. I was constantly on the watch for something new. It was all totally clear: the Western Allies were maintaining the military pressure relentlessly in order to obtain the unconditional surrender of Germany. Nothing suggested we might achieve a separate peace at the last minute. To the very end, Hitler could not understand why the British would not unite with him against Bolshevism.

Since February, my work hours could not have been considered normal. They were adapted to Hitler's rhythms, in which night became day, and day became night. The last situation conference seldom began before midnight and lasted into the early hours.

The cellar and bunker rooms were filling noticeably. It seemed to me that all members of the state and Party leadership were being given quarters here, in addition to their junior adjutants, who inhabited the catacombs in the New Reich Chancellery. The first rooms that one reached at the end of Kannenberg-Allee were those of Luftwaffe adjutant Nicolaus von Below, Otto Günsche and General Wilhelm Burgdorf. In this stretch were also to be found the domains of Martin Bormann and his co-workers – the half-brothers Wilhelm Zander and Alwin-Broder Albrecht.

Much further on were the rooms of the female secretaries – Gerda Christian, Christa Schroeder, Traudl Junge and Johanna Wolf. These were adjacent to the offices of Himmler's liaison officer Hermann Fegelein, General Hans Krebs and Major Bernd Freytag von Loringhoven. Finally, rooms had been allotted to Vice-Admiral Hans-Erich Voss, diplomat Walther Hewel and Hitler's pilots Hans Baur and Georg Betz. The remaining rooms were for the house staff. Right at the end of this cellar, behind the officers' mess and the garages, were the living quarters for the staff of the motor pool and the office of Hitler's driver Erich Kempka. In one of the large cellar rooms with access to Voss-Strasse, an emergency hospital had been set up. Many civilians sought treatment there – the dressing station was quickly filled to overflowing. I only came to this part of the catacombs once, and briefly.

So, there we sat – like the German people – in cellars, and above us the land lay in ruins.

Chapter 13

Bunker Life: The Last Fortnight of April 1945

SOMETIME IN MID-APRIL, 'BUNKER life' began. Hitler descended into the place where he would die. Eva never left his side, and lived from then on in his dressing room. All situation conferences were now held in the Führerbunker map room and the bunker telephone switchboard had to be manned around the clock. Our SS bodyguard commander Schädle came up to me. I already suspected what he was going to say: 'Misch, you are going down there with them.'

Reluctantly, I made my way with my sleeping mat into the new subterranean kingdom. On the way down into the Führerbunker, every step reinforced my bad feelings about the move. I was never claustrophobic, but since those days down there I understand the fear of confined spaces. While most of the steel doors were open most of the time, the last door down into the Führerbunker itself was always kept shut. In front of this last door, one of the bodyguard, occasionally with an RSD colleague, would be seated at a small table. The RSD were principally responsible for guarding the second exit – the emergency way out.

As I unrolled my sleeping mat for the first time in my new workplace deep underground, it occurred to me that we were now finally buried alive. I had my telephone lines, however. Now in the truest sense of the word I was going to 'be on the phone all day' – it was my only contact with life outside the bunker. I was surrounded by cold, damp, glaring-white artificial light. To know that Hitler had to live and suffer under the same conditions was of little comfort. Or should I say gave me no comfort? Now it was no longer the time to think of others, not even the Führer. One had one's own problems to attend to.

Whenever possible I would go up to my old service room to sleep; only when there was nothing else for it did I lay out the mat in the bunker. Usually, I would be too dog-tired to notice whether my 'bed' was really comfortable or not.

In a cellar room, directly under the entrance for vehicles, a dining hall had been set up. The kitchen staff had a big field kitchen in which they cooked tasty dishes for all the Reich Chancellery staff and the military hospital. Hot food was available all day – one could fetch it at any time. Only occasionally did I join the female secretaries to eat at the long wooden table in the corridor of the ante-bunker. Every day I could have eaten there the meals prepared in the small corner-kitchen of Frau Manziarly, Frau von Exner's successor, but that kind of diet-food was not really my thing.

I had no scheduled meal time. When I wanted my lunch break I would call my deputy Retzbach at the New Reich Chancellery switchboard, who would then come down. He did not like to be my No. 2. No wonder. There was a gloomy, depressed mood everywhere to be sure, but in the deep bunker it was worse. One could see the same thoughts in the eyes of everybody who had to come down to this – this funeral vault.

In it I lodged. Because of where my workplace was situated, I could see whoever entered or left the Führerbunker – all the comings and goings. From now on, everybody who wanted to see Hitler had to come past my telephone switchboard. Beyond the situation conferences there were only short audiences. None lasted more than twenty minutes. Everybody wanted to get out of the bunker as quickly as possible. Even Mohnke, my former company commander, who had driven me to the Reich Chancellery on my first day there five years ago, could not find the time to exchange a few words with me after seeing Hitler. Adolf Hitler, Eva Braun, valet Heinz Linge, Professor Theodor Morell, maintenance technician Joahnnes Hentschel and I – we were the inhabitants of the Führerbunker.

20 April 1945

It was Hitler's last birthday, his fifty-sixth. To congratulate him, Reich Youth leader Arthur Axmann had some young, highly decorated SS soldiers and about twenty Hitler Youth parade in the garden of the Reich Chancellery. I only heard about it, but saw nothing of it. I never went up the whole day. I sat at my switchboard and just could not get away from telephone calls bringing birthday wishes. Hentschel's diesel engine and my head throbbed in competition. The ventilation system ran incessantly.

After a reception at the New Reich Chancellery in which, among others, Goebbels, Göring, Himmler, the Bormann brothers, Speer, Ribbentrop and some generals such as Wilhelm Burgdorf and Hans Krebs took part, Hitler came down to the bunker and held a situation conference in the map room. There was no trace of any festive spirit – the birthday was finished with.

The only word to describe the military situation was 'catastrophic'. Days before, the 300,000 men of Army Group B had surrendered in the Ruhr Pocket. Their commander, Field Marshal Walter Model, shot himself shortly afterwards. The British and Americans were at the Elbe, while the Soviets were close to the gates of the Reich capital.

For the imminent division of Germany into a northern and a southern part, Hitler had ordered Grand Admiral Karl Dönitz, commander-in-chief of the Kriegsmarine, to take command of the northern sector, and the commander-in-chief west, Field Marshal Albert Kesselring, to take over the south. The final order was 'resistance to the last man'. A small assortment of Wehrmacht soldiers and Waffen-SS, Volkssturm pensioners and Hitler Youth against millions of Red Army men – what could be hoped for?

I heard the participants at the situation conference urging Hitler to direct the final struggle from Obersalzberg and leave the bunker while there was still time to get out of Berlin. Until then I had been counting on our going to Berchtesgaden, but Hitler would not be moved – he wanted to remain. Now I had to do some rethinking. I did not succeed. What would it mean for me? All I wanted was what most of the others wanted. You could see it in their eyes; they all wanted to get out of here, out of the bunker, out of Berlin.

Göring in his effeminate uniform looked very nervous all day. Apparently, he was worried that he might not be able to get away in time. Finally, he took his leave of Hitler under the pretext that important tasks would be awaiting him in southern Germany. Hitler let him go without raising any objections or passing a remark. He seemed to look upon this *sauve qui peut* mood as if he were a disinterested spectator.

I was hoping that perhaps there might be somebody who could change his decision. My mind was racing, while telephone calls interrupted from time to time. Until this day, Hitler's birthday, on which under code-word Clausewitz the State of Alert had been added as preliminary stage to the declaration of a State of Emergency, I had always gone home to see my wife and daughter after duty. During this State of Alert that was no longer possible. On my advice, Gerda had taken Gitta to her parents' house at Rudow from our marital flat into which she had moved back. I strained every brain cell trying to think of some way to get my family to safety, away from the Russians. In the bunker the export-model version of the Volksempfänger radio set was to be found everywhere. Goebbels was speaking through it. I did not listen to what he was saying. If he had known that at home I regularly listened to BBC London . . . Da Da Da Daaaaah . . .![1]

---

1 The BBC used the opening bars of Beethoven's Symphony No. 5 in A minor, opus 67 as its recognition melody ('V for Victory'); by the *Verordnung über ausserordentliche Rundfunkmassnahmen* listening to enemy radio stations was punishable by imprisonment.

In the evening, Eva gathered the remaining guests of the birthday reception upstairs in the Führer-suite. The bunker was almost empty. Only I remained at my work post, and Hitler in his room – the last celebration in the Reich Chancellery took place without the Reich chancellor.

21 April 1945

During the morning, the Reich Chancellery came under heavy artillery fire. In the deep bunker one heard nothing; only when a shell came down near the garden exit did the walls tremble for a second or so.

On this day I saw Hitler only briefly on a few occasions. Linge had awoken him to report about the shelling. 'The boss' could still not credit it that the Russians were at the gates. Over the last few months he had grown increasingly distrustful of his entourage, and now, shortly before the defeat, this distrust reached its zenith. Behind every contradiction he detected treachery; everywhere he suspected disinformation. He was fidgety, nervous and looked depressed.

My colleagues and I knew that the fall of Berlin to the Red Army was only a matter of a few days. The Soviets had already fought through to the suburbs, and Bernau, about fifteen kilometres from Berlin, had fallen. Frenzied activity and total apathy alternated. Among ourselves we spoke openly of our hope that Hitler still might decide to leave Berlin, giving us the chance at the last moment to escape being trapped in the bunker. Only Goebbels kept pouring out his fantastic Final Victory scenarios. I noticed how he kept on at Hitler constantly as if trying to inebriate him one last time using all the tricks of the propaganda trade, something of which even the Führer himself now seemed to be in dire need. It no longer cut any ice with us.

The last months had not passed Hitler by without leaving their mark. Every defeat, every setback, every act of treason – real or imagined – from within his closest circle contributed to his clearly recognisable physical decay. Now his gait was sluggish, and he dragged a leg. The eyes often seemed to have no fixed point, while his sense of balance seemed disturbed. Above all, in his every movement he had slowed, and all in all he looked to me like an old man. His left hand trembled distinctly, something I had not noticed before, and though he did not fumble when accepting despatches, now he always used his right hand. Just as in better times, when he attempted to hide his need for reading glasses, in this case too he tried to conceal the visible signs of weakness by keeping the trembling hand out of sight as much as possible.

As for his physical and mental state, he continued to make a good show of it. Even we, those closest to him, could only assess his general level of morale and mood from the reactions and expressions of the other participants at the situation conferences – it was very rare that we noted anything. He wanted to keep up this discipline which he showed by day, but the rapidly increasing physical burden made it visibly ever more difficult. Morell was no longer able to control the wear and tear and was released after nine years' service: he trudged past me, carrying his packed bags and breathing heavily, on the evening of 21 April. Dr Ludwig Stumpfegger, one of Hitler's travelling physicians, took over his care.

My concern for my wife and daughter grew unceasingly. For some time much of the population of Berlin had taken up residence in the overflowing bunkers. Formerly, I had always been able to ring Gerda at her parents' house. Our private early warning system continued to function there. Some time beforehand, telephone technician Gretz had had some lines laid in the neighbouring houses. When I warned my wife of an alarm, she pressed a button and the neighbouring families knew of an imminent air raid and reacted at once. That was a great advantage in the competition for a place in the bunker. In this way, most still had enough time to reach the bunker before the deadly bombs rained down.

On this 21 April my attempts to telephone Gerda met with failure. I kept trying until midnight. Around the corner I could hear the sentry at the garden exit snoring. I discovered that something was wrong with the distributor box in the Berlin-Britz telephone exchange, through which calls went to Rudow and Buckow. Gerda's line remained intact but I could not dial it. I had an idea. I rang a colleague I knew well in the Reichspost distributor exchange in Munich. From Munich one could use a broadband cable to Berlin. This cable could handle 280 conversations at the same time. 'Can you ring a number for me in Berlin?' I asked. At that moment a female telephone operator who handled trunk calls switched into our conversation: 'That is no problem. I can connect you at once if you like.' I gave the lady the number and less than a minute later I heard Gerda's voice. She had not slept and was crying softly.

22 April 1945

The date that for me marks the end of the Third Reich was 22 April 1945. It was eight days before Hitler's death, and some time before the unconditional surrender. The German Wehrmacht capitulated on 8 May 1945 – but on 22 April, a Sunday, Hitler capitulated. This day scarred itself into my memory no less than the day in which Hitler took his own life.

Like all days since we began our bunker existence, 22 April 1945 had no beginning. At some time or other, the long sleepless night ended in morning. I had nodded off again and was trying to keep myself awake with cognac and chocolate. The situation was more hopeless with every passing minute. To the north of Berlin, Soviet troops had advanced to Pankow and the frontline already ran along Gesundbrunnen and Bernauer-Strasse. To the east of the city, the Red Army had reached Karlshorst and Friedrichsfelde and had penetrated the inner defensive ring. Hitler's hoped-for breach between the Western Powers and the Russians had not come about, and neither had the attack by General Felix Steiner.[2] Around midday, preparations were made for the situation conference. Keitel, Jodl, Krebs, Burgdorf

---

2 SS-Lieutenant General Felix Steiner had instructions to assemble northeast of the city a troop that would relieve the siege of Berlin. No such troop was formed by Steiner.

and Bormann were already in the Führerbunker. The commanders-in-chief, who had removed themselves from Berlin, were represented by their adjutants: Dönitz by Vice-Admiral Hans-Erich Voss; Göring by Brigadier Eckhard Christian; Himmler by Major General Hermann Fegelein; and Ribbentrop by diplomat Walther Hewel. I had the commander-in-chief of Ninth Army, General Theodor Busse, on the line, and I connected him to Burgdorf. Busse reported: 'The bitter fighting has as its hallmark the increasing excessive demands made of the troops and the irreplaceable losses in men and materials.' I listened into the whole conversation – contrary to regulations. I was hoping to find a few sparks of hope, but I found none.

The telephone rang again. Our chief Franz Schädle was on the other end of the line. I had been noting down the main points of reports mentally. For this reason, I extracted only fragments of what he was saying: 'Machine – fly out – place reserved. Fetch your wife.' Suddenly I was wide awake. A place had been reserved for my wife and daughter in one of the last aircraft to leave Berlin. They could fly out. To Berchtesgaden. It was almost incredible. I was quite overcome; in all the chaos somebody had thought of Misch, the bunker telephonist.

I was released from duty, and a colleague from the motor pool drove me to Rudow. Berlin was deserted; nobody was about. The man drove as fast as the ruined streets allowed. At our flat nobody was at home – doors and windows gaped open. The Russians blew up closed houses at once, they said. I guessed that Gerda and Gitta would be in an air-raid shelter about four hundred metres away. I had myself driven there, looked for them and happily found them very quickly. Gerda fell into my arms straight away. Her reaction to my life-saving news came as a terrible blow to me. She shook her head. No, she could not fly out, she said. Brigitta, our one-year old daughter, had a high fever. Furthermore, she did not want to leave her parents alone in Berlin. I tried to persuade her, mentioned the atrocities committed by the Russians against civilians in East Prussia, of which I had heard. I failed to convince her. 'It is the last chance, Gerda,' I implored. 'The very last!' But she had decided. She shook her head sadly and pressed her emergency bag into my hand. 'Here, take this with you.' I could not remain any longer, got back into the car and tossed the bag onto the back seat – my mind a blank.

It would be many long years before I saw Gerda and Gitta again. I missed the personality of my daughter developing, never heard her first words, missed her schooling, knew nothing of her joys and troubles as a young girl. Gitta was told about her Papa, but not about Misch, Hitler's bunker telephonist. We were never able to regain what we had lost.

Back at the Reich Chancellery I reported immediately to the chief of the SS bodyguard, Schädle, in the upper region of the cellars: 'My family won't fly.' He did not pursue the matter, but said merely: 'Then I must offer the seat elsewhere.' I nodded and resumed my duties. 'Is there anything for the boss?' anything for me to take down?' Schädle had nothing for Hitler.

There was great activity in the Führerbunker. This surprised me. 'The boss has released everybody,' Retzbach whispered. What was behind it all? During the situation conference, Hitler had finally uttered the magical sentence, and since then it had been repeated in incredulity to everybody creeping around the bunker: 'The war is lost.' Those present at the situation conference, the colleagues of the SS bodyguard and RSD, the servants and other personnel – all now knew about it. Hitler had given up. 'The war is lost.' In 1943, these words had dropped from his lips in a moment of weakness and almost nobody had noticed them, but this time it really did mean the end. Whatever was done from now on was merely preparation for the abdication.

'The boss is staying in Berlin,' my deputy told me and gave me a penetrating stare. We all knew what that meant. He would kill himself. If the worst came to the worst, then that was an option for him – he had mentioned it several times. 'All the others can go,' Retzbach went on, 'Hitler said, "Nobody is now duty-bound to anything."'

Nobody is now duty-bound to anything. Nobody doubted that Hitler was absolutely in earnest, that he had spoken the final word. The activities attached to this fundamental change tumbled out one after another at once. Hitler himself had various files brought to him, looked at some papers and finally engaged in conversation with chief adjutant Julius Schaub.

I remembered the emergency trunk which I had left upstairs in the cellars of the New Reich Chancellery with Schädle. I went up to him again. Dozens of cases were being carried past me. In curiosity, I asked Unterscharführer Hans Hofbeck of the RSD what they contained. 'Those are the official papers of the past two months. They are going on the aircraft,' he replied. In these zinc cases were to be found all the transcriptions of the latest situation conferences. A valuable freight. The cases were set aside, piled into imposing towers. I put Gerda's emergency bag somewhere between them. It had to be taken to safety absolutely without fail, but I had no idea what it contained. In my disappointment at Gerda's reaction to the possibility of evacuation I had quite forgotten to ask her, and to this very day I still do not know.

I had just put the bag aside when Schädle approached me again. I suspected what he was going to tell me. Exceptions to Hitler's general release were naturally those who were indispensable for the immediate continuation of bunker life. After Retzbach's statement it was clear to me at once that I would not be among the lucky ones released. 'Misch, you are naturally still needed!' Schädle said. I gave him a weak nod. Therefore, on my way to the Führerbunker I passed excited people. Beucks the telegraphist almost ran past me. He had an important message for Heinz Lorenz, deputy of Reich press chief Otto Dietrich. Not five minutes later, Lorenz came to my small telephone switchboard. A signal emanating from the Western Allies had just be intercepted, he told me. According to what it said, they were hoping that Berlin could hold out another fourteen days against the Red Army so that they could encircle it and take the Reich capital together. He had to take this signal to the Führer immediately.

For the Soviets to conquer Berlin single-handed seemed to be a thorn in the sides of the Western Allies. I awaited Hitler's response with interest. When Lorenz reappeared at my side, I asked him for the outcome. 'Too late,' he had said, making a dismissive gesture, 'Hitler merely said, "What difference does that make? The war is lost. They should have reported themselves much earlier."' Hitler saw the report as confirming his conviction that the Allies would eventually tear themselves apart, but too late. Meanwhile, it was too late for anything.

The Ju 352, a machine from the Führer-Staffel, took off two hours later as planned. Pilot Friedrich Gundelfinger, with whom I had made many courier flights over the last few years, rang before take-off to advise that he was intending to fly the aircraft to Reichenhall in Bavaria. My colleague Willy Arndt, Hitler's favourite servant, had taken the seat originally set aside for Gerda and the infant.

Some time later, a report reached me that this very plane had been intercepted by the Allies and been forced to change flight plan to Cologne. Gundelfinger had not complied and finally the aircraft had gone down near Dresden.[3] According to the reports, there were no survivors. The news did the rounds in a flash, mainly because Willy Andt had been on board. When I talked to a British officer about this aircraft years later, he stated frankly his suspicion that it had been shot down by the British. I had been that close to putting my wife and daughter on a death flight.

Meanwhile, Hitler had appointed my former commanding officer Brigadier Wilhelm Mohnke as battle commandant of the Zitadelle,

---

3 The machine crashed near the village of Börnersdorf near Pirna/Dresden. There was probably only one survivor. He did not know the other passengers, and this created problems of identification because the bodies were so badly charred. Thus initially it was suspected wrongly that the secretaries Christa Schroeder and Else Krüger had been on board. Christa Schroeder, *He Was My Chief*, London 2009, p.180. It remains unclear when exactly the plane crashed and if important documents, which according to Flight Captain Hans Baur had been entrusted to the safekeeping of Arndt by Hitler, were lost. The mystery surrounding these missing files provoked the 'Hitler-diaries' farce in 1983.

the innermost government quarter. *Kampfgruppe Mohnke* led by him had its command post in the cellars of the New Reich Chancellery. The force was 4,000-strong and embraced all Waffen-SS units in Berlin, including the Wachbataillon. From these units, two regiments were formed with battalions and companies, while smaller groups of the Wehrmacht, Luftwaffe and a formation of Axmann's Hitler Youth made up the numbers.

While I tried to ring Gerda, hoping that she had perhaps left the air-raid shelter, somebody else had a quite different vision of how he was going to save his family. Dr Goebbels wanted to save his wife and children not *in* the world but *from* the world after the defeat; he added them all to those condemned to die in the Reich Chancellery.

Staff members who had long since been given shelter rooms in the ante-bunker had now to abandon them for the Goebbels younger generation. Goebbels himself moved into the room directly alongside my telephone switchboard, which Professor Morell had vacated the previous evening. There was no direct entry into it from the corridor. Goebbels therefore had to come through my workplace to enter or leave his room.

I thought it was complete madness to bring six children to live in this sarcophagus. When, instead of the Soviets, this little gang came storming into the deep bunker for the first time I did not know whether to laugh or cry. At least twice daily they visited their father, and when he left the Führerbunker they would romp around in the corridor. The atmosphere in the bunker did not dampen their high spirits in the least. They played, laughed, sang, were cocky and carefree, as all children are. Again and again I had to remind them: 'Enough, this is not a playground,' though it was more effective for me to say: 'Be quiet, children, your Uncle Adolf is sleeping. Under no circumstances must he be awoken.' Günther Ochs, Goebbels's valet, would then take the five girls and one boy up to the civilians in the New Reich Chancellery cellar.

Late in the evening I rang Gerda's number again. The line was working, I heard the ring tone, but nobody picked up the phone. Gerda, my parents-in-law and the child must therefore still be in the air-raid bunker, and they would not leave it until the end. I tried to sleep at my switchboard and left my sleeping mat rolled up. Dr Goebbels might wander through my workplace at any moment. What would he think if he found me asleep!

23 April 1945

Now and again, when I could no longer tolerate the dismal, suffocating narrowness of my telephone cubbyhole, I would go up to my old service room in the adjutants' wing not far from the cellar exit and rest there for a little. In the bunker I was the only person who kept watch day and night at the switchboard – except for the short meal breaks when my colleague Retzbach covered for me.

Late in the afternoon, Hitler suddenly left his rooms. Slowly, very slowly he plodded past me at the switchboard, the Alsatian dog Blondi never leaving his side. Together with some of the SS bodyguard he went upstairs into the Reich Chancellery garden to breathe fresh air for the last time. These were often wonderful spring days against which backdrop this hell played out.

Shortly afterwards, there was some excitement. Göring had managed to fall into Hitler's bad books at the last moment. I thought it had to do with a telegram from Göring at Berchtesgaden, but I could not obtain the precise details and was having difficulty concentrating on my telephone calls. The Krügerin – our nickname for Bormann's secretary Else Krüger – came to my switchboard and told me excitedly that Martin Bormann was sounding off about 'high treason'. He had dictated a radio signal to her, which had to be transmitted upstairs. Not until later did I find out that, as a result of Hitler's statement on 22 April that he had no more orders to give, Göring had taken that to mean that he was ready to initiate the procedure for his successor. To all appearances Göring was already in the starting blocks, ready to take over from Hitler in the event of his apparent inability to govern, as was prescribed for such a case. Chief intriguer Bormann had seen through Göring's little game, however, and more than ever Hitler was ready to listen to shocking accusations of betrayal, conspiracy and sabotage.[4]

Meanwhile, Albert Speer, Herr Artistic Genius, had arrived. He was the Armaments Minister, but looked completely out of place in the bunker. While waiting he paced the corridor, then finally went in to see Hitler. He stayed until the situation conference with General Krebs. Later that evening, Eva Braun wished to see Speer. She came to me at the telephone switchboard with her request to pass on the message. Speer was staying in the upper levels of the catacomb.

Finally, I got through to my wife on the telephone. It was the last time for many years that I would hear her voice. That same evening her father died, but I was not informed. He had left the air-raid bunker prematurely with two other people, because he was worried about our unlocked property being exposed to looters. A shell landed among them and blew all three to shreds. What remained of him is buried in the garden.

24 April 1945

The ranks of the faithful around Hitler dwindled. Meanwhile, the female secretaries Christa Schroeder and Johanna Wolf had been flown out. Traudl Junge and Gerda Christian remained.

Frau Christian – Dara – was Hitler's favourite secretary. She had a sense of humour and the swift Berliner retort; 'the boss' liked that. But why was Frau Junge still here? Traudl Junge was always the spare wheel. I never knew Hitler to call her as his first choice for dictation; she was only used as a reserve if another secretary could not come.

---

4 In an opening telegram, Göring had requested Hitler's agreement to take over the leadership of the Reich as from 2200 hrs. In a second telegram Göring had ordered Foreign Minister Ribbentrop to Berchtesgaden for the succession. This convinced Hitler that Martin Bormann was right when he said that Göring's request to Hitler had actually been an ultimatum.

Albert Bormann had brought her one day from the Munich Party HQ when Dara took leave for several months after her marriage.[5] When I saw Frau Junge, Fräulein Humps as she then was, for the first time, at Berchtesgaden, it really gave me a shock. She had an incredible squint. Soon afterwards, they operated on her eyes and now one could look at her.

The Red Army was occupying ever more city districts. The airfields at Gatow and Tempelhof fell on this day. For this eventuality, Hitler had arranged for a new airstrip on the Charlottenburger Chaussee,[6] between the Victory Column and the Brandenburg Gate, to be installed as a reserve. He was hoping to use it to fly in reinforcements for the defence. About two hundred naval ratings arrived by this route from Dönitz in the middle of the inferno.

Hitler met me in the corridor. He now looked like the kind of figure who one imagines lives without daylight and fresh air. Pallid, stooped, uncertain in his gait, he shuffled past my switchboard like a man in prison allowed to walk up and down the corridor once every couple of hours. Like a murderer in the death cell. This was quite in contrast to Eva. She continued to take care with her appearance as before, put rouge on her cheeks and dressed as though she found herself in a villa of the nobility and not in a tomb with furniture relics of long bygone days. I liked that. One must almost make the point that

---

5 Misch recollects that, when he enquired, Albert Bormann replied that he had brought Traudl Junge from the Munich Party Chancellery as a conscript for essential service. She says in her memoir: 'My sister Inge was then making a living in Berlin as a dancer at the Deutsche Tanzbühne. One of her colleagues was related to Albert Bormann and through him one fine day I received an offer to go to the Führer's Chancellery in Berlin ... I accepted and went there ... I often asked myself why they had sent for a secretary expressly from Munich and even conscripted her for essential service.' See Traudl Junge, *Bis zur letzten Stunde – Hitlers Sekretärin erzählt ihr Leben*, Munich 2002, p.37. In an interview with André Heller, Junge said she had asked a female friend with links to Albert Bormann to solicit from him a position for herself. See the documentation in André Heller and Othmar Schmiderer, *Im toten Winkel*, DVD 2002.

6 Today, Strasse des 17 Juni.

Eva was the only one to remain cultured. She reminded me that we were not dead yet. Apart from her appearance, everything there had to do with death. Everywhere only the past, the end, defeat. All faces were grey, only Eva's lips were not. Until then, I had not anticipated that there was still something important to come in Eva's life – she did not have much time left.

Since Hitler had announced the end, on 22 April, it had been clear to us that by it he meant his own end. Everybody seemed to be occupied with the question of what was the best method of suicide. I heard that Dr Stumpfegger would distribute cyanide capsules. None was offered to me. I did not need poison. I kept my Walther PP on my switchboard table with the safety catch off. Should the time come, I would shoot myself in the head.

Those among us, who were here by virtue of their services being indispensable, knew only too well that the only hope of saving our own skins would come after Hitler's death. Therefore we waited for it. After that, there would be three choices: to die by one's own hand; to run up a white flag at the telephone switchboard and surrender to the Russians; or take a chance on flight. I wavered. On the one hand, I thought my hour had now come and felt dull and empty; on the other hand, strategies to save myself darted through my head. My will to survive had not yet been extinguished, but once it was I would end my life with the Walther PP. And if Hitler waited too long? Should I then simply stand up, walk out of the Reich Chancellery and try to get through to my wife and daughter? What chance was there of that? Wandering through the ruins, the Gestapo would soon pick me up. To be hanged as a coward and deserter – that I did not want. Everything revolved around two questions: When would Hitler kill himself? When would the Russians arrive at the bunker door?

It was the same for my colleagues. In any case, there were not many of us left behind. Without saying as much, we were all waiting for the same thing. When would Hitler finally release us? We waited hour by hour, day by day. Quite a few were praying – some for the first time in their lives. I was ever more isolated in the Führerbunker. None of my colleagues let themselves be seen down there unless it was absolutely necessary. Only my relief came regularly. In recent days, I had not seen my good friend Helmuth Beermann; meanwhile he must have been flown out. The same went for Albert Bormann, who also had not taken his leave of me.

Eva Braun and Magda Goebbels often sat in the corridor discussing the day's events, the bunker and above all, naturally, Hitler and Joseph Goebbels. I heard how that they gave each other courage not to leave their respective men but to die with them: 'We have lived with them. We shall die with them.'

The telephone rang ceaselessly. Many troubled civilians called. As I mentioned, the number of the New Reich Chancellery was in the telephone directory and even the number of the Führer's flat was not a secret. Whoever knew it could pass it on. My colleagues above often redirected the calls to me.

Once I had a woman on the line, screaming and crying. She was in such a state of distress I could hardly understand her. Her neighbour was being raped, she sobbed. 'Help, help! – come and help us!' In the background I could hear terrible screams. 'One moment,' I said, I could not think of anything else to say, I just wanted to be rid of the call. Dr Goebbels stood nearby. I beckoned to him, holding out the receiver. 'Civilians!' Goebbels handled every one of these appalling calls, including the one with the rape.

Between the situation conferences the mood was especially depressing. Everybody whispered. I did not wish to be infected with this sepulchral mood and spoke deliberately in loud tones and very audibly into the mouthpiece. This brought a little normality into the eerie atmosphere. In the evening there was another situation conference.

25 April 1945

I was glad to be constantly occupied. It helped me a little to forget the times. In the evening, signals were sent to the commander-in-chief

Twelfth Army, Walther Wenck, and to Jodl. The relieving attack that had been hoped of Army Wenck, however, never came.

26 April 1945

The battle for Berlin entered its final phase. The Reich Chancellery lay under an artillery bombardment all day. Despite having plenty of filters, occasionally Hentschel had to close the fresh air ventilation system because it was sucking smoke into the interior.

Despite the incessant artillery fire, I continued to spend my breaks upstairs. I simply had to leave that coffin now and again, otherwise I would have gone completely mad. I now decided myself when I would have a break, but with Retzbach's approval. On this day too, after lunch, I went to my service room. At the entrance to the adjutants' wing a Volkssturm man lay dead. He had probably been hit by falling masonry during an air attack. Dead tired I stepped over the corpse and dragged myself to the bed. It was my last time upstairs before Hitler died.

In the evening, the female pilot Hanna Reitsch[7] and Luftwaffe General Robert Ritter von Greim[8] arrived in the bunker. Hanna Reitsch was a real she-cat. I knew the gifted and bold pilot from her several visits to Hitler. It was she whom he had chosen in 1944 to find the fault in the V-1 flying bomb.[9] This missile, on which such great hopes rested, was not working correctly and the fault had to be sought in flight. Therefore, a converted version with a cockpit had to be constructed. When Hanna Reitsch was suggested as pilot, Hitler growled 'Can't a man fly it?' but finally he agreed. Reitsch found at least one of the causes of the malfunction: a cable in the guidance

---

7 Hanna Reitsch had the Iron Cross, First and Second Class.

8 Greim (1892–1945), see biographical entry, p.227.

9 The V-1, *Vergeltungswaffe*-1 (weapon of reprisal), known internally as FZG 76 *Flakzielgerät* (flak target device), was Goebbels's propaganda term for the Fieseler-103, an unmanned aircraft armed with explosives (the first semi-guided missile).

system of the machine* was disconnected, and there was probably a whole series of other problems.

Because Gatow airport had been in Soviet hands for some time, Reitsch and Ritter von Greim had had to land their Fieseler Storch[10] on the Charlottenburg Chaussee, which had been renamed East–West Axis in 1935. Greim was wounded in the leg, as the aircraft came under fire when landing. My SS colleagues brought him in to see Hitler on a stretcher. While they spoke, Hanna Reitsch spent the time with me at the telephone switchboard. I looked at the Iron Cross, First Class resplendent on her roll-neck sweater. Günther Ochs, Goebbels's valet, fetched three wine glasses and filled them up. Outside, the last battle of the war raged, and we sat there in a kind of church-hush drinking a glass of wine. When Frau Goebbels appeared, Hanna Reitsch asked her straight away about her children. She pleaded, using her silver tongue, to be allowed to fly the five girls and one boy out. Nobody need know whose children they were. 'If necessary I will fly in and out of here ten times,' she implored the mother. Finally, she made it clear: 'What you decide for yourself is your affair. If you want to stay with your husband, then do so. But the children . . .' All to no avail.

Meanwhile, the talk between Hitler and Ritter von Greim had finished. Greim looked almost jolly as he hobbled out. Hitler had promoted him to field marshal and commander-in-chief of the Luftwaffe. Göring had been replaced and relieved of all his offices. Later, Hitler had him arrested, together with all his entourage at Obersalzberg. Greim and Hanna Reitsch spent the night in the ante-bunker.

27 April 1945

Report followed report unceasingly. At first, we were told that Wenck had made a decisive advance and was twenty kilometres from Berlin.

---

10 The Fi-156 was a high-wing, single-engined propeller aircraft developed at the Fieseler Works, Kassel, and called the Storch for its high, fixed undercarriage.

* Not a rocket 'Rakete', propulsion was by ram-jet. (TN)

Goebbels announced that Berlin must be held without regard to the losses. I did not hear any more. I functioned as if hypnotised. Wenck's advance meant for me just another prolongation of the tough wait for Hitler to kill himself.

The radio contact to Wenck was continually breaking off, and soon the report was received that the advance had stopped. The offensives to the north and south of Berlin were also unsuccessful. If such a thing was possible, all this compounded the depression in the bunker. According to Hitler and Martin Bormann, the failure of the offensives could only be explained by treachery – treachery extending up into the closest circle. The remaining SS bodyguard and I meanwhile went over the countless senarios in which the Russians stormed the bunker.

In the afternoon, Hitler wanted to speak to Himmler's liaison officer Hermann Fegelein. After Fegelein's marriage to Eva Braun's sister Gretl, the ladies' man was to a certain extent Hitler's brother-in-law to be. We of the SS bodyguard had no doubt that, by means of his marriage to a Braun, Fegelein was aiming to inveigle himself into the close circle around Hitler. Marrying a Braun, however, had not proved as useful as he had hoped.

On this 27 April Fegelein could not be found in the Reich Chancellery cellars. I was told to call all known telephone numbers he used in order to contact him, but found him present at none of them. An RSD squad finally located him at his flat on the Bleibtreu-Strasse, a side street off the Kurfüstendamm. Martin Bormann was waiting in the corridor to the Führerbunker when the RSD men returned without Fegelein, to make their report. I stood listening as they told Bormann that they had found Fegelein at his flat, but he had declined to accompany them to the Reich Chancellery. What were the RSD men to do? They were simple soldiers, in SS uniform admittedly, but without rules – mere police. Fegelein, on the other hand, had the rank of a brigadier. He was not obliged to follow the instructions of these RSD men. Fegelein had been under the influence of alcohol, lightly clothed and not alone, the report went on. They had not recognised the lady accompanying him as his wife. She was probably a radio announcer from Deutschlandfunk, as I later learned. In any case, according to the RSD men, Fegelein had then made the vulgar observation: 'What is all this shit about, anyway? It doesn't involve me any more.'

Bormann scowled when he heard that. 'Go back there immediately! Arrest him and bring him here,' he stormed. Meanwhile, Fegelein had decided to come to the Reich Chancellery under his own steam. I understood that all kinds of valuables had been found in his flat, jewellery maybe, and a lot of money including British pounds sterling. Apparently, he wanted to withdraw secretly. Later, on my way to our commander Schädle, I saw Fegelein in uniform in the catacombs of the New Reich Chancellery accompanied by two RSD men. He was taken to Mohnke's command post for interrogation by Kriminalrat (detective chief superintendent) Peter Högl.

I went back to my workplace suspecting that it was not going to be pleasant for Fegelein. I got one of the RSD men, Hans Hofbeck, to promise to keep me informed. Hitler concerned himself only briefly with the matter; he reduced his 'brother-in-law to be' to the rank of an SS private and ordered a field court martial. Fegelein was stripped of all orders and decorations. Hofbeck told me that after the interrogation Fegelein would await the judgement of the tribunal under Högl.

28 April 1945

At night I had much to do again. Several times I set up a line for Krebs to Keitel. In the early hours it became disconnected. Keitel was having difficulties with the commander-in-chief of Army Group Vistula, General Gotthard Heinrici. Heinrici probably ignored orders to mount a relieving attack and was immediately relieved of command.[11]

---

11 Against his own orders, General Heinrici had ordered the retreat of von Manteuffel's Panzer-Armee. Keitel met Heinrici personally but was unable to convince him to use his forces to mount an attack to relieve Berlin by opening a gap in the Soviet ring around the trapped troops. Heinrici considered this would cause

More bad news arrived in the bunker. The signals service took down foreign news broadcasts, which served as one of the main sources of information for the daily situation conferences. From a Swedish radio station we now learnt that Heinrich Himmler had made the British and Americans an offer to capitulate. It had been turned down on the grounds that the Western Allies would only accept unconditional surrender to them all including the Soviets.[12]

Himmler was probably trying to wriggle out of this when confronted. Then the BBC sent a Reuters report confirming all the rumours. The chief of the news bureau, Heinz Lorenz, took the report to Hitler personally. For a moment Hitler lost his self-control. It was loud – I could hear his voice above the telephone calls I was dealing with: 'Himmler of all people, Himmler of all people!' Snatches of his words could be heard throughout the Führerbunker area. The whole thing reminded me of his reaction to Hess's defection to Britain in 1941.

Hitler called Hanna Reitsch and Ritter von Greim to him. They were to arrest Himmler. I was totally downcast. I had been hoping secretly that Hitler would fly out with Greim. Now the last hope floated – or better put, flew away. Hitler was to remain in Berlin. I did not leave the bunker. Reitsch and Greim took off from the Charlottenburger Chaussee airstrip in order to meet Dönitz at Plön.

Hans Hofbeck appeared below again and told me more about the Fegelein affair. In the light of Himmler's efforts, Fegelein had been given short shrift. A search of his service room in the catacombs had brought to light certain files from which it was obvious that he must have known of the secret negotiations initiated by Himmler through the Swedish intermediary Count Folke Bernadotte. Thus, Fegelein

---

senseless losses. Keitel then relieved Heinrici of command at his own request. See Joachim Fest, *Der Untergang*, Berlin 2002, pp.111ff.

12 Himmler had attempted to negotiate with the Western Powers through the Swedish diplomat Count Folke Bernadotte and had even said he was ready to 'capitulate unconditionally'. See Joachim Fest, *Der Untergang*, Berlin 2002, p.114

was not merely guilty of planning to flee Berlin, but of high treason. The field court martial under Kriminalrat Högl condemned the husband of Gretl to death by firing squad. There was no direct order from Hitler. He had only ordered Fegelein to be reduced to the ranks.

Hofbeck now described to me in great detail the execution carried out immediately after sentence. An RSD colleague – Hofbeck told me his full name[13] – had shot Fegelein from behind with a machine pistol in the cellar corridor. Hofbeck imitated the raising and aiming of the weapon to shoulder height and then downwards and imitated the noise of the shooting: 'Ratatatata'.

29 April 1945

Shortly after midnight I saw a man in the bunker whom I had never seen before. Hentschel nearby seemed less surprised than I, as the man and two assistants walked calmly past us.

'Who is that then?' I asked Hentschel.

'That is the registrar.'

'The who?' I thought I must have misheard, but Hentschel repeated: 'The registrar!' He was the Stadtrat (city councillor) and Gauamtsleiter (NSDAP regional office leader) Walter Wagner, who had worked with Goebbels in the Berlin Gau leadership. 'The boss is getting married today,' the technician informed me. I also asked him to repeat this sentence as well.

In this manner I heard of the planned marriage of Hitler to Eva Braun. So at last. I saw Wagner disappear into Hitler's study, the two men who had accompanied him remained outside. Inside Eva and Hitler both said '*Ja*'. Apparently, Bormann and Goebbels were the witnesses. Towards half past one it was completed.

There were a few well-wishers present to toast the Hitler newly-weds: the Goebbels couple, Hitler's secretaries Junge and Christian, generals Krebs and Burgdorf, Colonel von Below and Hitler's

---

13 Misch did not wish to reveal the name of the gunman, out of regard for the latter's family.

diet-cook Constanze Manziarly. I remained at my workplace and considered how I should now greet Eva when I met her. 'Frau Hitler' – that did not seem possible. 'Frau Hitler' did not suit Eva, the Führer's girl, and neither did it suit Hitler to be a married man. The bodyguard speculated later that Hitler had only wanted to make Eva 'Frau Hitler' to preserve convention at the end – above all for Eva's parents, so that everything should ultimately be in order. The Brauns must not live with the shame of their daughter having died as a concubine.

Thoughts about the correct form of address for Eva Hitler and the whole marriage thing had long given way to the big question: When will we have the suicide? Sunk in contemplation, I failed to notice that Traudl Junge had quietly sat down on the only other seat by the telephone switchboard and begun to type up something from her dictation pad. 'My Political Testament' – I could not read anything else. Frau Junge typed three copies in a business-like manner.

While she was making the fair copies, Bormann and Goebbels appeared and gave her something more urgent to do. More urgent than Hitler's Testament? Yes, apparently so.[14] In the early morning, it was between five and six o'clock, the copies of this last Will were sent by courier – one to Dönitz, a second one to Schörner and the last to the NSDAP headquarters in Munich. Therefore, it could not be much longer now – and Hitler would finally put an end to himself. My telephone lines ran hot because of the failure to arrest Himmler.

Meanwhile, the noose around our necks grew ever tighter. It was clear to all that at any moment the Russians could storm the bunker. I still had lines to almost all Berlin, and so I rang civilians at random to find out where the Red Army was. I discovered later that the Russians were doing exactly the same in order to establish their own frontline.

---

14 According to Traudl Junge, Joseph Goebbels dictated his own Testament to her while she was working on the dictation of Hitler's Will. Goebbels' Testament was to have been an appendix to Hitler's. See Traudl Junge, *Bis zur letzten Stunde – Hitlers Sekretärin erzählt ihr Leben*, Munich 2002, pp.203f.

It was dreadfully stuffy in my small switchboard, and made me sleepy. I approved a few cognacs for myself.

My former company commander Mohnke was ordered to Hitler in his capacity as battle commander of the government district. How long can we still hold out, Hitler wanted to know. 'No longer than twenty, at the most twenty-four hours,' I heard Mohnke state. Without speaking to me Mohnke left the Führerbunker.

Shortly afterwards, I observed Professor Werner Haase, since 1935 Hitler's travelling physician, having a quiet conversation with Hitler in the lobby. Haase would usually be found operating on the wounded in the field hospital below the Reich Chancellery. He and Hitler finally emerged into the corridor and stood in front of my telephone switchboard. At that moment Feldwebel Fritz Tornow led in Blondi. Haase and Tornow then disappeared with the dog into the washroom about three metres from my post. The door was left open, and I peered in. Tornow held Blondi's nose up, and Haase thrust a pair of tongs inside the mouth to drop a small object inside. There was cracking sound and Blondi quickly collapsed. Hitler made a few steps forward and observed for a few seconds. Then he turned away silently and returned to his room. There was a smell of bitter almonds. After the dead Blondi had been dragged away, Tornow took her five pups, born at the beginning of the month, into the Reich Chancellery garden and shot them, dead. Now I could be sure. If Hitler had decided to kill his beloved dog, then it would not be long until he followed her in death.

First, I had to get away as soon as possible from this workplace stinking of bitter almonds. In the cellar of the New Reich Chancellery I came across the next macabre scene. Music and singing were coming from the room near the field hospital. The six Goebbels children were sitting together with their parents at a long table singing:

The blue dragoons they are riding
With drum and fife through the gate,

Fanfares accompany them,
Ringing to the hills above.

A young man, perhaps sixteen years old, provided accompaniment
with his accordion. A crowd of civilians, staff and wounded stood
around them. I understood: this was the manner and way in
which the Goebbels family took their leave – a last opportunity to
demonstrate the unity of the family. Unsuspecting and well brought
up, the Goebbels children concentrated on their song – I could not
bear to watch this activity any longer and was suddenly in a hurry to
return to the Führerbunker.

Events followed one after another in the next few hours. Towards
evening we sent a telex to Jodl. There were five questions:

1. Where are Wenck's spearheads?
2. When will they attack?
3. Where is the Ninth Army?
4. Where will the Ninth Army break through?
5. Where are the spearheads of von Holste?[15]

Some time towards 2300 hrs the report was received that Italian
partisans had shot dead Mussolini and his companion Clara Petacci
and apparently hanged them up by the feet. Somebody said there were
even pictures of it. Had Hitler needed a final shove in order to make
his own suicide a reality, that was probably it.

I was almost totally exhausted, but I kept working at the
switchboard. I wanted to listen to everything, know everything,
miss nothing. But it was a hard battle to fend off sleep. My forehead
fell forward against the junction box. Senseless, senseless, senseless.
Nothing else went through my head.

---

15 Major General Rudolf von Holste commanded XXXXI Panzerkorps to the
north of Berlin.

Chapter 14
Hitler's Last Day: 30 April 1945

S HORTLY AFTER ONE IN the morning, Hitler wanted to know if there were any fresh reports from OKW. There were none. Two hours later, around three o'clock, a long-awaited radio signal arrived from Keitel, which extinguished any remaining shimmer of hope. The attempt to break the encirclement of Berlin had come to a halt. Upstairs, they had to send another signal. Dönitz must take immediate action against all traitors ruthlessly and as soon as possible.

It was not until much later, around midday, that the Berlin city commandant, Helmuth Weidling, reported that the Russians were in immediate proximity to the government district.

Suddenly Hitler came shuffling along the corridor to my telephone switchboard and stood in the doorway. I rose, assuming he had a job for me. He looked me in the eyes. His gaze was lustreless but clear; nevertheless, it was not the old Hitler gaze. I had the impression he wanted to communicate something private. Before I could think how I should respond if he spoke to me or offered me his hand for the last time, he turned away without a word and shuffled back to his room. In a way relieved to have avoided an undesirable scene, I resumed my seat at the switchboard.

Now it would be soon. Towards 1500 hrs, I heard a quiet murmuring in the corridor. For the last time I heard Hitler's voice, and I also heard Günsche, Goebbels, Linge, Bormann and perhaps Axmann, but now

I am no longer so sure. Hitler was speaking quietly and unexcitedly. I pricked up my ears but could not understand anything precisely and had to concentrate on my work – telephone calls were coming in all the time. Now and again I stood up, went to the door, then turned back to take the next call.

I caught a last glimpse of Hitler as he disappeared into his study. Eva, now his wife, followed him. She looked pretty in her dark blue dress with a bright white frilled collar. She rode out the the last hours of her life differently from others who saw their end approaching. For me, she is the only one who went truly nobly to her death. In any case, Eva lived until death. She had married a dead man – in a mortuary.

Günsche closed the door behind Eva and Hitler and then came over to me: 'The boss does not want to be disturbed again.' The small farewell party broke up. The Goebbels couple and generals Burgdorf and Krebs were among them, Frau Manziarly and Hitler's secretaries. Traudl Junge almost rushed past me. Günsche whispered to me that 'the boss' had taken his leave of him with a handshake and released all soldiers from any erstwhile oath sworn to the Führer.

Now it was still, dead still. Besides Hentschel, there was an RSD colleague with me at the telephone switchboard. Günsche had asked him to stand by ready for the burning. I had already been informed that under all circumstances Hitler wished his body to be consigned to the flames. Günsche told me. The memory of Mussolini's body strung up for exhibition must have stayed with him – for that reason the funeral pyre seemed very important. We waited. For what? Hitler had asked Haase about various ways to commit suicide sparing oneself unnecessary suffering. Which would he choose? We all thought he would shoot himself. It was soon clear to us that we would probably not hear anything – the diesel motor in the adjoining room was far too loud.

I was nervous. Not for Hitler. Or not exclusively in any case. I whispered with Hannes Hentschel. During the lunch break I saw

Gestapo Müller[1] in the New Reich Chancellery accompanied by two high-ranking SS officers. All still in full uniform.

'Hannes, what in heaven's name is he doing here?'

Müller never came into the Reich Chancellery – I had never met him there even once. Were all eyewitnesses to be eliminated? What if the bunker had been so constructed that if necessary the whole thing could be blown up? Was the bunker provided with a time-fuse installation? Hentschel had been present when they built the bunker and so I asked him, 'Hannes, be frank with me, can the bunker be blown up?'

'Whatever next?' he said, trying to calm me.

Everybody was listening, but all we could hear was the humming of the ventilation system and the droning of the diesel generator. Nothing could be heard of the fighting above.

Waiting.

We had already been waiting since 22 April.

I needed to have something to eat, having postponed my lunch break repeatedly. Eat now? Yes. In any case, get away from here. I called the New Reich Chancellery and told Unterscharführer Retzbach to come down and relieve me. As soon as I had hung up I heard somebody shouting: 'Linge, Linge, I think the time has come.' Bormann or Goebbels, I am not sure which, was calling for Hitler's valet.* One of them must have heard something. At the telephone switchboard, nobody had heard a shot fired.

---

1 Heinrich Müller (1900–1945(?)) was head of Amt IV (Counter-terrorism), RSHA.

* Linge remembered it differently. 'As I was passing the lobby doors I smelt the burnt powder of a discharged weapon. I did not want to go in alone. I went to the conference room where some people were gathered around Martin Bormann. I gave Bormann a sign to accompany me to Hitler's study. I opened the door and went in followed by Bormann.' Heinz Linge, *With Hitler to the End*, London 2009, p.199. The three principal witnesses of the suicides to finish up in Soviet hands – Misch, Linge and Günsche – all disagreed on how the suicides were discovered and by whom, where Hitler was sitting, where the blood, if any, fell and who carried out which body and in what order. It would have been these discrepancies, if repeated to the Soviets, which led to all the tortures inflicted later 'to get at the truth'. Erich

I took a few cautious steps from my room into the corridor. Linge pushed me aside from behind, barged past me hastily. I do not know if he came from the washroom or the steps from the ante-bunker. Deathly silence. Linge placed his ear to the door of the anteroom. He and Günsche opened the first door to the anteroom. They advanced slowly to Hitler's study door. Nobody drew breath. The second door was opened. I took a few steps forward and craned my neck. I looked for only a few seconds but I have never forgotten what I saw.

My glance fell first on Eva. She was seated on the sofa with her legs drawn up, her head inclined towards Hitler. Her shoes were under the sofa. Near her – I cannot remember whether on the sofa or the armchair near it – the dead Hitler. His eyes were open and staring, his head had fallen forward slightly. I saw no blood.

I shrank back. All I wanted to do now was get away. Retzbach was in the corridor by the telephone switchboard having answered my call at once. I heaved a sigh. Hitler was dead, Retzbach had come. I had been relieved and had a reason to leave the deep bunker. In hurrying past I called to Retzbach that I had to go upstairs quickly to make a report to our commander Schädle. I rushed up the stairs, strode through the ante-bunker, ran along the bomb-damaged Kannenberg-Allee. Then I stopped suddenly. Hitler, the Führer, was dead. I had to return immediately, see what happened now, I did not want to miss anything. Back at the threshold of the study I saw that, meanwhile, they had laid Hitler out on the ground. Standing outside, I made way for the Führer for the last time. Linge, Günsche, Kempka and an RSD man I did not recognise wrapped him in a grey blanket and carried him past me. The blanket was too short to cover the body, and Hitler's shoes projected out from below it.

Kempka, who avoided Russian captivity, provided a fourth variation in his book *Die letzten Tage mit Adolf Hitler*, DVG Preussisch Oldendorf, 5th edn 2004, pp.95, 99) where he had the two bodies actually burning between 1400 and 1930 hrs, starting ninety minutes before the suicides occurred. (TN)

Goebbels stated that he would now take a long walk around the gardens until he was killed by the shelling. I went back to Retzbach to tell him I was going up again. He called after me that I should hurry. He looked distinctly unwell. No wonder. Our commander Franz Schädle remained totally calm as I delivered to him the news of Hitler's death. His features were as if carved in stone. He murmured only 'Hmm', and told me to return at once to my workplace. I made a detour through the kitchen, but found I had no appetite. I burnt my service identity document in the fireplace, where the field kitchen vat hung over it. My yellow 'Open Sesame' was now a worthless piece of a paper, and soon would have been a deadly one too.

The bunker corridor was empty again. Retzbach received me with the words: 'So, the boss is burning now.' For a moment I had the mental image of my service document flaring up in the flames.

'Go up there if you like.' He nodded towards the garden exit.

'No, I'd rather not, you go,' I replied.

'I'm off then.' Retzbach said that more to himself than to me. As if in a trance he stood, said something to take his leave and went away. I never heard anything from him again.

Hentschel and I sat together by the telephone switchboard. We just sat, not talking, not moving. Paralysed with anxiety. I imagined hearing the tread of the death squad's boots sent below by Gestapo Müller to shoot us. I released the safety catch of my pistol. I do not know how long we sat there, but Müller never came down.

After a while Günsche joined us and reported quickly on the burning. It had to be done quickly. It was more than just laying out the bodies, pouring petrol over them and lighting it, and it could not be done under permanent artillery fire. One should at least have dug out a small depression, I told Günsche reproachfully. He merely shrugged his shoulders.

Finally, those remaining gathered in the corridor, Mohnke among them, and Goebbels of course. What now? Soon we had a consensus: negotiate with the Russians. We had to connect a line to their field telephones. Linesman Gretz appeared with a giant drum of cable, pointed to two plug points on the junction box and said: 'Those two connections there – they have to be kept free under all circumstances. Now I'll go over to the Russians.' The Red Army was already in Zimmer-Strasse, not four hundred metres away.

Gretz was accompanied by some men from Mohnke's company. After a while he came back and I put the cable end into one of the free points. 'The line is dead,' I announced regretfully. Gretz checked it for himself and nodded. 'I'll go back over to them.'

It was not long before he returned and told me the reason why the first attempt failed: 'The cable wasn't earthed.' I plugged in the cable again, and this time I heard a Russian voice on the other end. 'Moment, moment,' I said, and connected the call to General Krebs, who was fluent in Russian. Before the war, he had been the military attaché in Moscow.

Out of curiosity I listened to the entire conversation but understood nothing. I spoke no Russian – something that would soon change. Apparently, Krebs agreed a meeting with the Russian general. After that there was a situation conference and a long discussion on what was going to be said at the negotiation.

Above left: Rochus Misch in front of the Mönichkirchen railway station, near Wiener Neustadt, 1941.

Above right: Rudolf Hess, 'the Führer's representative', flew to Scotland on 10 May 1941 to negotiate peace. His flight was considered treachery by the National Socialist government, which declared Hess mentally deranged.

Below: On the stairway leading to the Berghof, 7 June 1941, Hitler proceeds upwards with Tsar Boris III of Bulgaria (to his right): standing, far right, is Walther Hewel, chief of the personal staff of Reich Foreign Minister Joachim von Ribbentrop; second left is Albert Bormann, and below him Lieutenant General Adolf Heinz Beckerle, envoy in Sofia. In the driving seat of the Mercedes 770 is the head of the Reich Chancellery motor pool, Erich Kempka.

Above: The telephone exchange in FHQ Wolfsschanze, 1942–3, all carefully planned down to the last detail.

Below: Lazing at the Moysee near FHQ Wolfsschanze. Rochus Misch (nearest camera) with his colleague Karl Weichelt and a female stenographer.

Above: *Waiting for Mussolini at Bahnhof Görlitz, specially created for FHQ Wolfsschanze. The Italian dictator often arrived along this single branch line.*

Below: *The 'reception hall' for Mussolini's visit to Bahnhof Görlitz.*

Above: In order to defeat the plague of mosquitoes, head nets were issued. Here they are appreciated by Misch and some of his colleagues (from left): Misch's Berlin room-mate, the films controller Erich Stein; August Körber (without headgear); Rochus Misch; and an unknown RSD colleague.

Below: The FHQ Wolfsschanze chef (nicknamed 'Krümel' or 'crumbs' and formerly of the Kaiserhof hotel in Berlin) standing in front of the special train, Amerika, with Willy Arndt (far left) and Rochus Misch (far right).

Above left: *Rochus Misch sunbathing at FHQ Wolfsschanze, winter 1941.*

Above right: *Professor Theodor Morell, Hitler's personal physician from 1936, photographed in 1942.*

Below: *Hitler and Mussolini met at Schloss Klessheim (near Salzburg) in the Reich government guest house, on 10 April 1943. From left, front row: General Kurt Zeitzler, chief of the army general staff; Mussolini; Göring; and Hitler. From left, rear row: Dino Alfieri, Italian ambassador; Giuseppe Bastianini, Under-secretary of State at Italian Foreign Ministry; Paul-Otto Schmidt, chief interpreter at the Foreign Ministry; and (far right) Hans-Georg von Mackensen, German ambassador to Rome.*

Above: Rochus Misch took the cure for four weeks in July 1942 at very fashionable Karlsbad, as ordered by Hitler's personal physician Theodor Morell.

Below: FHQ Wehrwolf, which included a camouflaged blockhouse, was the largest of three such installations in the occupied Soviet Union.

Above: Hitler's study in a wooden barrack hut at FHQ Wehrwolf; photo taken by Rochus Misch, 1943.

Below: There was a lively trade between FHQ Wehrwolf staff and the local Ukrainians, in which fresh geese were exchanged for sewing needles.

Above: FHQ Wolfsschanze – The Mosquito Home! Rochus Misch on sentry duty in the winter of 1942 in Sperrkreis 1, the so-called Führer-Sperrkreis.

Opposite below: Hitler greeting General Ferdinand Schörner in the situation conference room of the bunker shortly before the end of the war; in the background is Hitler's chief adjutant Julius Schaub.

Below: The inner-circle at FHQ Wolfsschanze, 1942–3: (from the left) General Erhard Milch, Albert Speer, Hermann Göring, Heinrich Himmler and Colonel Nicolaus von Below.

Left: Gerda and Rochus Misch on the day of their marriage, New Year's Eve 1942. Misch wears the uniform of an SS Unterscharführer (corporal) – the white lacing on the collar and shoulder straps denoting NCO status. The decorations are: on the medal bar the Iron Cross II, Sudetenland medal and Austria-Anschluss medal; on the pocket the Infantry Assault badge and below it the Black Wound Badge.

Right: Rochus Misch photographed in July 1944 at the entrance to the situation conference barrack hut at FHQ Wolfsschanze. A few days later inside this hut Claus von Stauffenberg's attempted to kill Hitler. Originally the wooden hut was used by Albert Speer as an office.

Above: Rochus Misch on sentry duty in front of Hitler's bunker, 1944.

Below: Hitler's last visit to the troops, in Ninth Army HQ, Oderfront, 11 March 1945. Behind Hitler is General Ritter von Greim (with spectacles), to the right is General Theodor Busse, commanding officer, Ninth Army (also with spectacles), and between them is Luftwaffe Colonel Hans-Ulrich Rudel.

Above: The area in the Führer-bunker protected by gas-proof sluice doors, at the end of March and the beginning of April 1945. On the far left is Hitler's private physician Theodor Morell; near him (wearing a soft field cap) is Erhard of the SS bodyguard and naval attaché Rear Admiral Karl-Jesko von Puttkamer.

Right: A US soldier in the situation conference room holds the bunker key ring after the capitulation, in 1945.

Left: In the Führerbunker, in Berlin, a US soldier searches the bedroom of Eva Hitler née Braun, 1945.

Left: American forces search for the immolation site of Hitler and Eva Hitler by the Führer-bunker garden exit, June 1945.

Below: Plan of the ante-bunker and the Führerbunker, Berlin 1945.

Key to ante-bunker: *1.* Winter garden cellar; *2.* Festival hall cellar; *3.* Kannenberg corridor; *4.* Storage rooms; *5.* Laundry room/showers; *6.* Toilets; *7.* Larder and kitchen; *8.* Sentry position; *9.* Machinery room; *10.* Old Watch; *11.* Main entrance; *12.* Emergency exit; *13.* Waiting room; *14.* Personnel; *15.* Watch restroom; *16.* Stairway between bunker and Führer-suite; *17.* Gas-proof area; *18.* Accommodation; *19.* Dining room.

Key to Führerbunker: *20.* Concrete filling; *21.* Main bunker, first emergency exit; *22.* Drainage; *23.* Bathroom; *24.* Eva Braun's bedroom; *25.* Lobby to Hitler's suite; *26.* Hitler's study; *27.* Hitler's bedroom; *28.* Map room/situation conference room; *29.* Waiting room/anteroom to the situation conference room; *30.* Corridor and waiting area; *31.* Switchboard; *32.* Medical room; *33.* Bedroom (valet); *34.* Bedroom (Prof. Morell, later Goebbels); *35.* Anteroom; *36.* Führerbunker, second emergency exit; *37.* Observation tower (under construction); *38.* Ventilation shaft (under construction); *39.* Ventilation shaft for generator (under construction); *40.* Bunker walls; *41.* Kempka's house; *42.* Bunker access; *43.* Pergola; *44.* Foreign Ministry; *45.* Führer-apartment; *46.* Goods lift; *47.* Foundations (Old Reich Chancellery).

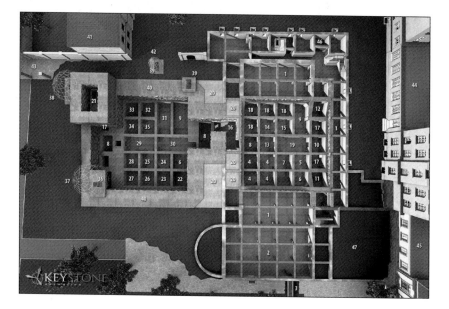

Right: *The ruined Reich Chancellery, around March 1945; to the right on the first storey was Hitler's suite.*

Below: *Location of the ante-bunker and Führerbunker (hatched area between nos 10 and 14) on the Reich Chancellery grounds.*

Key: 1. Central structure with marble gallery; 2. Entrance at Voss-Strasse 6; 3. Entrance at Voss-Strasse 4; 4. Barracks; 5. Car hoist to the catacombs; 6. Garden gate to Hitler's study; 7. Builders' entrance to Führerbunker; 8. Access lane to underground garage and Führerbunker; 9. Entrance to underground garage and for fire-brigade access; 10. Entrance to Führerbunker; 11. Kempka's house; 12. Greenhouse; 13. Cemetery; 14. Festival hall with winter garden; 15. Old Reich Chancellery; 16. Dining hall; 17. Propaganda Ministry; 18. Reich Chancellery extension; 19. Entrance to Wilhelmsplatz U-bahn (subway station); 20. Wertheim department store; 21. Leipzigerplatz; 22. Ministerial gardens; 23. Zoo; 24. Hermann Göring-Strasse (today Friedrich Ebert Platz); 25. Voss-Strasse; 26. Wilhelm-Strasse.

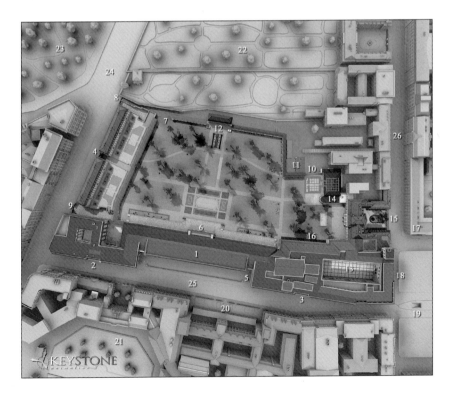

Above: Hans Krebs, chief of the Army General Staff (left) in front of the Soviet command HQ in Berlin, while waiting to proceed to the armistice negotiations. A few hours later he took his own life in the Führerbunker.

Below: 'The war is lost'. The Reich Chancellery in July 1945. View from the Foreign Ministry over the concrete roof of the Führerbunker with the exhaust pipe of the emergency generator. In the background is the 1935-built festival hall below which was the ante-bunker.

Above: A Russian soldier searching for remains of the immolated corpses of Eva and Adolf Hitler in early June 1945.

Right: In June 1945, US investigators examine the sofa on which the couple committed suicide. Rochus Misch had been an eyewitness on 30 April 1945: he saw Eva and Adolf Hitler dead in the Führerbunker.

Left: Hitler's desk inside the bunker.

Below: Hitler's bedroom in the deep bunker, 1945. On a cupboard lay volumes of a technical encyclopaedia.

Above: *After leaving the Borsig Palace through a cellar window in Wilhelm-Strasse (opposite the U-bahn station) on 2 May 1945 Rochus Misch crossed Wilhelm-Platz on his way to Kaiserhof U-bahn station (right in the picture).*

Below: *Rochus Misch and Michael Stehle in 2007.*

Chapter 15

Negotiations and the Goebbels's Children:
1 May 1945

E ARLY THAT MORNING KREBS went with some of Mohnke's
people to a place[1] determined by General Vassili Chuikov.[2]
Goebbels kept phoning Lieutenant Colonel Johannes Seifert,
at the Gau HQ. He was the sector commandant of Zitadelle, under
Brigadier Erich Bärenfanger, the commander of defence Zone A, and
General Rauch, responsible for defence sector Charlottenburg. My
head was spinning. Krebs came back after about four hours. From
what I could make out, the Soviets had insisted that the capitulation
had to be unconditional. They had no interest in any kind of separate
negotiation. Krebs handed over a piece of paper,[3] which Goebbels
studied indignantly. He would never sign anything of that kind, he
shouted, and Bormann, Burgdorf and Krebs agreed. This last chance
was therefore gone. For myself I still had a slight hope that Goebbels

---

1 This was the Hotel Excelsior, according to Joachimsthaler. The negotiations took
place in the provisional Tempelhof HQ of the Russians, Schulenburgring 2. See
Anton Joachimsthaler, *Hitler's Ende*, Munich 2004 (1st edn 1995) p.276.

2 In the battle for Berlin, Chuikov was commander-in-chief, Red Army 8.Garde-
Army, formerly 62.Army until renamed on 16 April 1943.

3 According to Joachim Fest, the Soviet paper contained these terms for
capitulation: '1. Berlin capitulates. 2. All weapons to be surrendered. 3. All soldiers
and officers are guaranteed their lives. 4. The wounded will receive treatment. 5. The
possibility of negotiations with the Allies by radio will be arranged.' See Joachim
Fest, *Der Untergang*, Berlin 2002, p.163.

would let me go. Now that Hitler was dead, according to Hitler's Testament Goebbels was the Reich chancellor and my new boss. There was no doubt that he would choose suicide now that we had the Russians' final decision. Therefore, what use was I here? Around me there were departures and escapes.

It was not Goebbels but Martin Bormann who approached me, however: 'You stay here. You have still got things to do.' From now on, all talk revolved around breaking out from the Reich Chancellery, which Mohnke was to arrange – but I was not to be included. 'Light, air, water, telephone and telegraphy – those responsible for these stay behind,' Bormann made clear.

I returned to my workplace. 'Things to do' there certainly were. Bormann was right. The telephone calls continued to pour in.

Towards five in the afternoon Frau Goebbels appeared at the telephone switchboard with all six children from the ante-bunker below. She pushed the eldest girl on the only chair, lifted the small ones on the table. Magda Goebbels then began changing one after the other into the same type of long white nightdress. She herself wore a brown dress with white trim hardly contrasting from her pallid face. She combed their hair and caressed the children gently. The nine-year-old Helga was crying. Frau Goebbels spoke softly and seriously with the children but was very tender with them. I sat with my back to her at my switchboard, heard her talking about Uncle Adolf as though he were still alive. I saw the children on the table, out of the corner of my eye. I tried to concentrate on my work and kept the headphones tight over my ears, even when I had no calls.

I knew that this was the final parting of a mother from her children, but I did not want to see it. Frau Goebbels was preparing her children for death. My telephone switchboard was the only place where nobody would bother her. Above in the ante-bunker they were excitedly making up the break-out groups.[4] There were civilians running about

---

4 The commandant of the Zitadelle, Mohnke, gave orders that all former members of Hitler's entourage still in the Reich Chancellery cellars and bunkers were to take

as well. Not much unsettled me in the sea of horrors except what was going on around me, which defied description. There I sat, until a short while ago the bodyguard of the Führer, Adolf Hitler, but I could not even protect these children.

I busied myself with telephone calls, kept myself facing my switchboard. The whole thing lasted half an hour. Then Frau Goebbels went back to the ante-bunker with the children.

I was still trying to rid myself of the thoughts as to what would happen upstairs next when Goebbels's personal adviser Dr Werner Naumann* entered my domain. 'If he had his way,' he said, indicating Goebbels's room with a thumb, 'the children wouldn't be here at all.' Naumann was certain that Goebbels wanted to have flown the children out, but had given in to the iron will of his wife.

'How . . .?' My voice broke, and Naumann understood.

'Dr Stumpfegger is giving them some sweetened water.'

My chest tightened; I felt ill. My daughter – she was just one year old.

Towards 1900 hrs Frau Goebbels returned alone from the ante-bunker. She was as pale as the harshly lit wall, her face frozen. Her eyes were red, but as she passed me in the lobby to Goebbels's room I saw that she was not crying. Only when she sat herself at the table did her body begin to tremble lightly. I saw her spread out a hand of cards and put them in order.

When I described this scene to my wife many years later she explained that Magda Goebbels was playing Patience. I did not know that game then. Dr Goebbels arrived and looked at her without speaking. I had calls waiting for him but did not tell him. His children were dead.

---

part in the mass break-out. See Ian Kershaw, *Hitler 1936–1945*, Stuttgart 2000, p.1,071.

* Werner Naumann (1909–1982) was state secretary at the Propaganda Ministry. He reached Argentina in 1946. See Camarasa Jorge, *Los Nazis en la Argentina*, Legasa, Buenos Aires 1992. (TN)

How can one murder one's children? How can a mother murder her children? All six? 'Misch, Misch, you are a fish,' I could still hear their joyful children's voices as they teased me, jumping past. Such lovely kids. How often have I been asked later what I thought when Hitler was dead. Finally, I thought, finally. The most dreadful thing I experienced in the bunker was not *his* death. The worst thing was the killing of these children. I know that I could have done nothing. Nobody could have dissuaded her from her decision. Not the secretaries, not Hanna Reitsch, not Eva, not even her husband. I came to terms with so much – but never with this.

I have been on the receiving end of much ill will for saying that I consider Helga, Hilde, Helmut, Hedda, Holde and Heide Goebbels to have been victims of the Third Reich. I stand by it. Later in captivity I met RSD colleague Hans Hofbeck. He told me that the bodies of the children had been specially laid out. The Russians had rounded up some Berliners from the street and led them past the corpses. The Berlin citizens are then supposed to have thrown stones and spat upon the dead children. Why would they do that?

Eventually Frau Goebbels rose and went upstairs. Alone, without her husband. That was the last time I saw her.

A short while afterwards I connected a telephone call from Busse to Burgdorf and listened in. Only later did I discover that they were related by marriage. Busse said it looked bad – there would probably be nothing for it but to accept captivity. Burgdorf should greet his wife for him. A week before such a statement would have been dangerous. It must therefore finally be over. After this call I plucked up courage to approach Dr Goebbels: 'Herr Reich chancellor, you will certainly know that upstairs they are putting together the break-out groups. I request permission to be allowed to join them.' Goebbels nodded: 'Yes, of course – but not yet. I shall let you know, Misch, when you can go.'

Now we were no more than a small company in the Führerbunker: Goebbels, generals Burgdorf and Krebs, Hentschel, Dr Naumann and myself. Now and again, we were joined by Goebbels's adjutant

Günter Schwägermann, the valet Günther Ochs and Dr Stumpfegger. Axmann, who had not been seen for some time recently, had meanwhile reappeared. His uniform was smeared with dirt. He had been reconnoitring escape routes, and apparently this had taken him through many cellar holes. Axmann offered to include me in his break-out group. I had still not been released from duty, however, and Axmann disappeared once more without speaking to me again. Actually, I was quite glad he did so, for there had been a rumour about doing the break-out with a panzer. I had little enthusiasm for the idea. If things went wrong we were likely to be fried in it! The alternatives I was imagining did not promise to be any more pleasant, but forcing a way through the Russians in a panzer was not my thing. I was to rue this decision, for it was the first of a string of bad decisions which led me into the Soviet torture chambers.

I kept looking nervously at Goebbels as he crept through the bunker rooms. Martin Bormann had come by one last time to take his leave of Goebbels and then of myself. He was wearing a hat, a long black leather coat, beneath it a paratrooper's camouflage smock. In his left hand was a briefcase, the right hand he extended to me: 'You are still needed. You will come afterwards. You know where: Weidendamm bridge.'

'*Ja, ja,*' I murmured.

He left the bunker with Dr Naumann and Dr Stumpfegger. Goebbels followed them, but turned back after a short while. 'Any calls for me, Misch?'

'*Ja*, Herr Reich chancellor. The Gau HQ, General Weidling and a call from Oberstleutnant Seifert,' I replied.

'Well, nothing much there,' he said and made a sign of refusal.

I dared to speak to him again about the break-out groups. Again, he comforted me. Over the next few hours I repeated my enquiry several times, each time feeling more worried. I could not leave without official permission from the Reich chancellor. I was stuck with it. My backpack stood below my table. On one of my last visits to my service room I had grabbed it and filled it to the top with crispbread, chocolate and a couple of packs of biscuits from the larder in the ante-bunker. If the time came when I had to look after myself I wanted to be prepared.

Once it finally fell quiet in the bunker – upstairs the break-out must already have begun – generals Burgdorf and Krebs sat talking to each other in the central corridor. Bottles and glasses stood on the table. I picked up a few phrases here and there, but concentrated on my work. Towards 2200 hrs I received a call for General Krebs, which I put through to the telephone in the corridor. I could hear it ringing from my switchboard. Nobody got up. I asked the caller to hold the line and went out to see where the general was. I had not seen him pass me to leave, and so he could not be far. When I came into the corridor I saw that both of them, Krebs and Burgdorf, were still sitting in the cocktail chairs there. They seemed to be asleep, which I did not find unusual because there was no distinction between day and night and we were all constantly dead tired. One slept when the eyes fell shut from exhaustion. I tapped Krebs lightly on the shoulder to awaken him. 'Herr general, you are wanted on the telephone.' In mid-sentence I realised the situation – Krebs and Burgdorf were both dead. I was shocked out of my wits. I felt queasy. I had not heard a shot. They must have taken poison not five metres from me. Without checking further, I left in order to inform Goebbels.

I had had enough of carrying dead bodies out. I remained at my post at the telephone switchboard and put through call after call to Goebbels. When I went out into the corridor later, RSD men had brought out the bodies of Burgdorf and Krebs, probably using the emergency exit to the garden. I had last seen Goebbels's adjutant Günther Schwägermann and the valet Günther Ochs shortly before the generals' suicides and even now there was no sign of them. I assumed they had joined one of Mohnke's break-out groups.

Long after midnight Goebbels gave me a sudden look as if he were seeing me for the first time. Perhaps the fact that he had to address his last words to a simple SS man of the erstwhile bodyguard humiliated him. 'The war is lost – *les jeux sont faits*.[5] We knew how to live, and now we have to know how to die. I do not need you any longer, Misch. Clear up here.'[6] Goebbels took a step towards me, looked steeply up at me again with that odd gaze. Then he gave me his hand, something he had never done before. His handshake was firm; his fingers cold. Without another word he withdrew into his room.

For a moment I felt relief. I thought no more of Goebbels or Hitler. I went back to the switchboard and plucked out all the plugs from the installation correctly, then with both hands tore free the cabling. Right, left, right, left. I could not do it fast enough. I did not overlook a single one, of that I am certain. A great cable salad piled up on the switchboard table. I was not conscious of the symbolic nature of this my last official act at the time, but with every cable I ripped free I felt a little freer myself. It was the end of my captivity in the Führerbunker. I was finally finished here. Now to get out.

---

5 A French roulette term; in British casinos *rien ne va plus* means that no more bets can be laid.

6 These 'parting words' appear in the memoir of Hitler's personal pilot Hans Baur as being addressed to him. According to Misch, Baur knew of them from conversations during their common period of captivity. See Hans Baur, *Mit Mächtigen zwischen Himmel und Erde*, Oldendorf 1971, p.283.

Chapter 16

Break-out and Capture

ON THE EARLY MORNING of 2 May 1945 the Reich chancellor of the German Reich released me from duty almost exactly five years after I had entered the service of his predecessor. All my thoughts were for my family, to whom I now wanted to make my way. I hoped that perhaps I would be able to reach some of the break-out groups heading for General Rauch in the north of the city. I grabbed my backpack lying ready and went over to Hentschel. 'Hannes, we are cut off, we should go.' Hannes wanted to stay behind to keep the military hospital supplied with fresh air and electric current. I took my leave of him. We exchanged duplicated letters for our wives to be delivered should one of us not be able to return to his family.

Much later, after my return from captivity, I asked Hentschel what had happened after I left. 'You were hardly gone five minutes than Goebbels was dead. Two hours later the Russians surfaced. You may not believe it but the first Russians into the Führerbunker were wenches.'[1] After that he went on to tell me that Goebbels had killed

---

1 There are major differences in the witness statements regarding the suicide of Goebbels. The majority believe that the Goebbels couple committed suicide in the Reich Chancellery gardens some time between 2030 hrs and 2200 hrs on 1 May 1945. See Ralf Georg Reuth, *Goebbels*, Munich 2005 (first edn 1991), p.614; see also Joachim Fest, *Der Untergang*, Berlin 2002, p.171. If the death of Goebbels occurred as early as this, it would mean that Misch and Hentschel remained behind in the bunker, both having been told they could go, until the early hours of 2 May and Misch missed

himself in his room in the bunker, his wife upstairs in the ante-bunker with her murdered children. Nobody wanted to chance dragging Goebbels's body up to the gardens and so an attempt was made to burn them where they lay. Obviously this was doomed to failure as there was not enough oxygen in the bunker to keep the bodies burning for hours. Others maintained that the Goebbels couple committed suicide in the gardens. Hentschel's version seems the plausible one, for in some photos taken by the Russians there are considerable traces of fire in the bunker central corridor. Furthermore, some strips of material are visible on his body in a famous photo. His clothing at least would have been totally destroyed if the bodies had been immolated in the garden. From what I observed in my last hours in the Reich Chancellery, it did not appear to me that husband and wife wanted to die together. After taking his leave of me Goebbels had withdrawn to his room in the Führerbunker, and Frau Goebbels had long since gone upstairs. I therefore consider it to have been more likely that they were separate when they died.

I went through the ante-bunker to my service room. In indecision I wavered between uniform or civilian dress. One thing was clear – I was not going to wear my immaculate service uniform while fleeing through the Russian lines. It was too elegant, and would have attracted attention, have betrayed the fact that, despite my low rank, I must have had an important function. I chose my front uniform. This made me look a bit more like a warrior. Since entering Hitler's service I did not have a steel helmet, and my only weapon was my Walther PP 7.65 mm, the same model used by Hitler to shoot himself.

As regards the military situation at this time, I knew little. By my watch it was four in the morning. I descended once more to the cellars and ran through the bomb-damaged Kannenberg-Allee already

---

leaving with the break-out groups, which he had intended to join. He and Hentschel might both have fallen asleep for hours, but Misch denies this. See Uwe Bahnsen and James P. O'Donnell, *Die Katakombe – Das Ende in der Reichskanzlei*, Stuttgart 1975, p.482.

flooded to a depth of five centimetres. Planks had been laid so that one could pass without getting one's feet wet. Through deserted floors I headed for Schädle's service room in the cellars of the New Reich Chancellery in order to report myself off duty.

'So here you are at last!' he greeted me, apparently so relieved to see me or anybody at all that he addressed me with the familiar 'Du' instead of 'Sie'. I told him of my release by Goebbels. My commander had no reason to doubt my words. Everybody else was long gone. 'But quick now.' Schädle indicated that I should follow him, and for the last time I went through the cellar labyrinth of the Reich Chancellery. He talked me through the route I had to go: first through the U-bahn shafts towards Friedrich-Strasse station, then over the Weidendammer Bridge across the Spree river. The others wanted to join up with the troops of General Rauch there; I should also try to.

Schädle had a leg injury and limped ahead of me through the endless corridors. Until a short while ago everywhere had been full of civilians, now gaping emptiness reigned. This seemed to me more eerie than the bunker atmosphere. Finally we reached a cellar window of the Borsig Palace on the corner of Wilhelm-Strasse and Voss-Strasse. From there I could get out into the open and reach the nearby U-bahn station on Wilhelm-Platz by the most direct route. I gave Schädle a questioning look. He understood what I wanted to know and shook his head: 'I cannot,' and pointed at his injured leg. He must have decided some time previously not to accompany the groups. We took our leave of each other. My commander wished me all the best. Immediately after helping me out, he shot himself in the New Chancellery.

Pushing rubble aside, I climbed out through the cellar window leading into Wilhelm-Strasse. I left the Borsig Palace on my stomach and moved into Wilhelm-Platz. The morning of 2 May 1945 was already dawning. Smoke rose everywhere from the rubble. A noticeable silence lay over the Platz, only in the distance could I hear dull rumbling, occasionally a round being fired.

Without cover I ran the approximately twenty metres to the entrance of the Kaiserhof U-bahn station.[2] On the stairway leading down I turned to look back. I felt that I needed this last look. I looked along Wilhelm-Strasse, then along Voss-Strasse, and finally up to the Reich Chancellery. The New Reich Chancellery had come in for a hammering: the caretaker's apartment was totally destroyed, but the façade of the Reich Chancellery still stood. I turned again and went down the steps into the U-bahn station. While doing so, I had to keep stepping over dead bodies – Russians, Germans, dead everywhere.

In the Tunnel

The station was full of people, all civilians. The scene was indescribable. The wildest rumours were circulating about the things the Russians were said to be up to in the already occupied districts of the city. The strangest thing below was that two young men were playing loud, happy Hawaiian rhythms on guitars. I could not believe it. Berlin was going down, not with drums and trumpets, but with guitar music. It was something totally unreal.

Through almost total darkness I felt my way along the U-bahn lines to Stadtmitte station, after which the line went north to Friedrich-Strasse station. There I met Hitler's former valet Heinz Linge; the caretaker of the New Reich Chancellery Ziegner; then a senior official who had worked for Goebbels – I think his name was Bader; and a colleague from the SS bodyguard, Untersturmführer (junior lieutenant) Helmut Frick. I had known him since 1938 but he had not been with us long. One day he had asked me how he could join the bodyguard. I told him that I could not really help, he should apply to the commander or Adi Dirr. I would soon discover why he wanted to join the bodyguard so urgently.

The group around Linge had broken out of the Reich Chancellery hours before me. We would have liked to have crossed the Weidendamm

---

2 Today Mohren-Strasse.

bridge from the Friedrich-Strasse U-bahn station, but this was out of the question. The bridge was under permanent fire. Russian snipers took aim at everything that moved. On this side of it was a wrecked Tiger tank, in front of it a female secretary from Hitler's private Chancellery, whom I recognised. She was dead. There were corpses everywhere. The fearsome hail of fire made any advance impossible. Weidendamm bridge was no longer an option. There was nothing else for it but to go back down into the U-bahn tunnel, which we had just left. There we met three grenadiers also fleeing northwards and joined up with them. We now had to cross the Spree underground.

On we went through Berlin's underworld heading north. Linge, Frick, the others and I, pack on my back, forced ourselves through a tunnel hatch, which was open by about fifty centimetres. What if the hatches closed when being flooded? I kept feeling for my Walther PP. In the case of flooding I preferred a bullet to drowning.

We came to Stettinerhof station. After a few hundred metres more we reached a spot where the tunnel roof had been penetrated by a bomb. The Russians were above the hole tossing down hand grenades every couple of seconds. These exploded with a stupendous noise. We attempted to estimate the distance in time between each – and then sprinted for it. Live or die, only luck determined which. I looked around. Frick was no longer with us. Strange, he must have set off on his own.

'Psst.' One of the grenadiers suddenly put a finger to his lips. 'Germans!' We listened. We heard German voices. On the wall we discovered stairs that led up to a ventilation shaft. This was where the voices were coming from. 'Right, we'll go up,' said another grenadier. He grasped the rails and went up first. Cautiously he reconnoitred the street through the bars of the shaft. 'Man, they are our people,' he called out in joyful excitement. General Rauch! I thought at once. Had German troops broken through the Russian encirclement around the government district and linked up with General Rauch's people? I was the last but one to climb up – only Linge was behind me. A moment later, I had scarcely raised my head than I felt a rifle butt poke me in the back. German soldiers who had broken through the Berlin Pocket – not on your life. Hope had been father to the thought. The German voices that had led us to think they were General Rauch's people were those of Germans taken prisoner. It was the end of my break-out attempt. Swiftly I tossed my pistol into the darkness below. We were in the hands of the Russians.

Captivity

The first thing I did was open the strap of my wristwatch. It was an expensive model from Switzerland, a limited edition of 2,000 made for the Foreign Ministry. Diplomat Hewel had presented it to me. They were intended as gifts to guests. I allowed the valuable timepiece to drop to the floor where I trod on it and slowly ground it underfoot. The watch shattered with the crunching. The Russians, whose wrists were graced by many similar pieces of booty, were not going to get this one. Linge tossed his watch away in a high trajectory. 'There it goes, the boss's watch,' he said. I did not know from this whether he meant that it was Hitler's watch, which he had taken from him at his death, or his own watch, a present from Hitler.[3] Just at that moment, as the watch flew through the air, the Russians shooed away an old woman who had wanted to give us some water. The watch landed near her. She bent down, picked it up and, unnoticed by the Russians, who had already turned away from her, tucked it into her pocket.

Shortly after, there was shooting. A completely crazy scene now played out before our eyes. A Red Army soldier guarding us perched on a heap of rubble suddenly opened fire on a group of his own comrades some distance away. He fired a salvo at the lower ledge of a window front on which some Russians were leaning. Some returned fire. They were actually picking each other off. Utter madness. They must have been drunk out of their minds. This was too much for Linge. He stared

---

3 According to Heinz Linge it was a watch engraved with his name, which had been a gift from Hitler. See Heinz Linge, *With Hitler to the End*, London 2009, pp.211.

at the ground. 'I am going to shoot myself now,' he said in a choked voice and with trembling hand raised the pistol which he had kept hidden from the Russians until now. I knocked it out of his hand. 'Don't be stupid. When you can, do the same as with the watch,' I hissed at him. Linge's Walther PP now followed his watch through the air. About an hour later we decided between ourselves that it would be better if we did not remain together so as to reduce the risk of being recognised. All the time I had known him I had not built up a real relationship with Linge, and was cautious with him. He squeezed himself through to some of our fellow sufferers at the collection place about fifty metres away from me.

Towards evening we were led off towards Berlin-Buch, where we spent the night in a meadow under the open sky. I did not see Linge again. We got into the train at Wartenberg. When we reached Landsberg an der Warthe there were thousands of soldiers in the reception camp set up there by the Russians for POWs picked up in and around Berlin. I looked around, hoping to find someone whom I knew. Here I actually did come across some of my colleagues.

I talked about the burning of Hitler's body with Hans Hofbeck, the RSD secretary who had kept me informed about the business with Fegelein. He told me that, at the moment when the bodies of Hitler and Eva were burning, two civilians had appeared on the Foreign Ministry wall. They were in the wrong place at the wrong time and had to pay for it with their lives. Apart from those whom Hitler had selected for the purpose, there were to be no witnesses to the immolation.[4] Hofbeck had established from their papers that they were Poles. What they were doing there and where they came from could not be determined.

Later the Russians persisted in showing a photograph of a body found in the Reich Chancellery garden, which they took initially for Hitler. From the photo produced for me it was obvious that the

---

4 Misch was told by Hofbeck who ordered these civilians to be shot and who the shooter was, but preferred not to disclose it.

assumption was incorrect, the man was wearing darned socks. Probably he was one of those unfortunate civilians, and had a moustache just like Hitler's.

Behind a barbed wire fence I suddenly noticed Helmut Frick, whom we had lost in the U-bahn tunnel. He stood among soldiers who belonged to the NKFD.[5] Now it was clear to me – he must have been working for the other side for some time.

From Landsberg we went to a transit camp at Posen. One day on the march there I recognised Hans Baur, Hitler's pilot, sitting in an open field. I knew him well from the many flights I took with him while accompanying Hitler as courier.

'So how are you?' Nothing any more ridiculous to say did not strike me.

'You can see, Misch,' he replied, pointing to what remained of his right leg. 'Amputated. Without anaesthetic. With a pocket knife.' The leg had had a wound about ten centimetres below the knee and had been sawn off.

'Is there anything I can do for you?' I asked. He mentioned fresh dressings and a bowl of water. While I was washing it and renewing the bandages he told me he did not have it so bad. He frequently got clean dressings and two adequate meals daily. Crutches as well. I stayed with him, tended his wounds regularly and massaged the leg. At Posen he was interrogated on a number of occasions.

In October 1945, he asked me one day: 'Herr Misch, I am probably going to be transferred to a military hospital in Moscow. I assume that the conditions there are going to be better than in a POW camp. Wouldn't you like to accompany me? I can choose an attendant.' It did not take me long to make up my mind. In my total naïvety I thought it would be a good idea to join up with Baur, that it would be better for

---

5 Nationalkomitee Freies Deutschland. The NKFD was an association of German POWs and German Communist exiles in the Soviet Union who fought against Nazi Germany.

me at his side than in a Russian POW camp in some inhospitable place in this gigantic country.

'Yes, thank you, I would like to – I shall accompany you.' Baur nodded. The Russians still did not know who I was.

A few days later we were brought to Moscow, or at least to Mozhaisk at first, a good hundred kilometres west of the Soviet capital. We would soon be proceeding to the military hospital, they said, and some time later a transport was made available for Baur and myself. However, instead of the military hospital we were brought to the notorious Butyrka prison[6] and to interrogation in the NKVD secret police prison at Lubyanka. Hitler had once referred to this place as 'the rat trap'.

---

6 The Butyrka was a holding prison in Moscow for convicted political detainees in transit into the Gulag system.

Chapter 17

My Nine Years in Soviet Captivity

FLIGHT-CAPTAIN BAUR AND I shared a cell that was bitterly cold and unheated. Baur received no more dressings. The wound could not heal properly under these conditions. We persisted in our requests for medical treatment, but these were turned down.

In December, there began endless inquisitions by the Stalinist interrogation officers. Baur was beaten and mistreated. Then he made the portentous statement: 'For that you should ask my attendant. He knows more about it than I do.'

Then it was my turn.

Baur and I were separated – now we were both tortured. I quickly saw what the point of it all was: the Russians could not believe that Hitler was dead.

'Where is Adolf Hitler?'

'Dead.'

'Where is Adolf Hitler?'

'Dead.'

'You lie. The dead man is his double.'

The questions had no end: 'How did Hitler leave Berlin? Where is he now?'

Thus it went on and on. Our interrogation commissar was initially Colonel Savalyev. The Soviet Interior Ministry[1] had long known that

---

1 The building at Moscow's Lubyanka Square No. 2 was until 1991 among other

what I said was correct. They had the information on Hitler's suicide. I noticed particularly how they made a big gesture by tearing the transcripts of my statements down the middle, but in the end they kept them. Later, the Russians held up to my face what I had said. They did so in the pretence that they thought it was all lies and had to interrogate me from the beginning all over again. As they apparently kept everything I said and compared the documents, they knew all along that I was telling the truth. Yet my tormentors – colonels Stern, Savalyev, Schweizer, Gagaze and Seltenvahr[2] – would not let up. Stern and Seltenvahr were Jews. They never let a word drop about death camps – nobody ever mentioned them. All they were interested in was Hitler's death. If they had wanted to learn anything from me at this time about concentration camps they would have been disappointed, for I knew nothing then about what went on in them.

During the interrogation I was beaten repeatedly about the face, and my feet were trodden on. Once I was given an injection, and next day I had a high fever. The interrogators fetched me out all the same, made me show them the site of the injection, which now was painfully inflamed, and then they tortured me there.

---

things the central prison of the Soviet secret service.

2 These names were written by Rochus Misch from memory. Stalin had ordered the NKVD to ascertain finally if and how Hitler had committed suicide. At the end of 1945, under code-name Operation Myth, People's Commissioner Sergei Kruglov was given the assignment by Interior Minister Beria of assembling officers fluent in German. Linge also remembered interrogators Colonel Wolf Stern and Professor Savielyev. Misch knew the latter as Savalyev; to other prisoners he also mentioned Dr Savelli. The prisoners themselves gave this most brutal and cynical of interrogators the nickname 'Lamefoot' on account of his limp. Linge also mentioned interrogators Schweitzer and Klausser, although the latter also gave prisoners his name as Klaus or Krause. Seltenvahr and Gagaze known to Misch were not mentioned by other prisoners, though Linge remembered a Lieutenant Colonel Georgadze. This was the cover-name of Fyodor Karpovich Parparov, who worked out the interrogation protocols for Stalin at the end of the 1940s. Seltenvahr was probably the cover-name of twenty-three-year old Lieutenant Smirnov, who was in charge of questioning Rochus Misch.

On other days the interrogating colonel would take a book or hole punch from his table and throw it at me. Often I had stand near the wall and then they would hit my head against the wall from behind. If I turned round they would hit me in the face. Always when I thought they had enjoyed themselves enough they would start all over again. Finally, I was told that members of my family were present in the jail, and they were not having it any better than I. I could go back to my wife, however, as soon as I told the truth. There was always somebody waving a pistol in my face.

In February 1946, I was put into a cell so cold that a layer of ice had formed on the walls. The iron bedstead was equipped with a very thin mattress and a blanket 150 x 50 centimetres. One had to choose whether to rest one's head or feet on the frosty iron. My clothing was taken away, and I was given ripped dungarees and shoes fit only for the rubbish dump. I had no socks or rags to wrap around my feet.

I shared this cell with another inmate, Robert Koch. This prisoner got a bed, a greatcoat, double blankets and officers' food. He was not allowed to give me anything from the latter. I found out later that he was probably a stool pigeon – his privileges were an extension of the torture. I hardly ever spoke to him.

I was deprived of sleep over a period of forty days. Only on Saturday and Sunday nights could I use my bed. On the other days I would be hauled out of my cell at 2200 hrs for questioning, which however never began before midnight. The two-hour wait I had to spend in a cell sixty by sixty centimetres, in which it was possible only to stand. Often the interrogation would be cancelled, and I would then spend the whole night standing up. I can still hear today the rattle of keys and the crash of the cell door when I was fetched.

The interrogation methods, or rather the torture, were increased. Now I was stripped naked, laid out on a table and whipped. A cat o' nine tails was used to flay my testicles, my head and the soles of my feet. If I slipped off the table, the whipping would be continued on the floor. Now and again, lying in my excrement, I would lose consciousness. Then they would wake me up to give me an ice-cold shower while somebody kept hitting my head against the wall tiles. Often I would only come to in my cell, or find myself redressed and lying on a stretcher in some room or other. Two guards would then tow me back to my cell or, supporting me under the armpits, drag me back like a wet sack. They liked a good laugh: 'You know what you look like? Really gorgeous – like a bird of paradise.' They had looked up this term specially in the German dictionary. A female doctor painted my wounds with some kind of green paste.

My ordeal lasted a week, ten days, twelve days. I no longer felt human, and I longed for death. On the twelfth day I asked for a piece of paper. Before I went insane, I wanted to leave them something to remind them I was a human. I was given the paper and I wrote to the responsible Minister of the Interior, Beria:

> My statements are true and correspond to the facts. The interrogators do not believe me. I continue to be mistreated in an inhuman manner during the interrogations, but I hold to the truth. Apparently the idea is to beat me to death; as a soldier I request you order that I be shot dead.

I gave the paper to a guard. I was immediately led into the interrogation room. 'So he wants to be shot dead, does he?' The officer aimed two pistols at me, then let them drop and shook his head with a grin: 'You can die, but we will beat you to death, no, half beat you to death slowly.' Then I was given more of the cat o' nine tails, but this time without being undressed.

Back in my cell I was not aware that this would be the last night of the heaviest torture. My written request had actually been forwarded to the addressee and is now to be found in the Moscow archives, where the BBC discovered it. Next day, I was given a wonderful meal. I never touched it. I just wanted to die.

Seven Weeks in Berlin

From the end of March until April 1946 I was well fed and given reasonable clothing. At the end of April I was taken to Berlin by train. Baur, Linge, Günsche and I were to be held in readiness as witnesses at the Nuremberg Trials.[3] The train journey lasted at least a week. The daily rations consisted of 400 grams of bread and nothing else. When I arrived at the Lichtenberg women's prison in Berlin I had not had anything to drink for two days, over the whole stretch since Brest Litovsk.

I was locked in a bare cell, my belongings were removed, including my cutlery. I had only been there half an hour when a Russian guard came in and punched me in the face, causing an injury from which I bled. Another Russian appeared and said to him: 'Leave him, he is not a bandit.' I requested some water. *Nyet*. I got some watery soup on the second day. It arrived in a twelve-litre jug. There was no spoon. From now on, this jug served all my needs – eating, drinking, urinating, defecating.

I was kept locked up for seven weeks. I made several protests at the conditions. I got a severe chill, for which a German doctor treated me. When I mentioned the unreasonable hygienic conditions he said with regret: 'I am sorry, but I cannot do anything for you. It is beyond my sphere of influence.' Once during an interrogation by a Soviet lieutenant colonel I made a complaint. He let me describe the conditions fully and then promised: 'That should not be. I shall bring those responsible to account and ensure that you receive the treatment you are entitled to as a detainee – not an accused but a witness.' Nothing changed.

I insisted on being allowed to see my wife and daughter, otherwise I would not say anything and let myself be shot. Again and again, I was given the comfort of a promised imminent visitation. Once they even

---

3 The Nuremberg Trials against the principal Nazi war criminals were held between 20 November 1945 and 1 October 1946.

sent a young lady to my cell to shave my face: 'Your wife will be here soon.' But these promises were all empty.

I understood that they took Linge to what remained of the bunker. Everything was sketched and measured, and forensic scientists examined the blood stains. I was not required to attend.

One day we were informed that we would not be needed as witnesses at the Nuremberg Trials. I never heard a word during all this time about concentration camps and Hitler's mass murders, nor about how the trials were going. 'Crown witness – *nix*, *nix* – Allied decision.' I could hardly credit it that I had spent seven weeks only a few kilometres from my family, had not seen them and would now be taken back to Moscow. By the end, I was totally debilitated, physically and psychologically.

Nine Years' Gulag

Back in Moscow they took me first to Butyrka prison. There I had some luck in sharing a cell with the ex-diplomat Gotthold Starke. Twenty years older than I, he had served in Moscow under the ambassador and 20 July conspirator Friedrich-Werner Graf von Schulenburg, with whom he had been active. Starke received special rations and got so much that there was enough for me. This time there was no bar on his letting me have a share. He even got cigarettes.

When we heard somebody being put into the neighbouring cell we attempted to make contact by Morse code. I knocked: 'Please, who there?' No reply. Apparently, the occupant of the neighbouring cell did not understand Morse code. It was ten days – I had kept up my dour attempts – until he understood. Then finally he tapped back: 'Slow.'

Again I rapped on the cell wall, this time with longer intervals between the individual letters, and several times over. Finally the answer: 'Here Lithuanian Rittmeister (cavalry captain) von Wolfshausen. Am three years here, last two years alone.'

I was thunderstruck. Starke saw the blank horror in my eyes. 'What is it? Tell me what he answered.' I told him and he gasped. 'Three years? What in God's name is going to happen to us here?'

Starke was the son of an evangelical bishop at Runowo in the Posen district, and very devout. He urged me to send the man some words of comfort: 'Just be patient. God will help.'

Back came: 'Here no God – here NKVD.' A Russian female physician said something similar to me later when we were talking about religion and belief: 'Jesus suffered much, but he was never in the Soviet Union.'

We contacted the cavalryman again in Morse code, asking if he was a smoker. Yes, but they did not give him cigarettes. 'The next toilet visit, watch out,' I tapped. It went well. We left him some cigarettes on the toilet. It apparently amused the guard, for he gave our co-prisoner a light himself.

Diplomat Starke had seen a few things himself after war broke out. In 1939 he had been chief editor of the newspaper *Deutsche Rundschau in Polen* at Bromberg[4] and had experienced there the butchery which went down in history as Bromberg Bloody Sunday.[5]

The cavalryman in the adjoining cell had not exaggerated about spending three years there. That was exactly how long I was kept in the military prison in Moscow. The tortures of my initial period there were luckily over. I now had many long talks with a certain Colonel Stern. He came from Vienna, and this reminded me of my first courier run for Hitler.

Thank God they gave us books. They had brought a whole library from Posen, we were told. A small, dressy woman distributed reading material every ten days. Starke thought she had something to do with

---

4 Bydgoszcz (formerly Bromberg) was Prussian from 1772 to 1807, from 1807 to 1815 part of the Duchy of Warsaw and from 1815 to 1920 the Prussian province of Posen, but after being annexed to Poland by the Treaty of Versailles following WWI remained a centre of German life in Poland.

5 'Bromberg Bloody Sunday' was a bloodbath occurring on 3 September 1939, in which many Germans living in the town were massacred. Nazi propaganda used the incident as a retroactive justification for the attack on Poland and inflated the number of German victims. Gotthold Starke was taken away by the Poles in connection with 'Bromberg Bloody Sunday' but later freed by Wehrmacht troops.

the would-be female assassin of Lenin.[6] I read books about the Teutonic knights, maybe by Heinrich von Plauen, then Karl Marx, finally poems and dramas by Theodor Körner.[7] The poetry was of bombastic style, not really my kind of thing, but under these circumstances I sucked them in, even liked the sentimentality of the words:

In the Night
I am close to you, only a thin wall
Separates me from you.
Perhaps you are dreaming of me already in the soft shivers of sleep . . .

It was your spirit, and sacred on my cheek
I felt your kiss;
I knew the greeting
Of the kissing song on your lips.

It was your spirit! It was the breath of love!
You were thinking of me!
O, that it remain eternal, eternal, eternal,
The glorious night!

Thus at least my thoughts could wander a little. Once I tried counting up how many books I had read and gave up when I reached two hundred.

For some time I shared the cell with Dr Richter, the former business director of the Adam-Opel Works – they had finally separated me from Starke. Dr Richter never returned home and died in Soviet captivity.

---

6 On 30 August 1918, an attempt was made to assassinate Lenin, but he escaped wounded. Fanya Kaplan was arrested as the perpetrator and executed by firing squad after being interrogated. Her exact involvement had not been conclusively determined, nor how the library-trolley inmate remembered by Misch might have been somehow involved with her.

7 Theodor Körner (1791–1813) was a German poet. Kurt Huber, member of the Weisse Rose resistance group quoted the first line of Körner's poem *Aufruf* (1813): 'Let's go, my people! The flame signals are smoking!'

After my return to Germany I visited his widow at Rüsselsheim. She invited me to spend a couple of days in the firm's guest house. I told her of the time her husband and I were together.

For a while a Japanese general was my cellmate. He was not the only Japanese there. I made an effort to learn a few words of Japanese so that I could at least say 'please' and 'thank you' and such like. We got on quite well. I remember an Estonian chess master. I have no idea how many games I played with him, and on the occasion when he saw that I could mate him in three moves – it was pure coincidence – he refused to speak to me for three days.

After three years in Moscow I was transported by cattle truck to a camp near the town of Jezkazgan.[8] The trip took thirty-two days and nights, and whoever survived it to reach this steppe prison in central Kazakhstan had withstood a journey under the most inhuman conditions. It was not possible to sit upright in the wagon– one had to lie the whole time with the head drawn in. I had terrible stomach pain. Moreover, my travelling companions were exclusively convicted Russian criminals, and so I had no chance of conversation.

I spent two months in the special camp, then I was taken on to Karaganda in Kazakhstan. The word 'Karaganda', which translates as 'black stone', comes from a particular light, porous coal which is abundant locally.

In POW camp 7099/1 at Spassk, the main camp of the Karaganda Gulag, I was declared capable of work. With eleven other prisoners I lived in a stretch of prison territory in which one could move about more or less freely. We twelve made up a repair squad. We were transported by narrow-gauge railway several hundred kilometres into the town of Rudnik. On the way we heard continual shooting. Our supervisors were amusing themselves shooting snow hares. At Rudnik we repaired public buildings, I worked as a painter. It was a comparatively pleasant activity. We twelve were watched by only one

---

8 The Steppe-ITL (Special camp No. 4) existed between February 1948 and April 1956.

supervisor and we had enough to eat. We were able to prepare semolina or similar for ourselves on a small stove.

Then I was confined to camp and could not travel out to work. Why, I have no idea. I succeeded in getting round the ban by borrowing the work card of another prisoner who remained in camp. The guards were constantly being changed, and nobody knew who was who. We were counted off in fives and that was it. At the work sites I was often given signwriting. 'Caution – crane swinging round' and such things I painted on sign boards in the finest script in German and Russian. It was almost as if I was employed in a Russian gulag in my profession of artistic painter. We were even paid 460 roubles. Of this 400 roubles was retained by the camp administration, but the rest was paid out. With this money one could buy things in the camp shop – margarine, for example. Margarine was important, for 'Butterbrot' – the Russians actually used this German word – was paradoxically only dry bread without butter. An almost pure Butterbrot was 'Butterbrot mit Margarine'. It was German margarine, a Russian at the till told me, but expensively wrapped in Russian paper.

Here in Karaganda I met Sepp Platzer, the former valet of Rudolf Hess, and heard the whole story of his former chief's flight to Britain.

I received mail for the first time in October 1948: a letter from my wife and one from my aunt. In September, I had written to Aunt Sofia for her birthday on a double-sided card, which had been handed out to us and on which we had to write our return address. This was the first sign of life from me that anybody in my family had received. Now finally I had a reply.

In a judgement of 21 December 1949 based on a mass trial[9] of German POWs in their absence, I was sentenced to death. I cannot remember exactly how I received the news since I had not been

---

9 Between 1949 and 1950, POWs were condemned to death in Soviet mass trials to get round the obligation to release them under the agreements signed by the Allies with the German Federal Republic. See Wolfgang Schuller, 'Opfer der sowjetischen Terrorjustiz', *Frankfurter Allgemeine Zeitung*, 5 November 1992.

informed of any trial or hearings, and so it provoked no emotion. To be threatened with death in the camps was nothing unusual. One judgement here, another there. In 1950 the penalty was commuted to twenty-five years' forced labour. My crime was 'supporting the Nazi regime'.

In 1950 I went from Karaganda to Borovichi[10] which, bearing in mind the great distances in this country, was not far from Leningrad. There I met Flight Captain Baur again, but was soon separated from him after it was noticed that we knew each other. Baur was transferred to a neighbouring prison.

At the beginning of my stay at Borovichi I came into close contact with the Knights Cross holder de la Rocca of the Spanish Blue Division.[11] The conduct of the Spanish in captivity impressed me very much. They were composed of two groups of enemies. The first was the so-called Red Spanish, anti-Fascist, who had fled to the East at the end of the Spanish Civil War or, perhaps as children, had been taken off there by their guardians. Their lot in Russia was a hard one, locked up in camps and put to forced labour.[12] The Spanish from the Blue Division, with a fascist and anti-communist background, had fought for the Germans as volunteers. Nevertheless, when any Spaniard was taken off for interrogation, then the others accompanied him and also reported. Without exception. There were no Blue or Red Spanish any more, only Spanish. They stuck together. The Japanese too. There was little the Russians could do about it – they could hardly shoot them

---

10 Borovichi (Oblast Novgorod) is about 270 kilometres southeast of Leningrad. From May 1943 until it was closed in August 1953 it housed five thousand German prisoners, of whom four thousand died there.

11 The Blue Division was an infantry division of Spanish volunteers incorporated into the German Wehrmacht from 1941 to 1943 on the Russian Front. Captain de la Rocca fought with the remains of a company in the final battle for Berlin.

12 Many of these Republican Spanish fled only as far as France, where they were interned. Most of them then worked on building the U-boat bunkers along the Biscay coast, 1941–3. See Lars Hellwinkel, *Hitlers Tor zum Atlantik*, Christoph Links Verlag, Berlin 2012. Later many were sent to Mauthausen concentration camp.

all. The same kind of thing did not exist among the Germans. If one of us was taken off for questioning, he went alone; no compatriot bothered himself about him.

I saw another death sentence looming when I was accused along with de la Rocca of having fomented a mutiny. For weeks they always gave us only maize pulp to eat. Maize pulp, maize pulp and more maize pulp. Despite the memory of worse times of hunger which we experienced in Borovichi, we could not bear to smell, see or eat maize. The very sight of the pulpy serving made us want to throw up. The other prisoners got the same. Somebody had pointed to de la Rocca and myself as the troublemakers. Shortly before a real revolt broke out, the camp administration had a change of heart; the maize pulp came to an end and they served up something else.

At Borovichi I met Rommel's former chief of the general staff Alfred Gause. I have already mentioned what I learned from him about Rommel's involvement in the attempted assassination of 20 July.

As had been the case at Karaganda previously, mostly I was not able to leave the Borovichi camp. I was given a job as nurse in the camp hospital. A young Jewish female doctor worked there. It was thanks to her that a small camp orchestra could practise in the hospital. One day she had a patient who said he was a lead violinist. She knew how to prove it, she said, and felt for a gristly area on the neck. Violinists developed this gristle, she explained. She found the proof, and from then on the violinist could practise with his musician colleagues in the hospital. One day after we had just finished treating a patient with a serious boil on his back, I saw tears in the eyes of our female surgeon. When Dr Schwarzer, a German colleague, asked her what the problem was, for the little operation had gone off well, she broke down: she would not be coming back. 'They are deporting all of us to the Amur where there are only swamps and mosquitoes,' she cried. Still in tears she went on to say that Stalin was forcibly resettling all Jews in that region. I never saw her again.

After that, I went right through the country, spending years in various special camps. From Borovichi I was taken to Tushino near Moscow. There I spent a summer building wooden sheds. After a while we noticed these were surrounded by small, symmetrically arranged flower beds. Somebody pointed to them and said: 'Just look at those, only Germans make them like that. They can only be Germans working there.' We decided that after our shift we would leave a note under a beam. 'We are German prisoners of war – who are you?' We turned the beam in such a way that it would have to be repositioned to continue working on it, and the other prisoners would be bound to find it. Next day we had the answer: 'We are also Germans.' Not until some time later did we learn more details about these camp inmates: the Russians had brought a number of important scientists to Tushino. Every morning a bus took them to an institute or university to spend the day researching. Towards evening they would return to the camp to work a little at building sheds. They were a group of atomic physicists who had once assisted the Nobel Prize winner Gustav Hertz.[13] Once the Russians had sucked them dry of all their knowledge, many were simply tossed back into camp life. At Karaganda I had come across discarded researchers whom one could always recognise by their elegant dress, and they all wore hats.

A transport brought me one day from Tushino to Sverdlovsk in the Urals. The camp commandant was an army captain who had been a POW in Thuringia. He had all the former SS men separated out, which gave me a bad feeling. Then came the surprise: the SS men went into the food factory; the others had to break rocks. I also had to do

13 Gustav Ludwig Hertz (1887–1975) received the Nobel Prize for Physics in 1925. In April 1945, he was brought by a special unit of the Red Army to Sochumi on the Black Sea, where he led a project involving German specialists at the Physics-Mathematics Institute founded by the NKVD. At the end of 1946, Interior Minister and NKVD head Beria initiated the deportation into the Soviet Union of German technical specialists from all areas of research, technology, industry and armaments together with their families. At Tushino, specialists worked on rocket technologies.

this, but later. Often children would stand around, spitting at us and calling us 'Hebrews'.

In the camp there was a traitor who reported to the guards whenever anybody had helped himself during kitchen duty. One day Lieutenant Schmidt went up to this prisoner, whose name was Kruse: 'We know now that you are the traitor. Today you do not go to work! If you do, I shall kill you!' Kruse really should have taken the threat seriously. He turned up for kitchen duty and was helping carry the pea soup on a plank with another prisoner when Schmidt came up on him from behind and hacked off Kruse's head from his shoulders. That earned him the nickname Hatchet Schmidt. Thank God I was spared seeing it; over the next few days it was the number one topic.

Finally I got to Stalingrad. I did not know than that it would be the last place of my captivity. Only too often had I heard how transports of prisoners left the camp for an unknown destination and mostly went to the next camp, and the next and the next. This transport from Stalingrad at the end of 1953, however, really would bring me back to Germany.

Chapter 18

My Homecoming and New Beginnings

S HORTLY AFTER CHRISTMAS 1953, our train stopped in the Brandenburg POW reception camp at Fürstenwalde,[1] which had been set up by the NKVD. There we were relieved of our prison clothing and given normal civilian wear. Now we looked like real people again. Would they really let us go? We were supposed to get on another train for Friedland near Göttingen,[2] but did not trust the Russians. Near Fürstenwalde camp was a tram station from where a line ran into Berlin. Five fellow prisoners and I decided to defect at the next opportunity. We succeeded. All six of us got on a tram and then after nearly nine years I was back. Back in Berlin.

Spying through the misted windows of the compartment I was totally overcome. Suddenly, at the entrance to a tram station, I saw a sign that read 'Neukölln'. I heard myself say: 'This is the West – everybody out!' We stumbled through the guard's van, ran down the

---

1 At Fürstenwalde, the former barrack camp for POWs and 'foreign workers' had been converted in 1946 into a camp for displaced people. The reception of former POWs had been intended to occur here.

2 Where the demarcation lines of the British, American and Soviet zones of occupation intercepted, on 26 September 1946 the British had set up a collection centre at Friedland near Göttingen in which refugees of the immediate post-war period were accepted, fed and registered. In 1952 the German authorities took over the camp, which became the returners' camp in the West for POWs released from the Soviet Union.

steps from the platform to the forecourt and found a taxi stand. A colleague who was heading in my direction got into one of the waiting taxis with me. I told the driver my address without mentioning that I had no money on me. Without a word he took us. We might not be wearing prison clothes any more, but as returners from captivity we were easy to recognise. The taxi driver did not want the fare. First he set down my friend at Britz, then carried on to Rudow. I read the street signs, some with the names of flowers, and then the street in which I lived – had lived – a long time ago. The taxi pulled up at the number I had given. I was home.

There stood my parents-in-law's small house, which I had last seen on 22 April 1945 – it looked exactly as I had remembered it. My wife had lived there since the end of the war. The first person I saw at the door was my mother-in-law. Shortly after that, Gerda joined her. It was 31 December 1953. Our wedding anniversary. The eleventh, but of those we had not lived together for nine.

And now I was to learn that life had not stood still in my homeland. I shared this fate with thousands of others who came back from the war late. Gerda had begun a relationship with somebody else, my father-in-law was dead and naturally for my daughter Gitta – by now almost ten years old – I was a total stranger. The homecoming I had longed for was a very different thing from my daydreams because the homeland I remembered no longer existed. It was too much for me. I was on the Havel bridge and jumped into the ice-cold water. I remember nothing of the details, but I was saved. Gerda decided we should take the chance of a new beginning. Thus, the year 1954 began for me in Berlin, and I had to find my new place in it.

First of all, I had to attend to correspondence. I rummaged through my things for the letters my fellow prisoners had pressed into my hands. At the first opportunity, I sent them to their families. Gerda took them to the post office. Later I got busy sending small parcels to the comrades I had left behind in Russia. I packed thick paint brushes from which I unscrewed the brush-head and put a little note into the shaft which I hollowed out. I hoped in this way to be able to smuggle in news from the homeland without the censors finding out. In captivity we had promised each other firmly that if you got post from a former prisoner now at liberty – give it the most thorough going over! I wanted them to know that the politicians in western Germany were doing everything they could for their early release.

The Social Ministry sent our small family on holiday for six weeks. We went to Reisbach in Lower Bavaria. Late homecomers were given support in this way to find their way back into their families. Gerda had got through the difficult period just after the war in masterly fashion. In 1945 she had re-entered the SPD (German Socialist Party), in 1946 the AWO (Workers' Welfare) and in 1950 the DGB (German Trade Unionist Federation). In 1946 Uncle Paul, through his contacts with the post-war Bürgermeister Ernst Reuter,[3] had got her work in a US military office. She spoke English, and nobody cared when neighbours denounced her to the authorities as the wife of an SS man. Soon after that Gerda took up teacher training. In 1951 she passed her second state examination, and since then had been teaching at a school in Neukölln. Later she was even appointed headmistress.

What was I to do for a living?

I took an apprenticeship to be a draughtsman. That seemed to me to be a little along the artistic lines I had once travelled pre-war and therefore suitable. Only a few weeks later, however, I gave it up. The instruction went totally over my head – I was incapable of assimilating it. After almost ten years in Gulag it was difficult to peel off the prison clothing. I had not yet arrived home mentally – the homeland was a place I still did not know.

I was offered employment as a porter in a hospital. I turned it down. Push beds here and there? That seemed to be too undemanding an activity. I spent more than a year looking for something suitable. I

---

3 Ernst Reuter (1889–1953) was responsible for political affairs in West Berlin from 1946; in 1948 was Oberbürgermeister of the three Western sectors; and from 1951 until his death was the governing Bürgermeister of West Berlin.

received several offers, but nothing in Berlin. Some came from south Germany through old colleagues. Someone I knew from Swabia suggested I could take over as his commercial representative for rubberwear of all kinds in southern Germany. The assortment ranged from rubber rings for glass jars to Paris fashions. I would like to have accepted, but Gerda was not prepared to leave Berlin.

I came across Erich Kempka, Hitler's former chauffeur and motor pool chief. He was now a test driver at Porsche. He invited me to work with him, and I called on him in Stuttgart. Kempka got in touch with Jakob Werlin,[4] whom I had known in earlier times. Werlin received me in his six-roomed apartment in Munich. I could also be a driver, no problem, he gave me to understand. The day I met Werlin he had to go to Italy, and he offered me his flat to spend the night. Here again I would have to work in south Germany, and Gerda was not prepared to leave Berlin.

Finally I heard through acquaintances that a shop selling artists' requisites was up for sale – its owner now wanting to retire. 'That would be just the thing for you,' my friend said. It certainly would, but I had no money to buy it.

In the end I turned to a former general who helped late homecomers. He sent me to Gräfin von Isenburg.[5] She was the chairperson of an association helping former POWs to get back on their feet. Princess von Isenburg was especially impressed by my story and organised a meeting with politicians in Bonn. She accompanied me, for example, to a meeting with the CSU (Christian Socialist Union) deputy Kaspar Seibold,[6] and Seibold related my story to Finance Minister Fritz

---

4 Jakob Werlin, later chairman of Daimler-Benz AG, had a friendly relationship with Hitler. For getting him released from Landsberg on 20 December 1924 Werlin as the Benz & Cie AG representative in Munich placed a vehicle at his disposal. In the National Socialist period he became an SS-Oberführer and inspector-general for road traffic.

5 After the Second World War, Helene Elisabeth Princess von Isenburg (1900–1974) became the first president of the association Stille Hilfe für Kriegsgefangene und Internierte (Silent Help for Prisoners of War and Internees).

6 Kaspar Seibold (1914–1995), CSU deputy and member of the

Schäffer.[7] Finally, I was invited to a talk with Schäffer, who wanted to know all the details of my time with Hitler. Thus we spent half the day talking about that before we came to my present predicament. I assume that this conversation contributed to capital being made available a little later for a fund to support late returners.

I got a loan of 28,000 Deutsche Mark from the Grund-und-Kreditbank, and finally I was able to buy out the seventy-six-year-old owner of the artist and interior decoration shop at Kolonnen-Strasse 3 at Berlin-Schöneberg.

When my Aunt Sofia was looking for a flat, I asked my local postman if he could help. He asked around, and my aunt was very grateful to be able to occupy a new flat, also in Kolonnen-Strasse, before moving into the old peoples' home at Rudow, where she died aged eighty-seven. I liked us being close to each other and would regularly go there for lunch.

When I met my old colleague boxer Adolf Kleinholdermann around this time he made me an unusual offer: he had started up a small peanut-butter factory and would I like to buy him out. After the end of his active career as a sparring partner he had emigrated to the United States. His wife could not stand the New World and told him: 'Adolf, I am a Berliner, I want to go home.' With the peanut-butter recipe in his pocket, back they came. This favourite American spread was quite unknown to us, and Kleinholdermann's monopoly, which he had set up as soon as he arrived home, was now overwhelmed by demand from the Americans. The enterprise appealed to me, and so I became probably Germany's second supplier of peanut butter.

The recipe was top secret and very successful – the magic word being lecithin. The Americans stationed in Berlin could not get enough of it, and my production hardly met the demand. The only problem was

---

Parliamentary Council.

7 The CSU politician Fritz Schäffer (1888–1967) was in Konrad Adenauer's cabinet as federal finance minister, from 1949 to 1957, then federal justice minister until 1961.

German law. Under the food regulations 'butter' came from milk – an animal product. Peanut *butter* could therefore not be butter. There were difficulties with the ministries, and in the end the courts had to decide. The result was that I could continue turning out peanut butter providing I gave it another name. The business then began to get out of hand, taking up more and more of my time, competing with my shop. I had to choose between full automation and having peanut 'butter' as my primary occupation or giving it all up. At a trade fair I saw a modern bottling plant, which I would have to buy to meet the rising demand. It cost a fortune. I decided in favour of my shop, or rather Gerda persuaded me. I would really have liked to have gone on with the peanut-butter production. Shame about that.

John F. Kennedy

On 26 June 1963 I worked again as the bodyguard to a head of state. Well, almost. All the same it was remarkable. In connection with the J. F. Kennedy visit to Berlin I was approached by the CIA. It was explained that they wanted to put around the Schöneberg municipal government centre a ring of alert civilians who would be prepared to keep their eyes open and report anything suspicious. My shop in Kolonnen-Strasse was about two kilometres as the crow flies from the municipal centre. I was to pay particular attention to a certain road junction, and I was given a telephone number to call if I felt that I ought to report something I had seen. I have no idea why the CIA chose me, how they knew I would be reliable and that I had experience as a bodyguard. I did not enquire and simply watched more keenly than usual. Thus, not twenty years after the war's end, I protected the highest representative of the former enemy. In the event, there was nothing to report and I made no use of the telephone number.

I followed Kennedy's speech with its notorious sentence 'Ich bin ein Berliner' ('I am a doughnut' – the correct term is 'Ich bin Berliner') from among the milling crowd. Another detail to cause a grin was the reward I received for my services: for a year the CIA paid me, Hitler's former telephonist, my telephone bill.

Prince Philip

My wife continued her career in politics. She was a district councillor at Neukölln, and in 1975 was elected to the Berlin House of Deputies for the SPD.[8] More than once I begged her: 'Gerda, why don't you leave politics alone?' But it was in her blood, and I had no chance of deterring her. I just had to have some understanding. It was often difficult for me, as it must have been for her when I was in Hitler's service. It was not that I had problems with the aims and objectives that she represented; I simply did not like politics and politicians. And that has never changed. Reluctantly, I once again became an extra on the political stage. If there was an official event to which the marriage partner was invited to attend, obviously I would accompany my wife. I got to know the important names in the SPD, beginning with the Berlin senator Joachim Lipschitz,[9] with whom my wife had considerable contact during his time as district alderman of Neukölln; with the governing bürgermeisters Klaus Schütz[10] and Walter Momper;[11] even with Willy Brandt, who after being governing bürgermeister of West Berlin became federal chancellor, but I do not remember the date.

Nobody ever spoke to me about my past, but most knew. If I attended official functions there was a tacit agreement that I would never mention it. Thus, during the state visit of Queen Elizabeth in

8 Gerda Misch was a member of the Berlin House of Deputies 1975–8.

9 Joachim Lipschitz (1918–1961) was a municipal councillor for the Berlin district of Neukölln, and from 1955 an interior senator, first in the Senate of the governing bürgermeister Otto Suhr and then under Willy Brandt. Lipschitz founded the action Unbesungene Helden (Unsung Heroes) which publicly honoured citizens who had provided refuge for people from Nazi persecution.

10 Klaus Schütz (b. 1926) was an SPD politician; 1967–77, governing bürgermeister of Berlin.

11 Walter Momper (b. 1945) was an SPD politician; 1989–91 governing bürgermeister of Berlin.

1978, even Prince Philip was not aware with whom he was having such a lively conversation as he was led through the Charlottenburg exhibition. I might even suggest that the Duke of Edinburgh and I were in partnership that day: we were both the escort to our respective wives and made no secret of the fact that we had no enthusiasm for the collection of sculptures. Soon the small group surrounding the duke was agreed – we preferred the garden. The duke was grateful to be led out to be shown the parkland designed by Peter Joseph Lenné. He liked that much better.

Ghosts

For many years my past was buried. I had minimal contact with old colleagues. I met my former company commander Mohnke once on the occasion of a birthday reunion of Hitler's pilot Hans Baur. After that, Mohnke invited me on a number of occasions to visit Hamburg, but because of my business I could never get away, even though he lived to be ninety-six. Occasionally I met Helmuth Beermann, a colleague from the bodyguard. He lived near my relatives, and I was often able to make a detour to see him.

I had an attack of the horrors one day on account of a totally unexpected meeting. I was with my wife in a restaurant. When the waiter arrived to take our order, I recognised him as Hatchet Schmidt, the co-prisoner from the camp at Sverdlovsk who had chopped off the head of the traitor Kruse. It was apparent that he recognised me at once. This was not a story for my wife, and I did not want to burden her with it, and so I acted as if the waiter were a stranger to me, and nothing in his tone made my wife think that Hatchet Schmidt was anything more than a waiter. However, I slipped him my address surreptitiously, and soon afterwards he visited my shop. Once he got back to the Federal Republic he had gone on trial for the business at the camp but had been acquitted.

Until the death of my wife in 1998, out of regard for her political involvement I kept in the shadows, gave very few interviews and never broached the subject of my past. For many years there was no special, or in any case no public, and certainly not a German, interest in my experiences. In the 1970s I gave the American historian and journalist James O'Donnell a long interview. He wrote a book[12] about the bunker experiences, although a lot of it did not seem to me to conform with how I had related it.

The books and documentaries known to me about the last days in the Führerbunker are all contradictory and excessive in number. There were really very few of us down below. If one counts up today how many have since 'inveigled' themselves into the bunker, there must have been a military company present. All of these had something to say. Supposedly, a hundred or so people were still living down there just before the suicides of Hitler and Goebbels. The fact is that nobody, absolutely nobody, spent time in the bunker who had not been expressly told to report there. Certainly, officers came down for the situation conferences, but then went up again as soon as they finished. My own commander, Schädle, never went down there, nor did RSD chief Rattenhuber. I can never recall ever having seen Hitler's pilot Baur in the bunker. I cannot insist that he was never there, but I certainly never saw him for myself.

People had to make themselves greater or lesser in importance to justify their presence. Otto Günsche, one of the few who really had something worthwhile to say, finally had enough of it and gave out no more information. He even withdrew from me because I gave his telephone number to somebody I considered trustworthy who then became very oppressive and unpleasant. Otto did not want to talk. I also stepped back out of the limelight under the weight of enquiries. In 1982, I gave an Australian film crew my first television interview, and after that I got some peace at last.

I managed my shop for interior decorators' requisites until my sixty-eighth year, when I sold it to a former co-worker. My wife had to

---

12 Uwe Bahnsen and James P. O'Donnell, *Die Katakombe – Das Ende in der Reichskanzlei*, Stuttgart 1975.

be cared for by me in the last five years of her life. It was difficult for me to watch my clever Gerda fall victim to Alzheimer's. The onset was harmless enough – she just started to slur the end syllables of longer words. Later she began to be anxious about public speaking. 'Rochus, I stand at the dais, and suddenly there is nothing there. Just emptiness.' At first I tried to play it down, but Gerda was too much of a realist not to notice that this was no normal ageing process she was undergoing. I cared for my wife at home until the last day of her life.

Rochus III

Now I live alone in the house of my parents-in-law. Over the years, unfortunately, I was never able to mend the relationship with my daughter. Those ten missing years could never be made good. The greater part of her childhood lay behind her when one day I returned bringing into her life not only her father but Hitler too. The latter stood like a wall between us. Gitta became an architect, and one of her major assignments has been the restoration of synagogues. She is certain that she has Jewish forebears on her mother's side. My daughter bore two sons relatively late in life – Rochus and Alexander.

Since the death of my wife I have faced the questions of the press and public. Many young researchers write to me, often with a whole catalogue of questions. A surprising number of enquiries reach me from eastern Europe and Russia.

One of the questions I am asked most frequently is: when did I realise that the war was lost? I then write back – often only months later – and I never forget to point out that war is the worst thing men can do to each other. War is nothing but mass murder. It was the worst then, it is the worst today. Everything, absolutely everything, happening in the world today can be watched from an armchair in the living room. No dictator can fool the people any longer. Everybody can keep himself informed. Yet people still fail to understand what war is. Will we never have good sense?

As I have discovered, my ancestor Paul Misch was a soldier in Wallenstein's army in the seventeenth century. My father and I were soldiers who served at the front in the world wars of the twentieth century: he died of his wounds; and I landed in Hitler's bunker and the Moscow torture chambers. For my grandchildren, the young Rochus and his brother, and to their generation, I wish nothing more than that they recognise what an uncommonly valuable challenge they have in today's democracy: to be able to go the way they choose. In my day I had no choice but to be a soldier.

Short Biographies

Amann, Max (1891–1957)

1914–18 war service as NCO; 1921 joined NSDAP; 1921–3 NSDAP business leader; 1923 involved in Munich Putsch, imprisoned with Hitler; 1922–45 business leader and director, Franz-Eher Verlag (central NSDAP publishing house producing *Völkischer Beobachter* and SS journal *Das Schwarze Korps*); 1933–45 president Reich press chamber, Hitler's personal banker; ensured that publishing houses classified as Jewish, and those in the possession of the SPD and KPD, went to the Franz-Eher-Verlag; with the so-called Amann decrees, the regional NSDAP publishing organs were largely deprived of power; 1948, in denazification trials, sentenced to ten years in work camp; released 1953.

Antonescu, Ion (1882–1946)

WWI, head of operational section, Romanian general staff; 1937–8 war minister; 1940 nominated head of government by King Carol II; headed a dictatorial system and engineered Romania's entry into the Axis pact; 1941 Romania allied with Germany to attack the Soviet Union; 1944 after secret negotiations with Antonescu's enemies by Michael I, successor to King Carol II, Antonescu was overthrown on 23 August 1944 and sentenced to death by the Romanian People's Court at Bucharest as a war criminal.

Arndt, Wilhelm 'Willy' (1913–1945)

Member *SS-Leibstandarte Adolf Hitler*; 1939–45 Hitler's valet and 'favourite' servant; killed in an air crash, 22 April 1945.

Axmann, Arthur (1913–1996)

1928 entered Hitler Youth; 1931 joined NSDAP; 1940 Reich Youth leader, previously deputy of his predecessor Baldur von Schirach; 1943 fought with 12th SS Panzer Division 'Hitlerjugend' in Normandy; in the battle for Berlin, led the Volkssturm, mostly underage Hitler Youth; 1 May 1945 escaped Reich Chancellery, declared dead officially, assumed name Erich Siewert and lived in Mecklenburg until arrested in Lübeck, December 1945; held by Americans; 1949 sentenced to three years' work camp in denazification trial as a 'principal perpetrator'; 19 August 1958 fined 35,000 Deutsche Mark by a Berlin court for 'Inciting Youth'; after two proceedings for bankruptcy, active in Spain 1971–6, where he was planning a leisure centre on Gran Canaria; subsequently lived in Berlin.

Baarová, Lida, née Lidmila Babková (1914–2000)

Czech actress; 1934 moved from Prague to Berlin; Ufa star (*Barcarole*, 1935); after her affair with Goebbels became public (ended on Hitler's intervention); she was expelled from Germany and returned to Prague; later acted in Italy under Federico Fellini, Roberto Rosselini and Vittorio de Sica; 1956 ended her film career; various theatrical engagements in German language area.

Baur, Johann Peter, known as Hans Baur (1897–1993)

1926–33 Deutsche Lufthansa pilot; 1933–45, Hitler's chief pilot and commander Flugstaffel Reichsregierung (Reich government); February 1945 appointed major general of the Polizei; 1945–55 Soviet POW.

Below, Georg Ludwig Heinrich Nicolaus von (1907–1983)

Colonel, Luftwaffe; April 1928 accepted as officer candidate, 112th Infantry Regiment (Halberstadt); until 1929 flight instructor, passenger pilot school Schleissheim; 1929–33 2nd lieutenant 112th Infantry Regiment; 1 July 1933 transferred into Reich Air Ministry (Staffelkapitän J.G. 'Richthofen' at Döberitz and J.G. 'Horst Wessel' at Düsseldorf); 16 June 1936 Hitler's personal Luftwaffe adjutant; co-signatory Hitler's Private Testament; 1946–8 British POW.

Bernadotte, Graf von Wisborg (1895–1948)

Nephew of Swedish King Gustav V; Swedish cavalry officer; 1943–8 vice-president and later president Swedish Red Cross; February 1945 negotiated with Himmler for release of Scandinavian concentration camp inmates (Operation Weisse Busse); 1948 UN mediator in Palestine; 17 September 1948 murdered in Jerusalem by militant leaders of Jewish terrorist group.

Blaschke, Hugo Johannes (1881–1959)

1908–11 studied dentistry in Philadelphia, USA and London (mandible surgery); 1914–18 military dentist in Frankfurt/Oder and Berlin; 1919–45 own practice at Kurfürstendamm 213, Berlin; 1930 treated Hermann Göring; 1933 joined NSDAP, contact with Hitler; set up dental surgery in the Reich Chancellery to treat National Socialist leaders; 1 May 1935 joined SS; 31 August 1943 nominated senior dental surgeon to staff, Reichsführer-SS; 9 November 1944 brigadier of Waffen-SS and physician for the SS; built dental surgeries at Dachau, Oranienburg and Buchenwald, but Blaschke had no knowledge of 'grievances' there; June 1946 to December 1948 detained; subsequently dental surgeon at Nuremberg.

Bormann, Albert (1902–1989)

Younger brother of Martin Bormann; banking professional; 1927 entered NSDAP and SA (Sturmabteilung); 1929–31 Hitler Youth Gau leader, Thuringia; 1931 active in Hitler's private Chancellery; 1933 head of private Chancellery, which from 1934 was classified as Principal Office 1 of the Chancellery of the Führer of the NSDAP; 1934 Hitler's personal adjutant; 1938 member of the Reichstag as deputy, Berlin-West; 21 April 1945 fled from Reich Chancellery to Obersalzberg; 1945–9 lived under false name as agricultural worker; 1949 surrendered himself; short period of internment.

Bormann, Martin (1900–1945)

Farmer; 1924 entered NSDAP; 1933 nominated NSDAP Reichsleiter, Reichstag deputy; 1933–41 staff manager in the office of Führer's deputy (Rudolf Hess); after Hess flew to Britain in 1941, on 12 May 1941 Hitler made Bormann chief of the Party Chancellery with the authority of a Reich minister; trustee of Hitler's private fortune and organisational leader for the construction of the Berghof (extorted land from the owner with threat 'sell up or concentration camp'); 12 April 1943 nominated as the Führer's secretary; 29 April 1945 witness at the marriage of Hitler and Eva Braun in the Führerbunker; 2 May 1945 suicide after escaping from Reich Chancellery (identified by DNA, 1998). Bormann was named as one of the twenty-four people at Nuremberg as a principal war criminal. On 1 October 1946 he was declared guilty in his absence and sentenced to death.

Bornholdt, Hermann (1908–1976)

Farmer; 1929 entered NSDAP; 1933 member of *SS-Leibstandarte Adolf Hitler'* (LSSAH), SS-Hauptsturmführer (= army rank of captain).

Brandt, Karl (1904–1948)

Surgeon; major general, Waffen-SS; 1932 entered NSDAP; 1933 entered SA; 1933 treated Hitler's senior adjutant Wilhelm Brückner; from 14 June 1933 Hitler's personal physician; 28 July 1942 commissioner-general for medicine and health; 5 September 1943 head of all medical supply and care organisations, and coordinator of medical research (initiator and accomplice in experiments on humans); end of war arrested by Allied forces at Flensburg; from 9 December 1946 to 20 August 1947 tried at Nuremberg (trials of medical personnel); sentenced to death; 2 June 1948 executed at Landsberg.

Braun, Eva Anna Paula, married name Hitler (1912–1945)

1928 convent school (commercial studies), Simbach am Inn; 1929 laboratory worker with Heinrich Hoffmann, Hitler's personal photographer; October 1929 first meeting with Hitler and frequent meetings in circle of the Hoffmann couple; 1932 and 1935 attempted suicide because of lack of attention from Hitler; 1936 moved into villa at Munich-Bogenhausen bought for her by Hoffmann at Hitler's instigation; frequent stays at the Berghof as Hitler's unofficial paramour; end of 1944 and beginning of 1945 several trips from Munich to Berlin to see Hitler; from March 1945 remained with Hitler in Berlin; 29 April 1945 married Hitler; in 1957 Berchtesgaden court determined that Braun entered suicide pact with Hitler and took cyanide at 15.28 hrs on 30 April 1945.

Braun, Margarete 'Gretl', married name Fegelein (1915–1987)

Younger sister of Eva Braun, 1932 female clerk to Hitler's personal photographer Hoffmann; 1943 trained at the Bavarian State Film School; 3 June 1944 married Hermann Fegelein; May 1945 at Berghof and pregnant at the time of her husband's death; 5 May 1945 daughter Eva Barbara Fegelein born (who committed suicide in 1975).

Brückner, Wilhelm (1884–1954)

Officer, Bavarian Infantry Regiment, WWI; end 1922 entered NSDAP; 1 February 1923 leader SA Regiment *München*; 9 November 1923 involved in Munich Putsch; short period of remand; January 1930 Hitler's adjutant and bodyguard, later chief adjutant until break with Hitler end of 1940; succeeded by Julius Schaub.

Burgdorf, Wilhelm (1895–1945)

1935 tactical instructor, War Academy, Dresden; 1 October 1942 deputy chief, army personnel office; from 20 July 1944 head of army personnel office; Hitler's chief Wehrmacht adjutant; 14 October 1944 gave Rommel choice of suicide to avoid his family being arrested (*Sippenhaft* = guilt by blood association) for his involvement in the Stauffenberg plot; co-signatory with Goebbels, Bormann and Krebs to Hitler's Political Testament; 1 May 1945 suicide.

Chekhova, Olga, née Knipper (1897–1980)

German actress of German-Russian origin; Ufa star; 1935 appointed state actress, Hitler's favourite actress; reported by British historian Antony Beevor to have been a 'passive' Soviet agent.

Christian, Gerda 'Dara', née Daranowski (1913–1997)

1937 personal secretary to Adolf Hitler; 2 February 1943 married Eckhard Christian, Jodl's adjutant; left service until end 1943; April 1945 successful flight from Reich Chancellery to southern Germany; held by US forces and interrogated; later worked in commerce in the Rhineland.

Darges, Friedrich 'Fritz' (1913–2009)

1933 joined SS; 1934 SS military academy Bad Tölz; 1935 platoon leader, SS-Standarte *Germania*; from August 1937 adjutant to Martin Bormann in staff of Rudolf Hess; October 1940 until 16 March 1942

Ordonnanz officer (young or low ranking adjutant, 2nd lieutenant to captain) with Hitler; drafted to front, 5th SS Panzer Division *Wiking*; 5 April 1945 Knights Cross; May 1945 captured by US forces; 30 April 1948 released; correspondended with Misch until 2007.

Dietrich, Jacob Otto (1897–1952)

Volunteer WWI; studied philosophy and political science; 1926 newspaper editor; 1929 joined NSDAP; 1930–1 deputy chief editor of Essen *Nationalzeitung* (National Newspaper); 1933 entered SS; 1931–45 Reich press chief NSDAP; 1937–45 state secretary at Reich Propaganda Ministry; 1938–45 chief of press, Reich government (Dietrich and Axmann, Reichsleiter for the NSDAP press, were Goebbels's most important rivals in the area of press policy); 13 April 1949 in the so-called Wilhelm-Strasse trials before the IMT at Nuremberg, sentenced to seven years' imprisonment; 1950 pardoned and released.

Dietrich, Josef 'Sepp' (1892–1966)

General, Waffen-SS; volunteer WWI; 9 November 1923 took part in Munich Putsch; 17 March 1933 on Hitler's instructions formed the SS-Stabswache *Berlin*; later commanded the *SS-Leibstandarte* of divisional strength; WWII Ardennes offensive, finished as commander-in-chief 6th SS Panzer Army; 1946 in Malmedy-trial at Dachau found guilty of war crimes by US military court and sentenced to life imprisonment. Released in 1955, he was rearrested and convicted by a West German court in 1957 of involvement in the shootings during the Röhm putsch of 1934. Released on health grounds in 1958, he died in 1966.

Dirr, Adolf 'Adi' (1907–?)

Blacksmith; semi-professional boxer; 1929 entered NSDAP and SA; 29 February 1932 one of the first eight members of the *SS-*

Begleitkommando (SS bodyguard); 22 April 1945 flew out from Berlin to Obersalzberg; detained until 1948.

Dönitz, Karl (1891–1980)

1 April 1910 entered imperial navy; U-boat commander WWI; 5 October 1918 until 15 July 1919 British POW; 1935 began the rebuilding of the U-boat arm; from 17 October 1939 commander of the U-boats (BdU); January 1943 took over from Admiral Raeder as commander-in-chief Kriegsmarine, promoted to grand admiral; 17 April–30 April 1945 also commander-in-chief Wehrmacht (North); 1 May 1945 commander-in-chief Wehrmacht and appointed Reich president in Hitler's Testament; 2 May 1945 set up caretaker German government; 23 May 1945 arrested at Flensburg; 1 October 1946 at the International Military Tribunal at Nuremberg sentenced to ten years' imprisonment for war crimes; October 1956 released.

Dörnberg, Alexander Freiherr von (1901–1983)

1919 Freikorps; studied law; 1934 entered NSDAP; 1936 Foreign Ministry, Berlin; 1938 entered SS; 1938–41 chief of protocol, Foreign Ministy and member, staff of Reichsführer-SS; Envoy Class I; 1945 detained; 1948 exonerated by denazification tribunal at Garmisch-Partenkirchen for 'active and passive resistance'.

Esser, Hermann (1900–1981)

Volunteer WWI; 1919 entered DAP (Deutsche Arbeitpartei/German Workers' Party); 24 February 1919 member, NSDAP; editor, *Völkischer Beobachter*; 1923 first head of propaganda, NSDAP; received three months' imprisonment for part in the failed Munich Putsch; 1933–5 head of Bavarian State Chancellery; 1933–45 Reichstag deputy and vice-president; 1939 state secretary at Propaganda Ministry; author of the anti-Semitic book *Die jüdisch Weltpest* published in 1939, two months after the November 1938 pogrom; 1945–7 detained by US forces; 1949 classified as 'principal guilt carrier' in denazification processes and sentenced to five years' work camp; 1952 released; subsequently lived in seclusion in Munich.

Exner, Helene 'Marlene' Marie von (b. 1917–?)

Trained at the University of Vienna as a cook–nutritionist; September 1942 until July 1943 specialist cook for dictator Ion Antonescu in Bucharest; July 1943 until dismissed from service 8 May 1944 (found to be of Jewish blood), special cook for Hitler.

Fegelein, Hermann (1906–1945)

1931 entered NSDAP; 1933 entered SS; 1939 Waffen-SS; commander SS Cavalry Brigade; 1942 inspector of mobile and mounted troops, SS-Führungshauptamt; 1943 commander, 8th SS Cavalry Division *Florian Geyer*, wounded; 1 January 1944 Waffen-SS liaison officer to Hitler; 3 June 1944 married Gretl Braun; 21 June 1944 major general, Waffen-SS; 27 April 1945 demoted by Hitler to SS-Mann; 29 April 1945 field court martial and executed.

Frick, Helmut (1913–?)

1931 entered NSDAP; 1933 '*SS-Leibstandarte Adolf Hitler*' (LSSAH).

Gesche, Bruno (1905–1980)

1922 entered NSDAP; 1928 entered SS; March 1932 in newly founded *SS-Begleitkommando des Führer* (Führer's SS bodyguard); 16 June 1934 until December 1944 commander SS bodyguard; then sent to front and demoted from SS-Obersturmbannführer (lieutenant colonel) to SS-Unterscharführer (corporal) for alcoholism; British POW; detained until 1947.

Goebbels, Joseph (1897–1945)

WWI volunteered but rejected as unfit (club foot resulting from osteomyelitis as a child); 1917 best school-leaving certificate of his year; studied German language and literature, history and ancient philology at Bonn, Freiburg and Heidelberg; 1922 graduated at Bonn; 1923 briefly employed as money market crier at Dresdner Bank; then unemployed and active as writer; 1924 co-founder of NSFP (substitute for banned NSDAP); private secretary of Gregor-Strasser (left, anti-capitalist wing of Party as opposed to Folkish-nationalist wing of Adolf Hitler); enticed away by Hitler, nominated Gauleiter of Berlin-Brandenburg; 1928 Reichstag deputy; most important speaker and NSDAP demagogue in the 1932 elections; 13 March 1933 Reich propaganda minister, president of Reich Chamber of Culture and Reich Cultural Senate; from 1942 Reich defence commissioner for Greater Berlin; 1943–5 Reich inspector for civilian air-raid precautions; 25 July 1944 plenipotentiary-general for total war; 25 September 1944 head of Deutscher Volkssturm in the Gross-Berlin Gau; 30 April 1945, 15.30 hrs made Reich chancellor by Hitler's Political Testament; 1 May 1945 committed suicide by taking poison.

Goebbels, Magda, née Behrend (1901–1945)

Daughter of unmarried servant girl Auguste Behrend, her father was builder and engineer Dr Oskar Ritschel; later her mother married the Jewish leather manufacturer Richard Friedländer, who adopted Magda and gave her his surname; 19 December 1931 married Joseph Goebbels; propaganda made Magda into the exemplary mother of the Third Reich; their six children were Helga, Hildegard, Helmut, Hedwig, Holdine and Heidrun; in 1939 some of them appeared in a pro-euthanasia film, contrasting them to the repulsive 'impaired' opposites; 1 May 1945 after poisoning all her children, Magda Goebbels took poison herself and also died.

Göring, Hermann Wilhelm (1893–1946)

1912 joined 12th *Prinz Wilhelm* Infantry Regiment at Mulhouse, Alsace, then German territory; WWI pilot training; commander Fighter Squadron No. 1 (von Richthofen's 'flying circus'); after the war exhibitions and commercial pilot; 1922 joined NSDAP; from

December 1922 leader of SA; 9 November 1923 wounded during Munich Putsch; given morphine to relieve the pain – became addicted; fled abroad (Austria, Italy, Sweden); end of 1927 returned to Germany (after general amnesty); stayed in rehabilitation centre for morphine addiction; after ban on NSDAP was lifted, was readmitted to Party and SA; 1928 lieutenant general; 30 August 1932 president of Reichstag; after Hitler became Reich chancellor, Göring was appointed Reich minister without portfolio and Reich commissioner for the Prussian Interior Ministry; 10 April 1933 minister-president of Prussia; 1933 Reich Commissioner for Aviation, Reich Minister for Aviation, Reich Forestry Superintendent; 1934 Reich Hunting Superintendent and Hitler's successor in the event of his death; May 1935 commander-in-chief newly founded Luftwaffe; 20 April 1936 general; 18 October 1936 head of the Four-Year Plan (taken over by Speer in 1942); responsible for founding the Gestapo and setting up the first concentration camp; July 1940 promoted from field marshal to Reichsmarschall of the Greater German Reich; 31 July 1941 passed Hitler's order to Reinhard Heydrich to extend the 'Final Solution' of the Jewish Question to all areas of Europe under German control. On 24 April 1945 he was arrested on the Obersalzberg on Hitler's orders for 'treason against Hitler's person and the National Socialist cause'. At the end of the war surrendered to US Seventh Army; 21 May 1945 placed in the secret US Camp 'Ash Can' at Bad Mondorf in Luxemburg; at Nuremberg Trials sentenced to death by hanging; took cyanide a few hours before his execution.

Greim, Robert Ritter von (1892–1945)

1911 ensign, Bavarian railway battalion; 1912 transferred to 8th Field-Artillery Regiment (Nuremberg); War Academy at Munich; 1915 trained as aircraft observer; 1916 trained as pilot at Schleissheim/Munich; January 1917 1st lieutenant; 1917 captain, Fighter Squadron 34; 1918 awarded Pour le Mérite; elevated to nobility 'Ritter von'; 1920 flew during the Kapp Putsch (attempt by Kapp and von Lüttwitz to overthrow the Weimar Republic); took to studying law; 1922 bank employee; 1924–7 in China to advise on building its air force; 1927 head of flying school at Würzburg; 1 January 1934 entry into Reichswehr (major); development of fighter squadron 'Richthofen'; summer 1935 inspector of fighter pilots; 20 April 1936 colonel and inspector of flight safety and equipment; 1938 head of Luftwaffe personnel office; 1 February 1938 brigadier; beginning of 1939 commander 5th Air Division; October 1939 commander 5th Air Corps; 19 July 1940 promoted to General of the Luftwaffe; 1 April 1942 commander-in-chief Luftwaffe Command East; 26 April 1945 commander-in-chief Luftwaffe and field marshal; seriously injured, when his aircraft was hit by ground fire while landing at Berlin; 24 May 1945 suicide in US custody before being handed over to the Soviets.

Günsche, Otto (1917–2003)

1934 entered *SS-Leibstandarte*; 1936 SS bodyguard; 1941–2 SS cadet school Bad Tölz; made his career in the SS; January–August 1943 Hitler's personal adjutant (as representative); fought at the front with *SS-Leibstandarte* Panzer Division; February 1944 personal adjutant to Hitler until his death; burnt Hitler's body; fled from Reich Chancellery; Soviet POW; 1955 transferred to German Democratic Republic prison at Bautzen; 1956 released; fled to West Germany.

Haase, Werner (1900–1950)

1918–19 military service; studied medicine and surgery; 1927 ship's doctor; 1933 entered NSDAP and SA; 1934 transferred into the SS; 1935 for a short while travelling physician on Hitler's staff; 1943 senior surgeon at the Surgical University Clinic, Berlin; April 1945 headed military dressing station in Reich Chancellery cellar; 2 May 1945 Soviet captivity; 6 May identified the bodies of the Goebbels's family for the Soviets; died of tuberculosis, probably in Moscow prison Butyrka.

Hammitzsch, Angela, née Hitler (1883–1949)

Hitler's half-sister, daughter of Hitler's father Alois and his second wife Franziska Matzelsberger; during WWI head of the Mensa Academica Judaica (a boarding house for Jewish students); 1924 (or 1925) moved to Munich; made Hitler's housekeeper there and later at the Berghof; mid-1930s moved to Dresden after a break with her brother; married the architect Martin Hammitzsch; spring 1945, brought from Dresden to Berchtesgaden by Hitler, to prevent her falling into Soviet hands; May 1945 her husband committed suicide.

Heinkel, Ernst (Heinrich) (1888–1958)

German engineer and aircraft manufacturer; the Ernst Heinkel Works were owned initially by the Luftwaffe, bombers being developed and built there, later the works passed to Heinkel; 1937 one of leaders of the military economy; 1945 a large part of the Heinkel works were destroyed or dismantled.

Hentschel, Johannes 'Hannes' (1908–1892)

1934 senior machinery foreman, Old Reich Chancellery; 2 May 1945 captured by Soviets; released 1949.

Hess, Rudolf Walter Richard (1894–1987)

1914 volunteer (infantry, later fighter pilot); 1920 entered DAP, then into NSDAP; November 1923 participated in the Munich Putsch; imprisoned with Hitler (Hitler dictated to Hess *Mein Kampf*); 1925 Hitler's private secretary; 21 April 1933 deputy NSDAP leader, Reich minister without portfolio; 1939 member of the Council of Ministers for Defence of the Reich; 10 May 1941 flew to Britain; 1946 sentenced to life imprisonment at Nuremberg war trials; 1946–87 served his sentence until his death at Berlin-Spandau (from 1966 the prison's only inmate).

Hewel, Walther (1904–1945)

1923 participated in the Munich Putsch; imprisoned with Hitler at Landsberg; worked in Indonesia for several years as employee of a British firm; member of Overseas Organisation of NSDAP; head of trade office and press departmental chief of NSDAP/AO Java, Dutch East Indies; 1938 head of personal staff, Reich foreign minister Joachim von Ribbentrop, and Foreign Ministry liaison officer to Hitler; 2 May 1945 committed suicide after escaping from the Reich Chancellery.

Himmler, Heinrich Leopold (1900–1945)

1918 officer cadet (no service at front); 1919 Freikorps Landshut and Oberland; studied farming; 1923 entry into NSDAP; took part in Munich Putsch; during ban on NSDAP joined front organisation NSFB; from 1925 NSDAP member again; 1927–8 representative of Reichsführer-SS; 1929 until 29 April 1945 Reichsführer-SS; 1 April 1933 political police commander in Bavaria, Gestapo inspector in all German provinces (except Prussia and Schaumburg-Lippe); 1939 Reich commissioner for the consolidation of German national characteristics; ran the SS and the concentration camp apparatus; architect of the 'Final Solution'; 29 April 1945 relieved of all offices by Hitler for attempting to negotiate a separate peace with the Western Allies; assumed a false name in an attempt to merge into German society; 23 May 1945 suicide after arrest by British forces and being identified.

Hitler, Alois; changed name in 1945 to Hiller (1882–1956)

Hitler's half-brother; illegitimate son of Alois Hitler, Senior and his second wife, Angelika Matzelsberger; early prison sentence for theft; emigrated to Britain, married Irishwoman Bridget Dowling (1911 had son William Patrick); 1915 returned to Vienna minus his family; married Hedwig Heidemann (1923 had son Heinrich); during the Nazi period ran a tavern in Berlin.

Hitler, Paula (1896–1960)

Hitler's full sister, sixth child of Hitler's father and third child of Hitler's mother; lived anonymously in Vienna using the name Wolf. Her contact with her surviving brother Adolf was slight; he had a disagreeable fiancé of hers sent to the front; 1945 detained by US forces; returned to Vienna; later lived out her life at Berchtesgaden.

Hoffmann, Heinrich (1885–1957)

Hitler's personal photographer; 1901–6 active with various photographers; 1906–8 head of two photo studios in Munich; 1909 opened his own studio; worked as press photographer; 1917 served in infantry in WWI; 1918 resumed as press photographer; 1920 entered NSDAP; took over anti-Semitic broadsheet *Auf gut Deutsch*; photographed Party bosses, including Hitler, during incarceration at Landsberg; 1929 introduced Hitler to his student Eva Braun in his studio; 1932 Heinrich Hoffmann Verlag involved in propaganda reports; made professor by Hitler; 1938 member of commission for the 'evaluation of confiscated works of degenerate art'; 1945 arrested by US army, sentenced to four years' detention and confiscation of his fortune by denazification tribunal; 1950 discharged; lived subsequently in Munich.

Högl, Peter (1897–1945)

SS-Standartenführer at his death; his final position equivalent to detective chief superintendent, Reich Security Service (RSD); 2 May 1945 committed suicide at Reich Chancellery.

Horthy, Miklos; officially, Held Nikolaus Horthy von Nagybanya (1868–1957)

Hungarian admiral and politician; WWI last commander-in-chief Austro-Hungarian navy; 1919 overthrew communist republic of councils under Bela Kun in order to bring back the monarchy; 1 March

1920 until 16 October 1944 Hungarian regent (provisional head of state representing the monarchy); 20 November 1940 Hungary entered Axis pact (with German Reich, Italy and Japan); 11 October 1944, after signing armistice agreement with the Soviets, deposed after coup initiated by Germans; arrested and brought to Germany; 1945 released by US forces; exile in Portugal.

Isenburg, Helene Elisabeth, Prinzessin von (1900–1974)

Wife of geneticist Wilhelm Karl Prinz von Isenburg (1937 professor of blood- and family research, Munich; pleaded the National Socialist racial cause); 1951 president of organisation to assist PoWs and internees; called 'Mother of the Landsbergers' for her efforts on behalf of National Socialist war criminals awaiting execution at Landsberg prison; her organisation pursued increasingly revisionist aims; November 1999 federal finance court recognised her organisation as a charity.

Junge, Traudl, née Humps (1920–2002)

1935 member of the girls' branch of the Hitler Youth, the 'Bund deutscher Mädel' (BdM); 1936 middle school and higher business school, then female clerk with VDM (German Metal Works), Munich; secretary to notary and assistant to chief editor of a trade journal for tailors; trained as dancer; 1942 applied for advertised post at Hitler's Chancellery, Berlin; 30 January 1943 appointed as one of Hitler's private secretaries; 1 May 1945 succeeded in escape from Reich Chancellery; 9 June 1945 taken prisoner by Soviets, rescued from a transport to the East by an Armenian interpreter; worked for administration at Charité University Clinic, Berlin; April 1946 fled to Bavaria to escape Russian occupiers, briefly interned by US forces; various employments as secretary.

Kannenberg, Arthur 'Willy' (1896–1963)

1931 ran the officers' mess at the Nazi Party headquarters, the 'Brown House' in Munich; 1933 house administrator Reich Chancellery (with wife Freda); 1945 detained in Bavaria; 1946 released; later innkeeper at Düsseldorf.

Kempka, Erich (1910–1975)

Motor mechanic; 1930 entered NSDAP and SS; 1932 driver with Hitler's SS bodyguard; from 1936 Hitler's personal chauffeur; 1945 detained, 1947 released; later test driver at Porsche.

Körber, August (1905–?)

1932 entered NSDAP and SS; 1934 LSSAH; later in Hitler's SS bodyguard.

Krause, Karl Wilhelm (1911—)

A carpenter and joiner by trade; 1931 Reichsmarine; 1 August 1934 entered Hitler's service as valet; 10 September 1939 during Polish campaign dismissed for making false statement; 2 November 1940 with LSSAH; December 1943 12th SS Panzer Division *Hitlerjugend*; (Hitler Youth) 1945 SS-Untersturmführer; POW; June 1946 released.

Krebs, Hans (1898–1945)

WWI volunteer; 1919 Reichswehr, Infantry Regiment; 1930 Reichswehr Ministry, Berlin; 1933–4 assistant to military attaché in Moscow; 1939 Führer-reserve, OKH, chief of general staff, III Army Corps; 1943 chief of general staff, army group centre; 29 March 1945 chargé d'affaires, chief of army general staff; co-signatory of Hitler's Political Testament; 1 May 1945 negotiated for surrender of Berlin with Soviets; on same day he committed suicide by cyanide capsule.

Lammers, Hans Heinrich (1879–1962)

1933 state secretary, Hitler's head of Reich Chancellery; 24 April 1945 arrested on Hitler's order in connection with Göring's alleged treason; death sentence suspended; captured by US forces; 11 April 1949, Wilhelm-Strasse trials at Nuremberg, sentenced to twenty years in prison for war crimes, later reduced to ten years; 1952 amnestied and released.

Ley, Robert (1890–1945)

Studied chemistry; volunteer WWI; French POW 1917 after being shot down; 1920 returned to Germany still seriously wounded; 1924 entered NSDAP; 1925 Gauleiter, Rhineland South; 1930 Reichstag member; 1931 Reich inspector of the Party organisation, Munich; 1933 head of Action Committee for the Protection of German Labour – purpose was to dissolve the trade unions, later renamed Deutsche Arbeitsfront (DAF); until 1945 headed DAF; shortly before sentencing at Nuremberg Trials committed suicide by strangulation, in cell.

Linge, Heinz (1913–1980)

A bricklayer by trade; 1933 joined *SS-Leibstandarte Adolf Hitler*; 24 January 1935 selected by Hitler as a servant; after training at Hotel Technical College, Munich-Pasing, became Hitler's valet; until 1955 Soviet POW; then worked in commerce.

Lorenz, Heinz (1913–1985)

Hitler's press secretary at FHQ; from 1937 close colleague of Otto Dietrich, NSDAP Reich press chief; responsible for foreign political reports; May 1945 detained by British; released 1947; then journalist.

Manziarly, Constanze (1920–?)

Austrian mother, Greek father; trained in special diet preparations at the Innsbruck Housekeeping School; 13 September 1943 employed at Zabel spa house, Bischofswiesen; September 1944 special diet-cook to Hitler; 2 May 1945 possible suicide after leaving Reich Chancellery.

Meissner, Otto (1880–1953)

Lawyer; from 1920 head of Reich president's office under Friedrich Ebert, Hindenburg and Hitler; 1937 state minister, chief of presidential Chancellery of the Führer and Reich chancellor; witness at Nuremberg; 1949 accused in so-called Wilhelm-Strasse trials, acquitted; May 1949 Munich denazification tribunals, classified as 'person involved'; 1952 process abandoned.

Mohnke, Wilhelm (1911–2011)

One of first SS men in Hitler's SS-Stabswache *Berlin* under Sepp Dietrich; October 1934–May 1940, commander 5th Company, *SS-Leibstandarte*; frequently wounded; 30 August 1944–6 February 1945, commander, *SS-Leibstandarte Adolf Hitler*; 20 January 1945 promoted to brigadier of the Waffen-SS; 23 April 1945, commander *Kampfgruppe Mohnke* with power of command over the defensive forces of the government quarter (Zitadelle); 2 May 1945–10 October 1955 Soviet POW; lived subsequently in Lübeck and Hamburg.

Morell, Theodor Gilbert (1886–1948)

Studied medicine at Giessen, Heidelberg, Grenoble, Paris and Munich (qualified in 1913); medical officer aboard ships at sea; volunteer in WWI; 1918 opened practice in urology and electrotherapy in Berlin; 1933 joined NSDAP; introduced to Hitler through photographer Heinrich Hoffmann; 1936 until 21 April 1945 Hitler's personal physician; 17 July 1945 interned in southern Germany; 1948 died in custody.

Müller, Heinrich (1900–?)

Skilled aircraft assembler; WWI volunteer; 1929 secretary, Munich Political Police; 1934 joined SS; transferred to Gestapo offices in Berlin; 1936 deputy head of political police in security police head office; end of 1938 joined NSDAP; 1939 director, Reich Centre for Jewish Emigration; director, Reich Detectives; October 1939 head of Amt IV (Gestapo) in the rank of SS-Oberführer; participant at the Wannsee Conference (decisive involvement in the planning and execution of the Jewish genocide); whereabouts unknown since 1 May 1945.

Naumann, Dr Werner (1909–1982)

State secretary, Propaganda Ministry; special plenipotentiary for Volkssturm; personal adviser to Joseph Goebbels; erstwhile member *SS-Leibstandarte Adolf Hitler*; appointed in Hitler's Testament as successor to Goebbels; night of 1 May 1945 broke out from Reich Chancellery with Martin Bormann and Axmann; 1949 trained as bricklayer under false name in south Germany; 1953 the Naumann-circle, named after him, proposed setting up another authoritarian state by infiltrating North Rhine Westphalia FDP; main candidate for the Right-Wing German Reich Party (DRP) in Lower Saxony (without success).

Paulus, Friedrich (1890–1957)

Final rank WWI Hauptmann (= army rank of captain); 1919 accepted into 100,000-man army; February 1931 tactical instructor, War Academy Berlin; 1935 chief of general staff, motorised troops; beginning 1939 chief of general staff XVI Army Corps and later of Tenth Army at Leipzig (after 10 October 1939 renamed Sixth Army); 3 September 1940 senior quartermaster at general staff and deputy to chief of the general staff Franz Halder; 5 January 1942 commander-in-chief Sixth Army, promoted to general of panzer troops; 31 January

1943 capitulated with the surrounded Sixth Army at Stalingrad; Soviet POW; 11 February 1946 witness at the Nuremberg Trials of principal war criminals; 26 October 1953 returned from Soviet captivity; lived in Dresden.

Rattenhuber, Johann (1897–1957)

1920 joined municipal police, Bayreuth; 1922 Bavarian State Police; 1933 adjutant to Bavarian police president Heinrich Himmler and set up the Führer Protection Squad; 1935 head of independent authority RSD (Reich Security Service); 2 May 1945 Soviet POW; released 1951.

Remer, Otto Ernst (1912–1997)

1933 Reichswehr ensign; 1939 Polish campaign, 1st lieutenant; 1940 took over company (commander in 9th Panzer Division, involved in Western offensive, Balkans and invasion of USSR; 1942 promoted captain, transferred to Division *Grossdeutschland*; beginning 1944 in rank of major transferred to Berlin, took command of Watch Battalion *Grossdeutschland*; 20 July 1944 put down attempted revolt after the Stauffenberg assassination attempt; promoted to Oberst (= army rank of colonel); November 1944 commandant Führerbegleit-Brigade; January 1945 promoted to brigadier; taken prisoner by US forces and handed over to the British; until 1947 POW; co-founder of Right-extremist parties; several trials and convictions for incitement, disrespect to the memory of the dead, incitement to racial hatred and denying the Holocaust; 1952 received a three-month jail sentence for calling the military resistance 'traitors'; fled to Spain.

Riefenstahl, Helene Bertha Amalie, 'Leni' (1902–2003)

1921–3 classical ballet training; 1925–31 actress (*Der heilige Berg, Der grosse Sprung*); 1932 debut as film director (*Das blaue Licht*); 28 March 1935 première of *Triumph of the Will*, a National Socialist propaganda film about the 1934 Nuremberg rally, in Hitler's presence (film won the German Film Prize 1934/5, the prize for the best foreign documentary film at the Venice Biennial 1935 and the Gold Medal at the Paris World Exhibition 1937); 20 April 1938 première of the films *Fest der Völker* and *Fest der Schönheit* (Olympia Films); in her film *Tiefland*, concentration camp inmates were used as extras; despite worldwide appreciation of her later work, remained for all her life a controversial personality and artist on account of her role in the Third Reich and her proximity to Hitler.

Rommel, Johannes Erwin Eugen (1891–1944)

WWI awarded Iron Cross First Class; during Polish campaign, commandant Führer-HQ; promoted to brigadier; February 1940 commander, 7th Panzer Division; 1941 major general; 14 February 1941 took command of Deutsche Afrika Korps;* following assassination attempt of 20 July 1944 suspected of involvement; 14 October 1944 offered suicide as a way to avoid trial and spare his family (see Burgdorf, Wilhelm); same afternoon took cyanide in the presence of two generals.

Schädle, Franz (1906–1945)

Lieutenant colonel; 1930 entered NSDAP and SS; 1933 *SS-Leibstandarte Adolf Hitler* (LSSAH); January 1945 until 2 May 1945 head of SS bodyguard; suicide Reich Chancellery.

Schäffer, Fritz (1888–1967)

1920 senior civil servant, Ministry for Education and Culture; 26 June 1933 arrested; 1934 released and admitted to the Bar; after 20 July 1944 rearrested and taken to Dachau; post-war, CSU politician; 1949–57 federal minister for finance; 1957–61 federal minister of justice.

---

* 1944 appointed commander, Atlantic Wall defences against invasion of French coast. (TN)

Schaub, Julius (1898–1967)

1920 entered NSDAP (Member No. 81); 9 November 1923 participated in Munich Putsch; SS member No. 7; end of 1940 personal adjutant to Hitler; May 1945 captured by US forces at Berchtesgaden; detained until 1949; acquitted on a charge of aiding and abetting murders; later, became a pharmacist in Munich.

Schmeling, Max (1905–2005)

Heavyweight boxer; world champion 1930–2; Schmeling's victory in his most famous fight on 19 June 1936 against the as then undefeated 'Brown Bomber' Joe Louis (knocked out in the twelfth round) was used by the Propaganda Ministry as 'proof of the superiority of the Aryan race'.

Schmundt, Rudolf (1896–1944)

Battalion, then regimental adjutant, WWI; awarded Iron Cross I and II; 1921 adjutant, Prussian 9th Infantry Regiment, Potsdam; 1921–31 staff officer, 1st Division *Königsberg*; 1931–5 personnel office, Reichswehr Ministry; 1936 major; 1935–6 company commander and general staff, 18th Infantry Division *Liegnitz*; 29 January 1938 Hitler's chief adjutant; 1938 promoted lieutenant colonel; 1939 colonel; 1942 brigadier; 194 major general; 1 October 1944 died of wounds sustained during the attempt on Hitler's life at Rastenburg 20 July.

Schörner, Ferdinand (1892–1973)

Studied philosophy and new languages; 1918 1st lieutenant; 1923 as adjutant of General Otto von Lossow involved in putting down the Munich Putsch; 1934 major; 1937 lieutenant colonel; 1939 commander, 98th Alpine Regiment (Gebirgsjäger), Polish Campaign; commander 6th Alpine Division; 1940 brigadier; 1942 general, Gebirgstruppen; 31 March 1944, commander-in-chief Army Group South Ukraine; 20 January 1945 commander-in-chief Army Group

Centre; 5 April 1945 field marshal; 30 April 1945 appointed army commander-in-chief in Hitler's Political Testament; 8 May 1945 informed of the German capitulation at his HQ at Bad Welchow; 9 May 1945 fled in civilian clothing; detained later in Austria by US forces; end of May 1945 handed over to the Soviets.

Schroeder, Emilie Christine 'Christa' (1908–1984)

1922–5 commercial training, Münden (Hanover); 1929 employed as stenographer and office assistant; 1930 employed by NSDAP Reichsleitung, Munich; 1933 accepted as secretary in Hitler's personal offices in Berlin; until 22 April 1945 Hitler's personal secretary; 28 May 1945 detained at Hintersee near Berchtesgaden as 'principal war criminal'; released 12 May 1948 after reclassification to 'collaborator'; various positions as secretary; 1967 accepted retirement.

Speer, Albert (1905–1981)

Studied architecture at Karlsruhe, Munich and Berlin; 1931 entered NSDAP; 1933 first personal meeting with Hitler; 1934 successor to Hitler's 'court architect' Paul Ludwig Troost; February 1942 Reich minister for armaments; May 1945 Reich trade minister in the Dönitz government; 1 October 1946 sentenced at Nuremberg to twenty years' imprisonment as a major war criminal; 30 September 1966 released from Spandau.

Speidel, Hans (1897–1984)

Volunteer, WWI; 1921 Reichswehr officer; studied political economy and history; 1930–3 general staff training; 1933–5 assistant to German military attaché in Paris; 1936 head of department, Foreign Armies West in Berlin; 1937 No. 1 general staff officer at Mannheim; 1940 French campaign; 1 August 1940 chief of staff to military commander, France; 1941 colonel; 1942 appointed chief of general staff, V Army Corps, Eastern Front; 1943 chief of staff, Army Group South; 1944 chief of the general staff, Army Group B and thus a close colleague of General Rommel; contacts to military resistance of 20 July 1944; September 1944 detained (army prison, Küstrin); 1945 freed by French troops; 1949 tutor at the University of Tübingen; 1950 military adviser to federal chancellor Adenauer; 1951 specialist, 'Amt Blank', cover-name for the later Defence Ministry; 1957–63 General der Bundeswehr; commander-in-chief, NATO land forces in central Europe; 1964 retired.

Starke, Gotthold (1896–1968)

1915–18 studied law and political science; 1922 refused to repudiate his Polish nationality, 1922 forced to leave Prussian state service; worked at Bromberg as chief editor, *Deutsche Rundschau in Polen*; 1941–5 head of eastern Europe section, press and reports department; at this time adviser to German ambassador in Moscow; 1945 Russian POW; 1955 returned with the last German POWs.

Stauffenberg, Claus Schenk Graf von (1907–1944)

1926 entered Reichswehr; ensign at Reiter (mounted) 17th Regiment, Bamberg; 1927 Infantry School, Dresden; 1928 Cavalry School, Hanover; 1 January 1930 2nd lieutenant; October 1936 general staff training, War Academy, Berlin Moabit; 1 January 1937 Rittmeister (captain); 1 August 1938 general staff officer, 1st Light Division; participated in occupation of Sudetenland and served with 6th Panzer Division (1st Light Division renamed) in Polish campaign; 1940 general staff officer, Western offensive; transferred to OKH (Army High Command); March 1943 staff officer, 10th Panzer Division; 7 April 1943 seriously wounded, North Africa; chief of staff, general army office, Bendler-Strasse; 1 July 1944 chief of staff to commander of reserve army, General Fromm; 11 and 15 July 1944 set out to assassinate Hitler but abandoned attempt; 20 July 1944 attempt to assassinate Hitler failed; arrested, tried and sentenced to death by field court martial, executed same night, at Bendler-Strasse.

Stumpfegger, Ludwig (1910–1945)

SS-Lieutenant General; 1930–7 studied medicine at Munich; 2 June 1933 entered SS; 1 May 1935 entered NSDAP; 1936 assistant surgeon, later senior surgeon to Karl Gebhardt at the Hohenlychen Sanatorium; member of the medical team at the 1936 Olympic Games; September 1941 appointed head of the surgical group on the command staff of the Reichsführer-SS; took part in medical experiments mainly on Polish women from Ravensbrück concentration camp; 9 October 1944 travelling surgeon on staff of the Reich chancellor; May 1945 committed suicide after breaking out of the Reich Chancellery.

Troost, Gerhardine 'Gerdy', née Andresen (1904–2003)

Architect; wife of Speer's predecessor Paul Ludwig Troost; 1932 entered NSDAP; 1934 continued her husband's architectural bureau after his death (Haus der Deutschen Kunst project, Königsplatz, Munich); 1935 board member in Haus der Deustchen Kunst; 20 April 1937 made professor by Hitler; 1938 advisory board, Bavaria Filmkunst GmbH; published book *Das Bauen im neuen Reich*, a standard work for understanding National Socialist architecture; after the war classified as 'lesser involved' at the denazification proceedings, Munich tribunal, fined 500 Deutsche Mark and expelled from her profession for ten years; after that, resumed her career.

Wenck, Walther (1900–1982)

1935–6 War Academy; Knights Cross holder; 1 March 1943 brigadier; April 1945 commanded Twelfth Army (intended for the relief of Berlin and so ordered by Hitler), but in view of the military situation continued west and surrendered to US forces; 1945–7 US POW.

Werlin, Jakob (1886–1965)

SS-Oberführer and Hitler's inspector-general for motor transport; board member, Daimler-Benz AG; member NSDAP and SS; 1945–9

US internment; later proprietor Daimler-Benz holdings at Rosenheim and Traunstein.

Wisch, Theodor 'Teddy' (1907–1995)

Brigadier; October 1933 company commander, *SS-Leibstandarte*; December 1939 battalion commander, *SS-Leibstandarte*; May 1945 in military hospital, British POW.

Wolff, Karl Friedrich Otto (1900–1984)

Officer, WWI; 1931 joined NSDAP and SS; 1936 head of personal staff, Reichsführer-SS; 1939 SS liaison officer to Hitler; September 1943, senior SS and police commander, Italy; 1945 publishing representative; 1964 sentenced to fifteen years' detention for complicity in murders in at least 300,000 cases (deportations to Treblinka); 1971 sentence remitted.

Woellke, Hans (1911–1943)

Field athlete; 1936 Olympic champion, shot-putt; in WWII captain, Waffen-SS police regiment; killed by Russian partisans; posthumous promotion by Hitler to major in municipal police.

Wünsche, Max (1914–1995)

Passed out from SS Junker School, Bad Tölz; April 1936 *SS-Leibstandarte*; 1 October 1938 until 1940 (with short break) in Hitler's bodyguard; afterwards Sepp Dietrich's adjutant with the *SS-Leibstandarte*; several front assignments; until 1948 British POW, later industrial manager in Wuppertal.

Index